T0145796

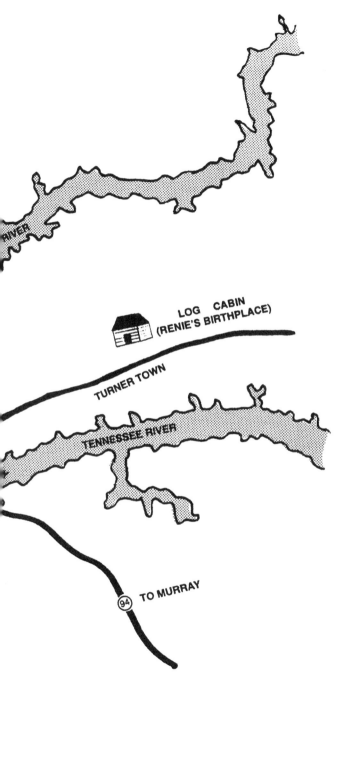

RENIE *from* GOLDEN POND

The Story of Lorene Turner Higgins

TURNER PUBLISHING COMPANY

TURNER PUBLISHING COMPANY

Turner Publishing Company Staff:
Editor: Randy Baumgardner
Designer: Shelley R. Davidson

Library of Congress Catalog Card No. 98-60900

ISBN: 978-1-68162-591-1

Additional copies may be
purchased directly from the publisher. Limited Edition.

Introduction

Renie from Golden Pond is the true life story of Lorene Turner Higgins. Her story begins with her birth, which was in a log cabin in the Fenton Community, located in Trigg County in what was known as "the land between the rivers." It continues to present time, where she now resides in Cadiz, Kentucky.

Lorene, whose pet name is "Renie", married at the young age of fifteen to Lawton Higgins, a seventeen year old moonshiner from the neighboring community of Oak Ridge. Needless to say, the continuing saga unfolds many humorous, heart warming and exciting events. The sweet innocence of the youthful lass depicts the overwhelming emotional trauma she experience as she copes with being married to a moonshiner; living with her mother-in-law, Ma Annie; after a year of marriage, giving birth to her first child, Virgil, who is deaf; and while he is a baby, having her second child, Doris.

History, culture and vivid geographic descriptions characterize the special breed of inhabitants in the various communities of the 'land between the rivers". The lost art of moonshining, along with many other common practices for survival, as well as entertainment among the rural Western Kentuckians of the early 1900s, the great depression, and World War II era's are shared as Renie's story progresses.

Lorene and Lawton were married eight years before she finally persuaded him to buy a home of their own. This, her dream home, and the one place she still calls home, was a two story house on the outskirts of Golden Pond, a small town in Trigg County. Renie describes, vividly, yet another emotional trauma, as she unveils the events that occur when they are forced to leave what had been her "dream home" for almost 30 years.

The chain of events that take place throughout the years as they enroll Virgil in the Kentucky School for the Deaf at Danville, Kentucky, Lawton's continuing career in the liquor business, along with dealing with failing health and adjusting to living in a new community, constitute a very unusual story.

About The Author

Barbara Hillyard was born and still lives in the Briarfield Community of Caldwell County, Kentucky. She and her husband, Jerry, have four daughters, Gerri, Lynn, Lori and Betsy; and three grandchildren, Matthew, Lindsay and Leslie.

For the past eighteen years, Barbara has been employed by Farmers Bank & Trust Company in Princeton, Kentucky. She is a Sunday School teacher at Donaldson Baptist Church, and her hobbies are spending time with her grandchildren, reading and writing. She is also known for her book, *The Antics of Liza Jane*, from which an excerpt, "Pie Supper Excitement," was published in *Back Home in Kentucky* magazine.

Acknowledgements

My personal gratitude is extended to a number of individuals for making this venture possible: first, to my family, who have urged, prodded and spurned me for several years to start "digging up bones" and put them in story form; then, to my many friends, each of whom wants the first volume; and finally, to Barbara Hillyard, who was brave enough to tackle my story. After nine months and many sessions, much patience mingled with warm friendship, she brought my story to life in script.

Dedication

Dedicated to Virgil and Shirley,
Doris and Kelsie,
My five grandchildren, seven great-grandchildren,
One sister still living, and
Those of my family now gone on…especially
Daddy.

Chapter One:

Lawton and Lorene

A chill, colder than the frigid February wind went over Lorene, leaving her frozen in her tracks! The dreaded sounds coming from the nearby woods penetrated the air, and echoed throughout the holler! Quickly, Lorene grabbed Dora May's arm to stop her incessant chatting! Dora May opened her mouth to speak, but catching the sounds at that moment, she became too paralyzed to move! Loud voices, along with the clanging of tin and the chop of axes rang through the early morning air as the two young women stared at each other, mouths open and eyes wide! They could hear Lawton's voice but other than an occasional oath, they could not make out what he was saying. They couldn't hear his cousin Jake uttering a sound, but muffled voices along with shouts and grunts were heard as the tools of the revenuers' slashed away at the still. Yes, Lorene and Dora May knew exactly what was going on. Fact was, somebody had snitched on Lawton and the revenuers had come in and was, at this very moment, chopping up Lawton's still! This was the dreaded time all moonshiners were sure to face sooner or later if they stayed in the business long enough. Lorene certainly wasn't prepared for all this and the timing could not have been worse.

"What are we a'gonna do, Lorene?" Lawton's older sister whispered.

"Well, I don't know what you're a'gonna do, but I'm goin' in there and give them infernal revenuers a piece of my mind!"

"Oh, no, Lorene, you can't do that, it'd just make things worse for Lawton. Besides, you're not in any shape to get yourself all riled up. The best thing we can do is get outta' here and the quicker the better. Why, they're liable to start a'shootin'. Common, let's go to the house," Dora May said in a low voice, tugging earnestly at Lorene's coat sleeve.

"I'm not goin' to the house. I've gotta help Lawton!" Lorene yelled, jerking free of Dora May's grip.

"Now, Lorene, you listen here to me," Dora May started, grabbing both of Lorene's arms and turning her right sharply to face her, "there's not a thing you can do in there cept' make matters worse. Now, I've been 'round this kind of business a lot longer n' you and I know how fixes like this turn out and I'm tellin' you, best thing we can do for Lawton is for us to turn around right now and get back to the house."

Dora May held her grip and her breath till the trembling Lorene sighed, let her shoulders slump and nodded her head. Big tears began to tumble down her cheeks as Dora May put her arm around Lorene's shoulders and started guiding her down the slope and back toward the creek, whose flat rocks the two of them had, only moments earlier, skipped so light heartily across.

"Oh, Dora May, what are we 'gonna do? With this baby comin' on anytime an' now, thanks to them blasted revenuers, no money comin' in, what ever are we 'gonna do?" Lorene sobbed as they made their way across the back porch and into the kitchen of the Ma Annie's house.

"Now, Lorene, there'll be a way, always is," Dora May answered, trying to be of some consolation to the distraught Lorene.

"You know they'll search the house. You know they will and that back room is full.

Oh, Lord a mercy, whatever are we gonna do?" Lorene moaned as she slumped her swollen body onto one of the six chairs at the long kitchen table.

"Now, Lorene, you gotta simmer down. You gettin' all worked up won't help nothing. I'll go get Mammy!" Dora May was saying, but she didn't have time to make the short trip across the yard to the little store Ma Annie owned and operated, for glancing out the back window she saw Lawton, Jake, three white men, none of whom she recognized, and two blacks coming across the back yard. Soon the three white men were ushering Lawton and Jake into the kitchen.

"Now, Higgins, the older man and spokesman for the group was saying as they paraded single file into the room, "you and you're partner stay put right here with Mr. Jessup, and me an Mr. Horning will do the search." He pulled a piece of paper from his coat pocket and continued. "Here's the warrant an' I've gotta do my job, er', mornin,' ladies," he nodded, looking rather startled at Lorene who was sobbing at the table and Dora May, standing at the window.

Lorene jumped up from the table and began wailing as she ran to Lawton, "Oh, Lawton, what in the world are we gonna do? What are they gonna do with you? They can't put you in jail. You can't go away, th' baby's likely to come anytime. You can't leave me here! We won't have any money! What are we gonna' do?"

Lawton did not say a word, but glared at the intruders, breathing hard, as his arm encircled his sobbing young wife, who was clinging desperately to him. The three revenue men were looking on, seemingly unable to muster the right words to fit the situation. Dora May moved from the window to Lorene and attempted to move her away from Lawton, but Lorene began to wail louder and cling faster.

The revenuers exchanged bewildered glances. Lawton looked mad enough to kill and swallowed hard, struggling with the rage inside him. Finally, the older revenuer spoke in a strained voice, "All right, Higgins, we found your still and busted it up good. I'd like to think we've put you out of business for good. Fact is, looks t' me like you're old enough to know this is no life for a family man. I'd advise you to take heed to what I'm tellin' you here, my boy. Now, due to the condition that this little gal you're married to is in, me and these men are gonna take your word that there's nothin' in the house and we won't use this warrant this time, but let me tell you something, my boy, if we make this trip out her one more time, I'll tear this place apart and bust ever dadblasted jug and keg I can get my hands on, an' you'll wind up with your hind-end in jail for a good long stretch. You better listen to what I'm sayin'. I'm tellin' you for your own good, boy. We've gotta take you in to file a report an' you know you'll have to appear in Federal Court before this is over. We won't keep you in jail, but we'll send the papers in and then they'll get back to me and I'll have to serve em' on you to go to court."

Lorene loosened her grip on Lawton and took a step back, watching him as he swallowed hard again while fire flashed in his eyes, but he still didn't say a word. Poor Jake had not moved an inch from where he stopped when they first entered the kitchen. Lorene wasn't even sure if he had so much as breathed. His color was ashen and there was a damp spot down the front of his pants. At this moment she almost burst out laughing, not just for the pitiful, yet comical sight of Jake, but because she was so relieved the sheriff and the revenue men had not searched the house. Now, maybe they would have enough "dew" in the back room to bring in money enough to last awhile, at least till the baby got here and till they knew the outcome of Lawton's trial in Federal Court.

The older revenue man, the spokesman for the group, glanced over the small group in the kitchen, then turned on his heel and motioned for the others to follow.

Lorene reached for Lawton again but he stopped her and said, "Now, Renie, I'll be back son's they get the papers filled out, quit worrin' an stay here with Dora May. I'll be back in a little bit." With that, all the men were gone.

Well, that's how it was, that first raid on their moonshinin' industry. The first, that is, since Lorene had married into the Higgins family. Lorene allowed it likely wouldn't be the last though, for she knew, sure as day, that Lawton Higgins wasn't about to stop making moonshine and that as long as there were others out there making it, too, there would always be somebody ready to snitch in an attempt to eliminate part of the competition. After all, Lawton did have the reputation of being a good moonshiner, and he did get a lot of business, despite the fact he was only eighteen years old.

Two days after the busting of the still, Lawton and Jake loaded up Lawton's '27 Chevy Coupe and headed out for Paris, Tennessee. This load depleted about a fourth of the inventory in the back room. Lawton allowed there was enough left to get by on till he found another spot and got the still back in working order. He figured that would give the "heat" time to cool, which would eliminate the major problem facing Lawton's livelihood for the time being. Lorene heard Lawton tell Jake he just might have to get on the good side of the sheriff and she knew exactly what he was talking about, for she had heard Lawton talk about how other men in the "business" were paying high priced insurance to keep the local law out of their woods.

Well, Lorene pondered on all these things with some disapproval, but kept her thoughts to herself. After all, life had been a lot easier for her here with Lawton. She had some store-bought dresses and underwear, a pair of nylon stockings and three pair of shoes, for the first time in her life. Why, Lawton had even bought her a red wool coat for Christmas. No, for a fact, Lawton definitely wasn't stingy with his money and he sure could be awful sweet at times, in that reckless way of his. He had a crooked grin and a certain wink that Lorene felt was just for her. Yeah, all in all, life wasn't all that bad for Lorene at the present time.

Some things about Lawton did get under Lorene's skin sometimes, though. Now, Lawton wasn't what you'd call a drinking man, even though, he did make the stuff, and every now and then he'd get a nip or two under his belt and get to bragging. In fact, the day after the raid, word got back to Lorene that he'd been bragging to some of the other men in the "business" about the revenue man taking his word that nothing was in the house and walking away without even using their search warrant. Well, Lorene sat him straight right fast that she had saved his bragging neck and not his word at all. Fact was, the revenue man said so himself, "Considering the condition that this lil' gal you're married to is in, we'll not search the house…" That's what he said.

Now, Lorene didn't just sit around and think up stuff to nag at her young husband about, but she wished they had a home of their own and didn't have to live here with Ma Annie, Dora May and her six year old daughter, Maxine. Dora May and Wallace Chambers were separated and they had moved back in with Ma Annie. Oh, it wasn't that Ma Annie treated her bad, not really, although she was awful bossy, and Lorene and Dora May got along pretty well, and Lorene did love little Maxine and Maxine loved her; it was just that it wasn't like having a place of their own. Sometimes she wondered if Lawton ever would leave his mama. She condoned everything he did. So did Dora May, Clara and Buina, his three older sisters. They all thought everything Lawton did was just

9

fine, moonshining, fast driving, even old girlfriends. Yep, they condoned it all. Lorene tried to console herself to the fact that Ma Annie likely had a hard time trying to raise a family, especially a boy, without a husband, and Lawton was the baby, the only boy, and it went without saying, he pretty much had his way all of his life. Lorene couldn't help but wonder if Ma Annie had bucked him a few times though, they might have a place of their own and Lawton might be making a legal living, and they wouldn't be having to fret over revenue men and what the out come of Lawton going to Federal Court would be.

Lorene vaguely remembered Harlan Higgins, Lawton's daddy who had died when Lawton was a small boy. One time when she was just a small child, she remembered seeing him sitting in the front yard of their home place in the Oak Ridge community and he was very frail and sickly looking. He was coughing a lot and Lorene saw him spit up blood. Years later, she learned he died of consumption. To Lorene's knowledge, Harlan Higgins had never been in the moonshinin' business.

Lorene sure wished there was a simple way for Lawton to get out of the moonshinin' business and find a place for them. She, in her young sixteen years of age, couldn't think of a simple way; never the less, she couldn't help ponder on the situation a lot.

The north wind drove winter's cold through the cracks around the window of the rambling old house. The boards creaked as the barren branches of the stately oaks, standing near the house, scratched like boney fingers across the shingled roof. Lorene sat with her elbows propped on the small table that set in front of one of the long windows in the stayin' room, her chin resting in her hands. She was watching for the black coupe to come winding up the lane, bringing Lawton home from Paris. The red glow from the sun was filtering through thin purple clouds as it sank lower and lower in the western sky. A cardinal and two blue jays fluttered about the crusty grass near the front porch in search for food.

Lorene's parents Duck and Ed Turner.

"He's had time to be back," Lorene mumbled to herself as she kept looking down the lane. "Is this the way I'm goin' to spend the rest of my life, waitin' and wonderin' when my man'll be gettin' home and if he's all right?" Well, whether consciously or subconsciously, Lorene's thoughts turned to lighter days, the days of her childhood.

Lorene Turner Higgins was born on April 22, 1913 in a one room log cabin in what folks called Turnerville in Trigg County, Kentucky. This was part of an area known as the land "Between the Rivers", the rivers being the Cumberland and the Tennessee. Edward Young and Oina Birdsong Turner were her parents. Most folks called her daddy Ed and her mama Duck, for Oina was short and plump. Lorene was the oldest of eight children. Jewel, sixteen months younger than Lorene, who they lost to influenza at the age of five, was the second child. While Lorene had dark hair, eyes and skin like her daddy, Jewel was fair with lighter hair and blue eyes like her mama. Two years after Jewel little Olin Edward, nicknamed "Shaw," came along and in another two years came Clyde. Tears welled in Lorene's eyes when she thought of little Clyde. They lost him to meningitis when he was only a year old. They had just lost Jewel a little over a year before. Lorene felt somewhat to blame for Clyde's death for the longest time. She was only around seven at the time. She had carried him out in the back yard to look at the new baby chicks one spring day shortly before he became sick and he, being a robust and very active baby, squirmed out of her arms and fell to the ground, landing on his head. Soon, the fever set in. In a matter of days he went from bad to worse and within two weeks he died. Some time after his death, Lorene confronted her mother of her feelings of guilt, but her mother assured her that the doctor said little Clyde had been stricken with meningitis and the fall had nothing to do with losing him.

Next to be born into the Turner family was Viona Katherine; then about two years later came Guy Crittenden, named for Duck's pa, and after Guy came baby Reba Nell.

Now, the Turner's were poor, but not unlike most families in the land between the rivers. They had few material things of which to boast, but growing up, Lorene did not realize they were poor. Fact was, it never crossed her mind. Her daddy was a farmer, as most in that area; he fished and cut timber in the winter and they moved around some, just within the community, though. Lorene guessed her fondest and most vivid recollection of an actual home place was in the Fenton school community. There they lived with her daddy's Great Uncle Joe and Aunt Rhodie. The house was a weather-boarded frame with two large rooms on one side, a dog trot and three more large rooms on the other. There seemed to always be a lot of noise, what with a house full of lively youngens, and it seemed there was a lot of love shared among all of them.

Lorene loved to be outside with her daddy. She didn't know if it was because she just loved the outdoors, or if it was a release from tending to her younger siblings, or if it was because she just loved her daddy so much; for all she knew, it was likely a combination of all three. Anyhow, she was out with Ed every chance she got. Her mother called her a "Daddy's Girl," and Lorene guessed she was, for she was forever tagging along behind her daddy. Most of the time he called her "Renie." Why, the first spring they lived at Uncle Joe's, he gave her all the chickens that were hatched outside the henhouse. Lorene loved holding the baby chicks and listening to them chirp as she smoothed their downy feather with her fingers. Lorene helped her daddy feed the stock, milk the cows, mend fences, clean the stable stalls, mend his fishing nets and lines, but there was one thing she flat out refused to have anything to do with, and that was the bucket of chicken entrails Ed saved for fish bait. Lorene smiled at the thought of their two faithful mules, Ida and Ada. They had hauled many a load in the buckboard, including the family. They had also pulled the plow, disk, corn driller and drag, many a day. Ed always fed them good and he'd rub them down after a hard days work. A good team of mules were hard to come by in those times, and he praised his good team of mules to other farmers every chance he got. Lorene's mama would say, "The way Ed brags on them two mules, why, you'd think he prided them more than me an' the youngens." Then she'd laugh, Lorene remembered.

Only a faint tinge of orange showed beneath the clouds by now and still no sign of Lawton. Lorene was getting tired of sitting in the same position for so long. It didn't take long for her back and legs to begin hurting, especially during the last couple of weeks. Ma Annie said the baby had dropped and this being her first, Lorene could deliver anytime now. Ma Annie ought to know, for she had been grannyin' in these parts for a long time. It was nothing for Ma Annie to be sent for in the middle of the night to help deliver a baby somewhere in the community. She always kept a fresh, white apron pressed and the glycerin within easy reach. Ma Annie was always quick to help at any accident or to attend the sick. People trusted her as much as they did most any doctor.

Lorene rose from the chair, stretched and rubbed her aching back, then went across the room to the fireplace to stir the fire, for she was chilled from her long stay at the window. She lit the coal oil lamp on the mantle, then turned her back to the fireplace to absorb the warmth of the now brightly flickering fire.

Chapter Two:
Moonshine

The land between the rivers, which had been Lorene's home for her entire life, was known for its green, rolling hills, dense woodlands and many creeks and springs. The area boasted of its agricultural industry. Many small farms were located there, most of which were locally owned and operated by individual families. Farming in the land between the rivers during Lorene's day was done by a team of mules or horses, a plow, rake, disk, corn driller, mowing machine and a drag. The farmers usually made enough in a good season to feed their stock, save seed for next spring's planting, and with the help of a garden and orchard, put food on the table for their families. Very little was bought at the local stores. Much of the time eggs, sweet cream or sorghum molasses would be traded at the stores for flour, coffee, sugar and salt. Most people took corn to the nearest gristmill to have ground into meal. One could consider these people to be a self-sufficient breed. It was a hard life, yet a satisfying one. Large families were the norm of every family dwelling in the land between the rivers; therefore, children, at a very young age, were expected to do their share with the chores and tending younger siblings.

The fertile, moist soil produced good corn, grain for hay, along with sugar cane. Due to the moist climate, few farmers raised tobacco, even though it was considered the money crop for most of the state. This unique and picturesque country was also rich in timber, producing many different kinds of trees. Among them were oak, cedar, pine, elm and walnut. All providing wood for homes, barns, and outbuildings, as well as cooking and heating. The supply of timber was so plentiful, many trees were felled each year to be cut and sold. Therefore, sawmills were a common sight in the land between the rivers. In fact, Lorene's uncle owned a sawmill. It was always a treat to go with Ed over to the sawmill and watch the huge saw transform the large trees into planks. She and her cousins would play in the big saw dust pile, behind the main building, being careful not to get the tiny particles in their eyes. There would be stacks of planks of varying lengths stacked neatly in sheds adjacent to the saw room. They were not allowed to play on the planks, for they usually belonged to a customer and too, there was the fear of the dreaded sprinters on the freshly cut planks.

Iron, another of this still somewhat remote and rugged land's natural resources, also brought money and jobs to the area. Yes, this unique area formed between the Tennessee and Cumberland Rivers was largely withdrawn from other communities, mainly, because of the barriers created by the rivers. Therefore, it's inhabitants were forced to be self- sufficient. Now, there's yet another industry that flourished in the land between the rivers during Lorene's day, that should not be over looked. This was the moonshine whiskey industry. This beautiful and resourceful region seemed to have the ideal environment for this making moonshine.

Now, moonshining, as all the other industries mentioned, carried with it some risks. In conjunction with farming, the weather played an important role in the process of moonshining whiskey, because corn was a necessary ingredient of this process. There was one other risk involved to which a moonshiner faced of which the farmer did not have to cope; this being the Federal government. You see, the making of moonshine

Replica of Lawton's still, used in modern-day parades, not for use!

whiskey for the sale of it, was, and still is, against the law. Fact is, the definition of a moonshiner is one who makes and sells illicit whiskey.

Now, the making of alcoholic beverages, according to historians, dates back as far as 6,000 B.C. How it was discovered is still, to this day a mystery, never the less, many men in the land between the rivers were known for miles around for producing some of the finest "dew" in the world. "Dew" is short for "mountain dew", as moonshine is often called. In fact, it's been said that Al Capone, the notorious Chicago gangster during prohibition days, bought quite a bit of the fine "dew" from some of the men between the rivers. So, the mystery of how or when the making alcoholic beverages came about was of little consequence to these moonshining business men. Most of the moonshiners in Lorene's younger days earned the title of being a "good moonshiner" by the trial and error method. As with anything else one attempts, a little common sense, practice and a little streak of good luck were the keys to success in the moonshining business. And, being on the good side of the law didn't hurt any either.

Well, Lawton Higgins was one of the men in the moonshining business, and he had the reputation for being a pretty good one, even before he was twenty years old. Lawton, didn't follow in his pa's foot steps, as most boys of the time did, for his pa wasn't known for ever being a moonshinin' man. Previous to Harlan Higgins death at an early age, he was just a farmer, so, his son Lawton came into the moonshinin' business on his own. It seemed Lawton just took to it on his own by watching and listening to old timers and others experienced in the" business." Some say he was a natural, for it got into his blood at such a young age. It seemed his theory was, "if a man had the guts and wasn't afraid to take the risk's it carried, he could make fast and fairly easy money."

Now, the process of making moonshine or mountain dew or white lightning, which everyone chose to call it, wasn't all that complicated. The secret was in the mixing and the timing, mostly the timing. You see, getting it aged just right was what gave the brew that special flavor and kick that brought the customers back, time after time. The necessary ingredients were simple enough, too; water, corn, sugar, unsulfured molasses and baker's yeast were the ingredients that went into every original "batch". The components that made up the necessary equipment were basically simple as well. Even the name of the properly constructed equipment was simple, it was a "still". Now a still was a contraption that had a "cooker", that being, a large copper boiler where the "mash" was put to heat. The mash, being a mixture of various amounts of the aforementioned ingredients, mixed and stored for several days or until fermentation took place, in a charred barrel, preferably oak. Yes, a charred oak barrel was considered almost imperative, for experienced men in the "business" seemed to think oak enhanced the flavor of the brew. Now, a fire was built underneath the cooker, which had to reach a temperature of one hundred and seventy-three degrees. The purpose of reaching this specific temperature was because alcohol vaporizes at one hundred and seventy-three, whereas water must be brought to two hundred and twelve degrees to vaporize, so, the separation began in the cooker. These cookers varied in size, depending on the individual operation. Copper tubing, better known in the "business" as a" worm," for it had to be coiled, was another necessary piece of equipment for the making of moonshine. The copper tube was attached to a hole in the top of the "cooker," allowing the alcohol vapors to funnel into the "condenser," or "cooler," as some called it. This was a barrel of cold water. The vapor ran from the cooker through the copper tubing, or "worm," into the" condenser" where it was cooled until it condensed, after which, it brought forth a brew that could put the "Partaker" in such an oblivious spirit it would ease pain, instill confidence, loosen the tongue, and contribute to a hangover identifiable only to "sick neigh unto death." This potent and much craved brew ran out the tube at the bottom of the barrel, or condenser, and into a waiting jug. These jugs were either stone or glass, ranging in a variation of sizes. Now, it was advisable to toss the first quart or so of the "dew," since it was likely to contain impurities. The next stage of the game was to "sample the goods." A reputable moonshiner always did a taste test before passing his "goods" on to his customers. Sometimes, more often than not, he'd call in an older, more experienced man in the "business", sometimes three or four, and it might take several samples before enough had run out to have that "just right" taste. Older or more experienced men in the moonshining business knew it was also, advisable at this time, to initiate the term, "sip" rather than "drink". A few moonshiners, just to make the "sampling" stage a little more lively, had been known to have a "green horn" or two to join in this testing stage. It, likely, went without saying, one of the old timers just happened to come in the buckboard, for you see, a "green horn" was one who hadn't yet learned the difference in the terms "sipping" and "drinking". Of course, no reputable moonshiner would want two or three "green horns" laying around the still sobering up. It wasn't good for business. Well, having been sampled and approved, which sometimes could take the bigger part of a night, and with those who had over indulged in the sampling safely carried home in the buckboard, the finished product was now ready to be stored in a dry basement or building or in the middle of a corn field, out of sight, of course, of those who didn't appreciate it's worth. The aging process could then begin its course.

The sound of someone coming in the front door brought Lorene to her senses as she continued warming her back side before the fire. "Must be Ma Annie comin' from the store," Lorene thought, as she turned from the fireplace and started into the kitchen. It was then she heard the sound of a vehicle coming up the lane. She knew from the sound of the engine, it was Lawton. A flood of relief came over her as she came into the kitchen. Lawton always pulled the car to the back of the house and soon he was bursting into the kitchen, all full of excitement! That was Lawton, always at the top when he made a good sale!

"Well, here's my two favorite women in the whole world!" he said, swooping Lorene off her feet in a big hug.

"Lord a mercy, Lawton Higgins, put me down! You're gonna cause me to have a miscarriage, grabbing me up like that!" Lorene yelled, breathlessly.

"Aw, Honey, it wouldn't be no miscarriage, it'd just be goin' ahead and gettin' that boy on out into the real world where he's belonged for a week or two, now," he said, laughing and kissing her square on the lips.

Ma Annie, who was coming through the back door, returning from her day at the store, grunted and said, "You two quit that and les' get some supper on the table. Dora May and Maxine won't be here for supper, Clara wants them to stay the night."

"Guess I'll be doin' up the night work with the lantern then, huh?" Lawton said, taking off his hat and coat and hanging them on the peg beside the back door. "Sweet thing, I sure miss you helping with the chores. Be glad when that boy gets here so you can help out again."

"Well, you won't be any gladder than I will. I'm awful tired of stayin' in the house all the time," Lorene replied, turning to the big wood stove in the corner of the kitchen. "What took you so dad-blasted long, anyhow?"

"Well, me an Jake ran into some fellers from Owensboro who seemed mighty interested in some of my "shine", and we all got to talkin' and before I knew it time had just got away. So, Sugar Baby, know what that means? It means more customers and that means mo' do' in de' pocket. An' that's exactly why it took me so long," Lawton answered, coming up behind Lorene.

"I can tell you one thing, pretty lil' lady," he went on, putting his arms around her from behind and waving a fist of bills before her face, "I'm gonna' buy you and that boy of mine two of the finest outfits we can find son's he gets here. Money will be no object, just anything you an that boy wants will be got!"

"Well, for all you know, Lawton Higgins, this baby just might be a girl," Lorene said matter of fact.

"Naw, Lorene, it's not gonna be no girl, it's a boy. I've told you all along."

"You're carrin' it to low to be a girl," Ma Annie chided in, setting the plates on the table. "Now, bring the beans and corn from the warming shelf. Lawton's wantin' to get the night work done up son's he can. I know he's tired and wants to get t' bed."

The three ate with Lawton talking ninety to nothing about the trip to Paris, Tennessee, Lorene would be glad when the baby came so she and the baby could make some of the trips with Lawton. She enjoyed riding through the countryside to other counties and towns and missed the trips very much, because Ma Annie had confined her to the house since Christmas. Ma Annie was afraid she might slip on ice or her time might come and no one around if she was at the barn or walking in the woods, as she had loved to do in the fall, so here she was, stuck in the house and flat out getting tired of it.

Lorene lay awake long after she heard the steady breathing of Lawton lying there beside her, her thoughts once again turning to her childhood. One particular incident came to her mind as she lay on her side looking out the window into the winter night. She could almost see her mother's face as she laughed and told the story.

"Well," Duck would begin, "your daddy an' me an' you had just moved into the little house your daddy had built on Grandpa Birdsong's place. We had to carry water from a spring several yards from the house and I had my wash kettle and tub up close to the spring, up behind the hen house and the lot there, where the chickens was. That morning I had to take you with me, for I didn't have anybody to tend to you while I washed th' clothes. It was early summer and good and warm, so I took a quilt and spread it down on the grass under a big oak tree, at what I thought would be a safe distance from the fire underneath the kettle. The pallet was fairly close to the chicken house, an' several of the chickens was a' peckin' around in the grass a short ways off. You was a' crawlin' a little, an' I was tryin' to keep my eye on you and scrub out the clothes at the same time. Well, I hadn't much more'n turned my back, not for more than a minute, fact is, I had just put you back on the pallet, for you kept crawlin' off, an' anyhow, I had no more than turned my back and I heard you a' gaggin'. Lord a mercy!!! It about scared me to death! I whirled around and ran to where you was, an' grabbed you up, an' you'll never believe what you was a' doin'. You was a' eaten' chicken doodie! Sure as the world you was! You was a' pickin' out the white and eatin' it and rakin' the black away. Well, I didn't know what in the world to do first! I finally grabbed up a rag out of the basket of cloths and commenced wipin' out your mouth. Well, of course, I had scared you to death for you started yellin,' and by that time I was so tore up I started in cryin'. Why, I didn't know but what chicken doodie was poison! I was beside myself, for sure! There we was, me wrestling with you and you a' kickin' and screamin' your head off, an' me tryin' to wipe out your mouth, an' all th' time I was a' squallin' as loud as you. Well, along about then I heard somebody hollerin'. I looked up and saw Grandma Birdsong coming across the chicken yard.

"What in the world is the matter? Is the baby hurt? Did she get in the fire?" Grandma was hollerin' at the top of her lungs as she started runnin' toward me n' you.

"Oh, Mammie, she's eat chicken doodie! She's done gone and eat a whole mouth full of chicken doodie! Will it kill er?" I yelled back. "She didn't eat the black, she just eat the white. Oh Lord, will it kill er?"

"Well, about then, Mammy stopped, clapped her hands an' threw her head back an just started dyin' laughing, in fact, 'bout made me mad, cause I couldn't see a thing funny about it. Then she finally came up and took you from me an' said, "Law, Law child, it won't kill her, likely won't even make her sick. But I'd say she's got a awful bad taste in her mouth though, and you've already about scared her to death with all your hollerin'."

Mammy couldn't hardly talk for laughing, an' she took the rag out of my hand an' started for the spring with you on her hip, talkin' to you to get you settled down. She said, "Now lets me an' you get down here to this spring and wash that stinkin' mess of your face, lil lady. Why, you've got it all over your pretty dress an' everywhere." When she came back up the slope from the spring I was still in a bad way, but I'd quit shakin' an' cryin' an' it was then that Mammy said something s' funny I couldn't help but laugh too, she said, "I'll say one thing, she's a pretty finicky eater, seeing as how she just ate the white and raked the black away. Then, Mammy laid her arm across my shoulder and declared we was the funniest sight she had ever seen. She stayed on and tended to you till I got the washin' on the line; guess she knew it might not get done if she didn't. Well, it wasn't no time till everybody in the neighborhood knew about you eaten' chicken doodie. At first I was so out done over it I couldn't hardly face people, but it wasn't long till I could laugh and tell it, same as Mammy."

Lorene chuckled to herself as she reminisced the story. She missed home and Mama and the kids, and especially Daddy. They weren't that far away, and they did get to visit the fifteen miles back and forth, often, but times like these really made her lonely for the security of her family. Lorene, after all, was but a mere child of sixteen herself.

The next morning Lawton and Jake went up to the still site to see what items were "salvageable" and what would have to be replaced. Lawton commented on having already picked out another spot up behind the corn field. There were some large rocks in a low place in a cedar thicket and although the creek wasn't as close as at the other still sight, the woods curved in around three sides of the cedar thicket and the rocks covered the other side, making it fairly secluded. It was farther on up the hill from the house and some trees would have to fall to make roads, both in and out, but Lawton allowed it was a pretty fair spot.

Dora May and Maxine were still at Lawton's older sister Clara's, who lived a short piece across the holler, and Ma Annie was tending the store across the front yard from the house. Lorene, once again, busied herself for an hour or so with the household chores. She was restless when she finished and decided since there was no snow or ice, she would go outside for some fresh air, whether Ma Annie liked it or not. She might even walk as far as the old still sight and see what Lawton and Jake had found out. Normally, Lawton didn't allow her around the sight, but since the revenue men and the sheriff had already busted it up, she didn't think he would care, so she put on her old coat, tied a wool scarf around her head, and went out the back door, so as not to raise any suspicion with Ma Annie.

The sun was out, its rays casting a glow on the frost covered weeds and grass along the path, creating the illusion of millions of tiny diamonds having been strewn over the ground. A chill was in the air, but the wind was calm. Somewhere in the distance, likely in the meadow where the cow and mules grazed in summer, a hawk made its squawking sound. "Probably got a rabbit," Lorene thought as she kept winding up the slope toward the woods. She could see a thin trail of smoke coming from the chimney of their new neighbors small house, which was nestled in a clump of oak and maple trees just this side of the ridge, some quarter of a mile away. A dog started barking somewhere, likely belonging to the neighbors, for soon, the low, throaty howls of coon hounds cut loose. The ol' man was already well known, round about, for his coon huntin' and his three fine coon hounds.

Lorene topped the slope and started down the incline to the narrow creek where light skiffs of ice were floating around the flat rocks where she and Dora May had crossed on that dreadful day of the raid. She paused at the edge of the creek to catch her breath for a moment and began watching the current swirl, lightly, around the larger rocks, then, ripple, playfully, over the gravel, sized rocks that lined the bottom. The water was clear and the sound of it's gentle splashing as it flowed down the shallow bed of the creek, again, brought back childhood memories, times when she and Jewel and other kids from nearby farms would wade in the narrow spring branch just below their house.

One particular time that came to Lorene's mind was the year Ed and Grandpa Birdsong made the decision to raise a crop of tobacco. That was the year Lorene and the rest of the family moved into the big house in the Fenton School community, with Ed's great Uncle Joe and Aunt Rhodie.

Duck was beginning to show with her fourth child at the time. Lorene would be six in the spring, Jewel was almost three and Olin Edward or "Shaw," as Ed had nicknamed him, because he knew an old man who was short and stocky and waddled when he walked, and the old man's name was Shaw. So, when Olin Edward began toddling, Ed laughed one day and called him Shaw, and the name stuck.

The Turner's, at the present time were living in a little two room house Ed had built on Grandpa Birdsong's place. During the winter months, Grandpa Birdsong would drop in and sit before the fire where Ed would be mending his fishing nets and lines or the tools he used for cutting timber. Grandpa Birdsong and Ed would talk; men talk, mostly, about fishing, politics, hunting and farming. Lorene was usually at her daddy's side, either helping or just watching. She was taught to refrain from talking or asking questions when company came so, Grandpa Birdsong, being company, she tried her best to be quiet and just listen. Well, one of those times during Grandpa Birdsong's visits the subject of raising tobacco came up. So, with more visits of considerable discussing and figuring, Grandpa Birdsong and Ed decided to put out a tobacco crop come spring. Lorene was very excited at this stage of the game, mostly because Ed was. He had explained to her they would have some money coming in around Christmas time. Now, Lorene didn't know anything about finances, and during those times she actually saw very little money, but she knew money could buy her a special treat at the Turkey Creek store or a new coat and a pair of shoes. So, her excitement was genuine.

Now, raising tobacco started long before setting time. First, a plant bed had to be burned. A plant bed, in essence, was a carefully prepared seed bed that was fixed in the early spring, usually in late February or early March. The size of the plant bed varied, for a small crop of tobacco, a bed six foot by twenty would produce plants for the initial transplanting, with enough remaining to reset plants that did not survive the first setting. Brush, logs and the bark from dead trees were piled on a cleared spot of rich ground and burned. This was usually an all day, maybe two day project. The wood ashes enriched the soil for the seeds, which were planted. The plant bed was then covered with canvas made of cheese cloth and tacked to logs that enclosed the bed. This covering protected the bed of planted seeds from heavy rains, late frost and strong sunlight. These beds remained covered about six weeks, in which time, the seeds had sprouted into plants about four or five inches tall. When the plants were a full six inches, they were ready to be pulled from the bed and transplanted into a well fertilized field. This was where Lorene's services began.

Grandpa Birdsong and Ed had prepared a half acre of ground on a ridge several yards from the spring branch. The ground for raising tobacco had to be on higher terrain than that for corn or grain, for tobacco, initially, was a dry weather crop.

That particular spring morning, the beginning of the tobacco setting day, the sun was out and the weather was warm enough for Lorene to go barefoot with her daddy to the plant bed. They had taken several baskets, a five gallon bucket for Ed and two one gallon buckets for Lorene. Ed Explained that the baskets were to be used to carry the plants they pulled from the plant bed to the patch, and the buckets were for watering the plants after they were set in the ground. Lorene couldn't figure out why they needed to water the plants, for she already had mud oozing up between her toes. However, she didn't question her daddy. She was, after all, so glad to be outside with him and relieved of the duty of seeing to her younger siblings for a day, that, she just did as her daddy instructed.

Grandpa Birdsong was over in the field, or patch, which most people between the rivers spoke of as a piece of ground where one raised tobacco. He was making the hills. Now, " hills" were small mounds of soil scooped up with a hoe and flattened on the top to accommodate each tobacco plant. They were in rows about two feet apart; this space allowing for the growth of the plant.

Ed had designated the edges of the plant bed as the place from which Lorene would help pull the plants, instructing her that they were tender and must be pulled gently, one plant at a time, bringing the whole root out of the bed, then held, roots down, in the other hand until she had pulled as many plants as her small hand could hold. The hand full of plants, would then be placed carefully into one of the baskets. This process would be repeated until the baskets were filled. It did not take long to fill the baskets. Ed filled two to Lorene's one, however, he complimented her on how well she was doing and told her he knew she would be just as good at dropping the plants on the hills.

They carried the baskets to the patch were Grandpa Birdsong had finished with over half of the hilling process. Ed knew Lorene could not carry the bushel basket down the rows, so he helped her arrange a couple of handful of plants in her long dress tail, by scooping it up to hold the plants like a large pocket. Ed instructed her to start a couple of rows over from him, and to watch him drop a few plants until she got the hang of it. She soon began dropping the plants along side of him, careful to drop then all in the same direction with the root landing as near the center of the hill as possible. All the while Ed, was watching, correcting and complimenting her. After the first row, Ed felt confident with Lorene's job performance and he pulled a hand carved, wooden "peg," about six inches long, from the hip pocket of his overalls and began gently poking the tender plants into the hills, making the hole, inserting and covering the roots of the plant, all in one motion, as he went. To rest Lorene from her chore, Ed would let her wade in the spring branch when she went to fill the gallon molasses buckets used to water the freshly set plants. A few times he had to call to her, for being the small child she was, he would catch her fishing for the tadpoles that played in the gently flowing stream.

The plants in the tobacco patch were half set by noon. Grandpa Birdsong had finished with the hills shortly before noon, and was now helping Ed "peg" the plants into the hills. When they ran out of plants, they would go back to the bed and pull more. This broke the monotony of walking and bending down the long rows of hills.

When Lorene, Grandpa Birdsong and Ed went to the house for dinner, Duck and Grandma Birdsong, who had come over with Grandpa Birdsong that morning, had put a good spread on the table. Much of the garden vegetables were in and there was enough ripe cherries from the tree beside the small shed behind the house, for a cobbler. Lorene ate and ate. Her busy morning had, really, whetted her appetite, however, by the time she had finished, she was beginning to realize her young legs were, pretty tired. Sitting there on the front steps with Ed and Grandpa Birdsong and with a full stomach she grew very sleepy, but she knew she must help finish the job. Despite her sleepy eyes and tired legs, she was still enthusiastic about getting to be outside with her daddy. After a short rest in the shade of the front porch, they, once again began the short trip through the field below the house, across the spring branch and up the slope to the ridge and the tobacco patch.

The first plants set looked wilted, despite the watering, for the sun had been bright and warm all morning, and Lorene was concerned they were dying. Ed assured her they would look spry again come morning.

Well, by the end of the tobacco setting day, Lorene's young legs were so tired and her feet so sore her daddy carried her to the house on his shoulders. He, then made another trip to the patch to bring back the baskets and pails. Grandpa Birdsong had headed in the opposite direction toward his house to do his nightly chores.

Ed did up the night work at the stable, while Duck warmed up supper and Lorene tended the little ones. They ate, then Lorene and the little ones got their faces and feet washed, their gowns put on, and they all went out on the front porch, in the thickening twilight, to allow the house to cool from the heat of the wood cook stove. Ed sat, once more on the edge of the porch with his feet resting on the top of the long, flat rock, atop another, which served as steps up to the porch. His back was leaning against the porch post. Jewel crawled on his lap and, within moments, was fast asleep, and little Shaw was right behind her. Duck carried Shaw into bed, then came back out on the porch and took Jewel from Ed's arms to do the same with her. Lorene moved from her spot by the door, where she had been playing with one of the old yeller mammy cat's six kittens, to her daddy's lap. He held her close and stroked her hair. She snuggled against him, enjoying the feeling of safety and security she found there on her daddy's lap. The soothing mono-tones of his gentle voice as he complimented her for her days work, along with the music of the katydids and the occasional glow of lightening bugs in the fast growing darkness of the warm June night, soon carried Lorene to dream land.

Lorene cherished those moments. Those times with her daddy, who was not just her daddy, but who had come to be her very best friend in the whole wide world, even to this day.

"Renie!" It was Lawton calling from the edge of the woods where he and Jake were emerging. "What in the world are you doin' out here? Hadn't you better be at the house. You alright?"

"Course, I'm alright, an' the house is the only place you and Ma Annie think I ought to be, an' I'm blamed tired of being in the house all the time," she answered, shortly, her mind coming back to reality.

"Aw now, Renie, I'm not tryin' to start a racket with you," Lawton went on as he and Jake stomped across the creek and up the slope toward her.

"Tell you what, you pretty lil' fat thing. You can ride with me an' Jake over to Golden Pond. We're gonna see a feller over there about gettin' some parts for the still," Lawton said, putting his arm around her and turning her toward the house.

"Oh, goodie!" Lorene smiled, excitedly! Her mood suddenly changing. "We'd bet-ter tell Ma Annie, though. If she went to the house for something, and I wasn't there she'd likely, have a spell, then I'd hear it for a week."

Lawton laughed and nodded his head in agreement, "Then we'll tell Mammy." He squeezed her against him and kept laughing as they made their way to the house. Well that's how it was, Lawt was always up there, always had the situation under control.

Chapter Three:

Jewel

Golden Pond, in 1929, was the largest and most thriving town between the rivers. Golden Pond was not only a valuable trading point there in the heart of the bustling community, but also the cultural and educational center that served a large scope of the country. Golden Pond boasted of a Baptist church, the Golden Pond Hotel, a gristmill, blacksmith shop, two restaurants, a pool room, lodge, two filling stations, a dry-goods store, general store, a post office and the Golden Pond School. The rest of the village was made up of residential dwellings, most of which were well kept; some, even enjoying the few luxuries available and "affordable" of the time.

History has it, Golden Pond got it's name possibly from several sources. Some say that when the sun rose over Jenny Ridge, the water in a large pond that once was located at the foot of the ridge turned to a shimmering gold color. Others say many goldfish swam in the pond at the time Golden Pond was becoming a settlement. And, still some old timers claim a wagon, traveling with a load of gold, turned over on the ridge and a good portion of the gold spilled into the pond. Well, the mystery of which is fact and which is fiction, or if any is fact, has not yet been revealed, maybe never will, but the questionable myth's as to how Golden Pond really acquired it's name still live on and will likely be pondered for generations to come, thanks to the old timers who passed on what had been passed on to them.

Lawton Higgins' black coupe came barreling into the town of Golden Pond that morning carrying himself, Lorene and cousin Jake. The town was a bustle, as usual, as the black coupe, with it's three passengers, cruised into the first filling station. Heads turned as the sleek little automobile came to a halt. Lorene could see Lawton grinning from ear to ear. Lawton sure took pride in driving a good automobile and his '27 Chevy coupe was one of the few new ones in the land between the rivers. Lorene knew Lawton didn't care if the looks were envy, rather than admiration, and most of them were. It just made him feel good to be noticed, whatever the reason. That's the way Lawton was, always wanting to be the center of attention.

Renie's mom Duck Turner, little sister Reba, and Renie, standing in front of Lawton's '27 Chevy Coupe; 1928.

Now, between the rivers, most everybody knew everybody else. Actually, most everybody was akin to everybody else, but once in a while, a "furriner," as local folks sometimes called people that lived outside the bounds of the rivers, migrated to the land between the rivers. It wasn't a settled fact as from where Heck Tate migrated, nor why he settled on the old Harrington place. Some said he inherited the small place, since old man Harrington wasn't known to have any kin living around him; others said, Heck Tate was working the old place on the shares for some of Old Man Harrington's people that lived somewhere East. Seems nobody knew for sure, and likely, nobody cared as long a he minded his own business and didn't bother nobody. Rumor was, that Heck Tate could turn out some pretty good "shine." Now, Lawton, far as he knew, had never sampled any of Heck Tate's "goods". Fact was, Lawton didn't even know where he lived or what he looked like, but he had heard of him, heard enough to know he had moved some extra barrels and copper tubing, along with his other plunder, when he migrated between the rivers.

"Hey Randal," Lawton yelled, hanging his head out of the car window. One of the three men standing in front of the filling station threw up his hand and came toward the car. Lorene didn't know any of the three, but it was obvious Lawton did and obvious also, they knew him.

"What's up Lawt," he asked, spitting an amber stream into the dirt as he approached the car. Before Lawton could answer, one of the two men Randal left standing in front of the filling station, yelled, "Hey Lawt, got any "shine" in that fine ride your drivin'?" He then threw back his head and laughed.

"Naw Roy, can't say as I have, but I can get you some real fast!" Lawton called back, laughing with him.

"May have t' take you up on that pretty soon," the one called Roy answered, while the other man nodded his head in agreement, a wide grin on his face.

"Well, you boys know where t' find me. I can get you some of the best in the country." Both men laughed, gave Lawton a wave, then went back to their conversation.

"I'm lookin' for a feller named Heck Tate. Somebody said he lived down on the ridge an might have some used 'quipment he might wanta sell, know him?" Lawton asked Randal.

"Yeh, reckon I've seed m' a time er two. Lives on the old Harrington place. Know where that is?" the middle aged man said as he peering in the car at Lawton's passengers, tipping his hat at Lorene.

"Yep, reckon I do. Thought that's who I was thinkin' he was, but thought I'd better make sure before I messed around and ran up on the wrong feller. I'm much obliged, an' you can fill er' up if you've got the time," Lawton answered, as he started the car to pull closer to the gas pump.

"Gotta lot more time n' I have money, for a fact," Randal answered, starting the pump. "I sure appreciate your business. Seems everbody's talkin' these days bout money gettin' scarce, they call it a depression we're bout to come into. They say, "Well, if money gets any more scarce with me, I'd call it starving t' death," Randal said, again spitting an amber stream on the ground.

Lawton laughed and answered, "Yeah, I've been hearin' a little talk of hard times hittin' the country, but I don't study much about it, myself, guess we'll know what they're talkin' about when it gets here. Figure when that happens, that'll be time enough to start worrin'."

Lawton paid Randal the three dollars for the gas and they left the filling station and continued East down Main Street, which was actually Highway 68. Lorene would have loved to have gone into the dry-goods store, but she didn't dare say so, for she knew Lawton was in a hurry and she couldn't have bought anything, anyway. They were having to use all the money they had to get the still back in working condition, and there was the uncertainty as to the outcome of Lawton's trial, soon to come. They cruised on through the small town, left the business section and entered the residential area. Lorene admired the neat houses, some even had sidewalks leading out to the street. As they continued moving East, she thought to herself, "this would be a nice place to live."

"Lawton, what's depression?" Lorene asked, as they left the town behind.

"Aw, I don't really know, just probably a bunch of politicians in Washington stirrin' up stuff, wantin' to raise taxes. It ain't nothin' you need to be worrin' your pretty lil' head about," he answered, laying his arm around the seat and hugging her close to him. With that, Lorene dismissed the subject of depression.

Lawton picked up speed once they were out of Golden Pond and they traveled some, seven miles before they turned off the main road onto a narrow, rutted lane. The lane was so narrow in fact, dried weeds along the side of the road brushed the car. A dense woods was to the right and Lorene noticed wagon tracks leading into the woods in several different places. A shallow creek ran along the other side of the narrow lane, edging a small bottom which held several rows of corn stubble jutting out of the half frozen, ground. They wound up hill on the bumpy, rutted lane for over a mile. The thin layer of creek gravel beneath the tires of the coupe was barely enough to keep them from miring down. Finally, they came to a clearing on which set a tiny, weather boarded shack. A thin trail of smoke was coming from it's rickety chimney. As they drew nearer, three coon hounds, four beagles and a big gray dog that looked like a long-haired wolf, came charging from under the front porch toward the car! They were making a terrible racket and showing their teeth! The hair on the big gray dog, which was leading the pack, was standing straight up! Lorene thought, without a doubt, it was the most fierce looking animal she had ever seen!

"Lord a mercy, Lawton. I'd be afraid to get out," Lorene was saying, when a tall skinny man emerged from the back of the house. He was wearing a greasy overall jacket and bib overalls, which were tucked in muddy gum boots. His hair and beard were long and as greasy as his clothes and a streak of amber was trailing down one side of the graying beard. Lorene thought he was about the ugliest man she had ever laid eyes on.

"Shet yer mouths!" he said, trying to yell above the incessant yelps and growls of the pack of dogs. "Git outta here! Now git outta here rat now and shet that racket up!"

"Got ya a bunch of dogs, there," Lawton called from the lowered car window, in that friendly voice of his that indicated he never saw a stranger.

"Yeah, reckon I do; do a lil' huntin' myself. You lookin' fer somebody?" the man asked, ambling closer to the car. Lorene noticed he had a sizable cud of tobacco in his jaw and his beady eyes glared at them through graying, bushy brows.

"Lookin' for Heck Tate," Lawton answered, starting to open the car door.

"Well, yer lookin' at m', an' who might you be?" was his stern reply.

"I'm Lawton Higgins from over at Oak Ridge. A feller name of Chambers said you might have some still equipment for sale," Lawton said, pushing the car door open a little.

"That's a might fine vehicle yer a drivin' fer a moonshiner in these parts," the lanky man said, spitting a stream to the ground, then wiping his mouth with the back of his hand. He then narrowed his eyes and let them peer slowly over the car till he spied Lorene and Jake. When he noticed Lorene's, very obvious, impregnated condition, he glanced back at Lawton, whose hand was still on the door handle and said. "Well, reckon yer who ye say ye ar. Git out. Yer woman can go up to the house with Annie Belle, thar," Heck Tate motioned toward the shack with his head, then added, "Feller can't be too kerful these days, revenuers ever whar, ye know. Common', I'll show ye th' stuff."

Lorene glanced toward the house, trying to decide weather to get out or stay put. The dogs were peering from under the porch where they had retreated when their master called them down. They had hushed their annoying yelps, but low, throaty growls could still be heard. A young girl was standing in the half-open doorway across the porch. Lawton caught Lorene's eye as he started to shut the car door and motioned for her to go on. Slowly, she scrambled across the seat and got out behind Jake, who was also eyeing the dogs as he stood holding the car door for her.

"Reckon Lawton don't care if we get eat alive," she mumbled to Jake as she stood up.

Jake grunted, then shut the door and started to join Lawton and Heck Tate. His eyes on the dogs.

"Them thar dawgs ain't a goin' a bother ye non, gal. Go on in th house whar it's warm," Heck Tate addressed Lorene, sensing her obvious fear.

The young girl standing in the door opened it wider for her to enter as Lorene approached the porch. The dogs held their peace, but kept looking from Lorene to the three men headed in the direction of a run down barn about thirty yards from the house.

The inside of the tiny house was as bad as the outside, but a fire burned in a small fireplace in the far end of the room, casting a cherry glow on the sparse plunder. The wide boards that made up the floor, creaked as Lorene walked over them toward one of the two cane bottom chairs before the fireplace, that the girl had motioned her to as she closed the door. Annie Belle followed her, sat on the other chair and immediately, they began a conversation. She was Heck Tate's only child, and her mother had died two years ago of a stomach complaint, just before they moved between the rivers from the Eastern part of the state, Lorene learned as their conversation progressed. It seemed to Lorene that Annie Belle was hungry to talk to someone and she could understand why. Lorene couldn't help but notice how pretty her small face was and how long and thick the amber colored hair was that fell over her tiny shoulders.

"We don't get much company, out here," she was saying as she smoothed her faded, feed sack dress across her lap.

"Well, it's sure an out of the way place, back here," Lorene answered, examining the young girl more closely. Her eyes were dark, shaded with heavy lashes; her nose straight and small. She had high cheek bones and a broad smile that revealed even, white teeth. Her small hands were chaffed and Lorene noticed her shoes were so worn, her socks were exposed at the toes.

"I see yer in the family way," Annie Belle said timidly, glancing at Lorene's swollen mid-drift.

"Due any day now," Lorene answered, placing her hands on the front of her coat. "Lawton, that's my husband, says it's a boy; the way he goes on about it, reckon it'd better be," Lorene answered, laughing. "This is my first."

Annie Belle laughed too, nodded and said, "I kinda figured it was. Yer man's shore got a mighty fine car."

"Yeh, he has," Lorene said shaking her head and smiling. "Says he has to have one he can depend on, in his business an all."

Annie Belle nodded her head in understanding.

Lorene and Annie Belle chatted until the men returned from the barn. Lorene liked the young girl and had enjoyed their short visit, in fact, she even promised to come again sometime.

Well, Lawton had found the parts he needed for the still and he and Jake loaded as much as they could in the back of the car. They would have to make another trip for the rest that afternoon. On the way home, Lawton allowed Heck Tate had charged so much for the parts, that he and Jake would have to make another delivery in a few days to refurbish his funds. He and Jake thought it was very amusing that old man Tate took them for revenuers. Lorene, reminded then that he had not told Lawton to get out until he noticed her in the car, and, that old man Tate would have likely sicked the pack of dogs on them before the engine stopped, had it not been for her.

Lorene kept thinking about the pretty, young girl as they sped along the countryside back to Oak Ridge. Annie Belle had told her she was fourteen, the same age Jewel, her younger sister, would have been had she lived. Lorene wondered if Jewel would have been kind and quiet like Annie Belle. She really thought she would, for even though she was only five when she died of influenza, Lorene remembered her mama saying more times than one, she was glad Jewel was meek and not a spitfire like Lorene. She would declare, she just didn't think she could handle another one like Lorene. Lorene, being barely seven at the time Jewel died remembered very few details of the sad event. She did remember they were living with Uncle Joe and Aunt Rhodie at the time. Lorene, being only sixteen months older than Jewel, remembered mostly the good times they had when Jewel became big enough to be her playmate. She remembered, too, how sad she was that she had lost her dearest playmate and how it hurt her to see her mama and daddy mourn so, over losing Jewel. It was several years after they had laid her to rest in the small Turner cemetery, that Lorene asked Aunt Rhodie to tell her more about her sisters illness and death.

It seems Jewel had started a fever one cold day in December of 1920, the year she was five. The flu had been raging in the community for some time; in fact, everyone in Lorene's family had it, except Uncle Joe and Aunt Rhodie. Although Aunt Rhodie had no children of her own, she was very good at tending the sick. Jewel was the last to come down with the flu. Aunt Rhodie had put her to bed and piled on her as many extra quilts as she could find, same as she had done for everyone else when they first came down with it. But, Jewel's fever did not begin to break after a day or two as did, the others. Duck, under the instruction of Aunt Rhodie, bathed her in alcohol, while Aunt Rhodie brewed some "sassafras tea" for her to sip, but nothing seemed to break the high fever that racked Jewel's small body. Ed, even made a trip to the store at Turkey Creek for quinine, of which they administered the prescribed dosage of a spoonful, but still, the fever lingered. On the third day of her illness, Jewel developed a terrible cough. She was so weak after a coughing spell, she could not raise her head from the pillow. Aunt Rhodie sent Ed to a bootleggers place about two miles down the holler for some whiskey, and from there back to the store at Turkey Creek for some rock candy. Aunt Rhodie mixed some of the candy with some of the whiskey and gave her a few sips to try and relieve her cough. Jewel slept most of that night, but come morning she was even weaker and the fever higher. By nightfall, her breathing had become so labored she could be heard across the room. It was then, Ed went for old Dr. Rollins who practiced at Golden Pond. It was not a long trip on horseback, but by the time Ed returned with the doctor, little Jewel was weaker still. Her breathing had become very rasping and shallow. The doctor examined her, then, with some difficulty, gave her some liquid calomel, a "purgative", mixed with some type of cough suppressant. He then instructed Duck and aunt Rhodie bathe her, once more in alcohol, at which time, he also motioned for Ed to follow him into the kitchen. The look on Ed's face when he and the doctor came back into the room, told Duck and Aunt Rhodie, too, without a word being uttered, the seriousness of Jewel's condition. Aunt Rhodie left the room to tend the other children, while the doctor, once more examined Jewel. Ed came and stood with Duck beside the bed.

When Dr. Rollins finished the examination he sighed, raised from the side of the bed on which he was setting and said, "The calomel should make her rest the night and will work her out good by morning. I'll come back in the morning to see how she is. I would stay on, but I have another call to make tonight."

Ed nodded his head and followed the doctor to the door, took some money from his pocket and handed it to him. He expressed his appreciation for Dr. Rollins making the trip, then closed the door behind him. Once again, he walked back to Jewel's bedside, where Duck was standing with silent tears streaming down her face. Ed put his arm around her shoulder, and gently guided her to the long window near the foot of the bed. Silently, they both stared into the winter darkness. A few flakes of snow could be seen from the glow of the coal oil lamp sitting on the small table before the window.

"I know the doctor thinks she's awful sick," Duck mumbled, almost as though she were talking to herself.

"Yes, he said she's a real sick little girl, but I think she'll be alright. We can't lose faith,' Ed said softly, trying to comfort his saddened wife.

Duck ignored Ed's gesture, but, turned slowly from the window and returned to Jewel's bedside. Ed went to the fireplace and laid more wood on the slowly dying embers, then, sat on the rocking chair and stared into the small, flickering, flames that were beginning to crackle around the logs. Neither spoke another word, and Duck did as she had done for the last three nights. She sat there at her tiny daughters side, bathing her forehead; trying every. little bit to get sips of water down her, and even crawling onto the bed beside her to cradle her in he arms when her breathing would become so labored, as she would try to cough. At times, silent tears would spill down Duck's cheeks and onto the covers as she silently prayed and nursed her small daughter, but none of her earnest efforts held the healing power for which all were praying. Around three o'clock in the morning, Jewel began to moan and thrash about in the bed, pulling her legs up against her stomach and shaking violently. Duck held her tightly in her arms trying to still the rage of the apparent convulsion Jewel was having. After several minutes Jewel became still. Duck cradled her lifeless form closer against her, seemingly trying to pour strength from herself into her gravely ill child. This effort was to no avail, for in the shadowy gray dawn of that wintry day, little Jewel Turner, lying there on her mothers breast, drew her last breath at the tender age of five, answering the call of Jesus when he said, "Suffer the little children to come unto me and forbid them not; for such is the kingdom of God." The rest of the household was awakened by the piercing cries of a mother in anguish..

Burning tears were welling in Lorene's eyes as the car came to a halt at the edge of the back porch on their return from Golden Pond. Lawton and Jake had talked back and forth across Lorene all the way, but she heard little of what they were saying, for something about the gentle young girl, Annie Belle, had brought little Jewel and Aunt Rhodie's story back, so vividly to her mind. It was as though she were there in Aunt Rhodie's house, experiencing it all over again.

Lorene crawled out of the car as quickly as she could behind Jake and ran into the house. The burning tears, now streaming down her face, spilled onto her coat. She had not wanted Lawton to see her crying, for he would be concerned and she did not, at that moment, feel like explaining. Entering the kitchen, she glanced around quickly and was thankful no one was in the house. She went, quickly, from the kitchen, through the stayin' room and into the front room she and Lawton occupied. She flung herself across the double bed, letting the silent tears emerge into sobs, seemingly, trying to drain the sad memory from her thoughts.

After some time, she sat up on the edge of the bed. She had been so distraught when she got out of the car earlier, she barely heard Lawton say he and Jake would be taking the parts up to the new still site, then heading back to Heck Tate's for the remainder. While sitting, she noticed a sharp twinge in the small of her back, but passed it off as being the result of the bumpy ride up the rutted, narrow lane to Heck Tate's. She lay down on her side, still able to see out the long window near the bed. The side yard rolled into a small meadow where trees lined the ridge beyond. Patches of the muddy water of the Tennessee River gleamed in the mid-day sunlight through their barren branches. It was only a few miles down the river where Turkey Creek emptied into the mouth of the river, that she and her daddy had spent many a happy afternoon sitting on it's shady bank fishing;.. she, using a limb with the line tied to the end, while her daddy used a cane pole. In the spring Ed had let her help him drill corn in the bottom land near the river, and early in the mornings they would set their fishing poles in the soft mud on the river bank, then, go on with drilling the corn. Lorene remembered being so excited she would just have to check their poles every time around! More often than not, there would be fish on the end of their line, but, sometimes, there would be only an empty hook. Yes, she and her daddy had caught several good messes of fish while drilling corn there in the river bottom in the spring. It seemed the tranquillity of the peaceful country side and thinking of by gone days with her daddy, brought comfort which diminished, somewhat, the sadness she had earlier felt. Still lying there, once more, her mind returned to childhood days. This time back to the year they moved in to the big house, with Uncle Joe and Aunt Rhodie, which was located in the Fenton School community.

Pleasant weather had given way to hot sultry days, that summer, allowing Ed, Grandpa Birdsong and Lorene's tobacco to thrive. Necessary tasks, including chopping weeds, pulling off the suckers and getting rid of the pesky, worms which ate holes in the large valuable leaves, along with favorable weather, were all part of producing a good tobacco crop.

Lorene went to the patch with Ed as much as her mama could spare her. She couldn't master the long handle of the hoe to chop weeds very well, but she did help by pulling some of the smaller weeds by hand. She did not mind the blistering sun, nor the gum from the tobacco leaves that left her hair and arms sticky. She wasn't tall enough to reach the suckers, since they grew high on the plant, but there was one job she was able to do, which took almost more willpower than she was able to muster. That job was getting rid of the worms on the lower leaves. She thought for a fact she was going to have to disappoint her daddy in this case, for try hard as she might, she just could not bring herself to reach onto the leaf, grab the long ugly creature and pinch it's head off, as her daddy and Grandpa Birdsong did. Ed assured her several times, the worms were not harmful to humans, but that did not give her the courage to touch one. To Lorene they were monsters! Why, some were as long and big around as her fore finger!

Now, Lorene surely did not want to disappoint her daddy, and, besides, she was afraid if she wasn't helpful, she would have to go to the house. So, after some thinking and searching around, she devised her own method of killing the pesky worms in their tobacco patch. She found a short forked stick, which she would, very carefully reach into the plant, and knock the hideous creatures off the leaf, then with her heel, grind them on the packed ground between the rows, until they were squashed. Her daddy would walk by chuckling, pat her on the head, and say, "You got him, didn't you Renie?" Lorene would grin and nod her head, ready to move, with stick in hand, on to the next plant.

In August, the tobacco was cut, put on sticks then housed. The only part of this process Lorene was big enough to be of help, was drag the long, slim tobacco sticks down the rows as Grandpa Birdsong and Ed cut the tall plants with a long, wicked looking knife. She would watch as they lifted the plants, one at a time, over the sharp spike they had fitted over one end of the stick. The sharp spike slit a hole through the stalk, and the plant was then, slid to the bottom of the stalk. This process was repeated until the stick held five or six stalks of tobacco. When all of the plants were cut and spiked, they were left in the patch for a few days to wilt and start curing. The number of days they were left in the patch usually depended on the weather. It was not advisable for the tobacco to endure a hard rain.

Housing the sticks of tobacco in the barn was the next step. First, they had to be loaded onto the buckboard, then taken to the barn and lifted, with the help of two or three other men, to the top of the barn where they were placed on tiers so the curing process could continue. Lorene could only sit in the buckboard and hold the reigns of the mules to keep them in place and watch as the men proceeded with the hard work. Yes, the job of housing tobacco, certainly, was for strong men who knew what they were doing. The tobacco would hang there until it was dry and brown, then, one rainy day when it came "in case," which meant, flexible enough to handle without breaking the leaves, as Ed explained, they would take it down, one stick at a time, just as they had put it on the tiers and put it in a large pile, then pull the leaves off the stalk, then, tie them up in "hands." This process was called "stripping". When every leaf had been stripped from the last stalk, the tobacco would, then, be ready to take to market.

"Phew, daddy, it sure takes a long time and a lot of hard work to make tobacco!" Lorene declared, as she and her daddy started to the house that afternoon.

Ed chuckled, tousled her hair and answered, "it sure does, Renie gal and you've been mighty fine help in that tobacco path, as good a help as anybody could want helping make tobacco."

Well, Lorene would soon be separated from her daddy the most of her waking hours for the next six months, except on Saturday and Sunday. She was to start school the last of August. She had voiced her opinion to her daddy, as to what she thought about being away from home all day every day. She had already made up her mind she wasn't going to like it, but, her daddy told her it was very important for her to get schooling. He also told her he expected her to behave herself properly, pay attention to the teacher and learn all she could from the text books. He went on to explain to her, he did not have the opportunity to go to school, very much, when he was young, and he had always regretted not having a good education. Lorene didn't understand why her daddy thought he had to be any smarter. She thought her daddy was the smartest person she knew. Well, if going to school and learning from the text books was what her daddy wanted, she guessed she'd just have to go and make the most of it. She knew it wasn't going to be easy, being shut up in the school house all day away from mama and the youngens, and most of all, her daddy.

It was almost five miles to Fenton School from where they lived, there on Grandpa Birdsong's place. No other children, of school age lived within three miles of them, so Lorene, would have to walk alone. Her mama was very disturbed that she would have to make the long trip alone. Well, the answer to a prayer came shortly before time for school to start....Ed's great uncle Joe and Aunt Rhodie asked Ed, Duck and the youngens to move in with them. They were both in failing health and needed help on their farm. Uncle Joe and Aunt Rhodie's three hundred acre farm was a couple of miles closer to the Fenton school, and there were several school age children living near by, with which, Lorene could walk. Ed would have to ride one of Uncle Joe's mules back over to Grandpa Birdsong's place to help strip out the tobacco, but he was more than willing to do so.

Chapter Four:

Virgil

D uck, who by now was well rounded out with her fourth child, was experiencing mixed emotions about moving from Grandpa Birdsong's to Uncle Joe and Aunt Rhodie's. It was hard to leave her own folks, however, she would be glad to be closer to Fenton School, and she had loved Uncle Joe and Aunt Rhodie ever since she had been in Ed's family. Having no children of their own, they had always treated Ed and his family special. Well, that was just how it would have to be, Duck pondered in her mind, for, the move would be beneficial to both her family and to Uncle Joe and Aunt Rhodie.

Uncle Joe and Aunt Rhodie had a big, old, rambling house. There were two large rooms on one side, a dog trot, then three more rooms of the same size on the other. Uncle Joe and Aunt Rhodie had been staying in the side with the two rooms for some time now. That left the other three rooms for Ed, Duck and the children to occupy. The house set high off the ground in the front and had a long porch with five steps leading up, which was shaded by several of the many oak and maple trees that grew in the sloping yard. The branch, which ran from the spring where Uncle Joe and Aunt Rhodie carried their drinking water, would make a fine place for Lorene and Jewel to wade and dip up tadpoles, for it ran near the house and Duck could watch them from the kitchen window. Across the lane that led to the barn was a large orchard with a variety of apple, peach and plum trees. A tall "damson" tree stood behind the smoke house, and numerous clumps of wild blackberry bushes rambled in a small field beyond the hen house. A black walnut, along with several hickory trees, grew in the edge of the woods beyond the barn. Lorene loved to gather nuts with her daddy in the fall. They would peel away the green outside shell and let them dry before they put them in grass, sacks or buckets to store inside the house. On cold winter nights they would crack them on the hearth before a cherry fire, then dig the savory kernels from the hull. Uncle Joe had four bee hives at the edge of the back yard. It fascinated Lorene to watch, at a safe distance of course, the bees swarm in and out of the hives as they hummed busily, weaving their cone's and transforming nectar from various blossoms, into the sweet, pungent honey.

Uncle Joe had kept his team of mules and one jersey cow, which, for the last three years, he fed from corn and hay he received as his share for renting his ground to a neighbor. He did not like that set-up very well, which was one of the reasons he wanted Ed and his family to move in with them. He felt confident Ed would take better care of his ground and farm machinery than the outsiders had. Aunt Rhodie felt, too, that as fast as Duck was having youngens, she could be of help with them and they in turn would be company and a blessing to her.

Ed and Uncle Joe set out, the day before they moved, to make a survey of what needed immediate attention around the place. The stock barn was in need of some repair, along with the hog pen behind the barn. Uncle Joe had not raised hogs in the last three years, but had been getting meat from a neighbor in exchange for corn. He really missed having hog killings, and thought the neighbor had some pigs they could purchase to get a new start in the swine business. There was corn in the crib and a sizable amount of loose hay in the loft. Ed figured it would be enough to last the winter.

In addition to the cleared land that was already being used to raise corn and hay for the stock, Ed thought the small creek bottom beyond the pasture field would make a good place for a sugar cane crop to use for making sorghum molasses the next fall. That pleased Uncle Joe, for the little bottom had laid dormant for several years. He declared also, there was nothing better than sorghum molasses poured over hot biscuits and butter! Ed agreed whole heartily.

A small wooded hillside, beyond the bottom, grew a lot of good pine, oak and walnut trees. Uncle Joe gave Ed permission to cut and sell some of the timber as payment for the hogs, and another cow. Uncle Joe said, with all the youngens, it was a settled fact they were going to need another cow. Money from the timber would also be used for any other supplies needed to get the old place back in good repair. A cedar thicket that stood beyond the barn would provide posts for repairing fences, yet leave plenty to sell if the need arose for more cash. Uncle Joe had kept most of his farming machinery, but some repair would have to be done on the corn planter and the rake. Ed noticed some of the mule's harness needed a strap or fastener here and there, but nothing major. These were all jobs he could do this winter. Uncle Joe had made commented that he and Ed would go take a look at the pigs and find another good milk cow, first thing, after Ed and his family were settled in.

Grandma Birdsong had given Duck an extra bed, complete with straw tick, feather bed and bolster pillow. Lorene and Jewel would have the middle room all to themselves. Lorene knew that would take some getting used to, for she and Jewel had always slept in the same room as their parents and Shaw. Ed had told them he was counting on them to act like big girls, and he gave Lorene the responsibility of making Jewel feel safe, because she was the oldest and it was her place to set the example. Because daddy wanted her to do it, that was what Lorene would try to do. Shaw would have new sleeping quarters, too. The three quarter bed Lorene and Jewel had previously occupied would be put in the corner of the stayin' room, across from Ed and Duck's big bed. After all, it wouldn't be long until the new baby would be needing Shaw's spot in bed with his parents.

It didn't take long for Lorene and Jewel to get used to their new sleeping quarters. Lorene had to admit she was glad there was a full moon that first week in their new home. With it's light streaming through the two long windows of the big room, it made it easier to adapt to the strange surroundings. Now as for little brother Shaw, well, his getting used to the new sleeping quarters was another story. Every morning, Ed and Duck awoke with Shaw either between them, at the foot of their bed, atop the covers or simply hanging on the edge of the bed in front of his daddy. Finally, after three weeks of interrupted sleep for Ed, Duck and Shaw, it was decided little Shaw was going to have to bed with the girls, at least one of them. Well, after two nights of Shaw in bed with Lorene and Jewel, Lorene took it upon herself to ask Aunt Rhodie if she could start sleeping in the extra bed in the stayin' room, where she and Uncle Joe slept. Aunt Rhodie readily agreed. So, Lorene left Shaw as Jewel's nighttime responsibility, which seemed to work out very well, for little Shaw really didn't mind with whom he slept, just as long as he didn't have to sleep alone. Lorene liked sleeping in the big bed in Uncle Joe and Aunt Rhodie's room. Aunt Rhodie would tell her stories about her childhood, as well as funny stories about Ed when he was a little boy. Once she finished the stories, she would tuck the covers tightly around Lorene and kiss her on the forehead. Lorene would snuggle into the deep, soft feather bed and soon be asleep.

There were fireplaces in the front and middle rooms of the side which Lorene and her family occupied. A flu in the kitchen provided the ventilation for their wood cook stove. Wide wooden planks, polished to a luster from many years of use, made the floors. The ceilings were high and there were two long windows in each room. Their meager plunder looked lost in the three big rooms, but Aunt Rhodie had left behind a dresser, a sideboard and a large rocking chair which helped fill the space, so Duck did not complain or ask for more. Yes, all in all, even considering the adjustments of living with someone else, the Turners were very happy, even quiet thrilled with their new home!

Classes began in Fenton School in late August and would be in session until February, with the exception of days missed due to bad weather. Duck, with Aunt Rhodie's help, had made Lorene several dresses from chicken feed sacks, along with, a couple of petticoat's and three pair of bloomers from sugar sacks, to start off her new school year. It was nothing in Lorene's day to have Gouldaux sugar printed across the front of ones petticoat or shining on the seat of ones bloomers as the girls donned their gaily printed feed sack dresses. Lorene was excited about all her new clothes! It was the most new clothes she had ever had at one time in her whole life. Ed, on his first trip to town after they moved, even bought her a new pair of winter shoes and a dark green, wool coat with matching hood. Aunt Rhodie bought her two pair of cotton stockings, a writing tablet and two pencils. After all this, Lorene was beginning to think school might not be so bad after all.

The Fenton schoolhouse was a one room frame building with two doors in the front and three long windows down each side. There were two outdoor privies out back; one for the boys, the other for the girls. The school yard was wide and spacious, boasting of several elm and hickory trees. A flat area above the front yard served as a baseball diamond and on the same side of the schoolhouse, near the building, was a cistern that supplied drinking water for the children and their one teacher.

Twenty two students would be using the wood and iron desk's that were arranged in several rows facing the chalkboard and the teacher's desk at the far end of the large room. A tall round stove made of tin that set in the center of the room provided their heat during the winter months. Each student brought his or her own lunch, either in a pail or paper bag. Lunches were basically the same: a sandwich of biscuit and middling or ham, a sweet potato, a piece of cake or fried fruit pies. Apples were usually plentiful in the fall, and were a part of most of the student's regular lunch diet. Occasionally, a peppermint stick might be found in the lunch bucket, along with an orange, if it were around Christmas. There was only one dipper for the three gallon water bucket, so for the sake of good personal hygiene, each student had to furnish their own cup. Some were metal folding cups, others had tin cups, while some drank from cups made from a sheet of folded tablet paper. The students ranged in age and size from first graders to eighth graders; the one teacher being responsible for unveiling book knowledge according to the needs of each particular grade.

Well, that first day at Fenton School was an educational one in more ways than book learning for Lorene. When asked about the experiences of her first day at school, she was quick to give her answer. Recess was her favorite time, for they played outside. The four neighbor children she walked to school with were the only ones she knew, but she learned pretty fast, with whom to play, and who to avoid, for she declared, there were some of the meanest boys in Fenton School she had ever seen. The teacher was constantly having to stay on to them to keep them from disrupting the whole class. The older boys kept pulling the younger girls hair and during lunch recess, two of the boys locked Lorene and another little girl in the privy and would not let them out till someone went for the teacher. Lorene came barreling out of the privy, when the teacher finally opened the door, and gave the older boys a piece of her mind, using some choice words she shouldn't. Her unbecoming language and name calling almost caused her to spend the last recess sitting in the hot school room, along with the mischievous boys. In addition to the aforementioned calamities, someone stole one of the pencils Aunt Rhodie had bought her, and one of the smaller boys pushed her down on a rock when they were playing tag, which skinned her knee, getting blood on her dress. Well, as for learning much from the textbooks that first day, she hadn't, but some other lessons she did learn. She learned to put all of her supplies out of sight when she wasn't using them, so as not, to tempt anyone. She learned she had to out-run the boys at playing tag to keep from being pushed down, and to refrain from reprimanding any misbehaving students herself, that responsibility belonged to the teacher. That was Lorene's detailed report of her first day at the Fenton School. Her daddy assured her, as he kissed her goodnight, that things would get better as time went along, and Lorene sure hoped so.

Lorene was awakened by the sound of a door closing. She sat upright in the bed, trying to determine what was going on. Glancing toward the window, she noticed the evening shadows were lengthening fast. "I must have slept the entire afternoon," she thought to herself. She wondered if it was Lawton who came in the back door, returning from old man Tate's with the rest of the parts for the still. She didn't allow it was though, being Saturday he would likely hang around Golden Pond till dark. She climbed from the bed and as she stood a sharp tinge went through her back again, much sharper than the one earlier in the day. She stood still, waiting for the discomfort to diminish. After a few moments it had subsided enough for her to start across the room toward the kitchen. Hearing voices as she went through the stayin' room she knew it was Dora May and Maxine and not Lawton who had awakened her coming in the house. Dora May was starting to fix supper and Maxine bounced to greet Lorene as she entered the kitchen. Lorene played with Maxine for awhile then started helping Dora May finish the supper, still nursing a dull ache along with an occasional sharp pain in the small of her back, but she did not mention it to Dora May. Ma Annie soon came in from the store and Lawton made it home just as Lorene and Dora May were finishing up supper. Soon they all sat down to eat. Lorene only picked at her food, for she was feeling so miserable she just wasn't hungry.

Lawton went to the barn to do up the night work while the women cleaned up the kitchen. Soon after supper Lorene excused herself and retired to lie down, still not mentioning the discomfort she was having in her lower back.

She had not gone to sleep when Lawton came into the room some time later. She did not know if the pain was keeping her awake or the long nap she had that afternoon, or maybe a combination of both. Lawton put some wood on the fire, then sat in one of the rocking chairs before the fireplace to take off his shoes. It was then that Lorene told him of her condition.

"Reckon it's the baby comin'?" Lawton asked, coming over to the bed.

"I don't know, but I don't want to say anything to Ma Annie about it, at least not yet," Lorene answered.

Lawton nodded his head but said, "You know Mammy could deliver this baby as good as Dr. Rollins."

"I know she could but mama wants me to have the doctor and you know we've done settled on that, besides, I don't feel like talking," Lorene said as he lay down beside her.

Well, Lorene got very little rest that night. The ache was so bad during the night that she got up and sat before the fire. Lawton heard her get up and offered his help if there was anything she needed. She told him to get his rest, she was all right, but by daylight she was hurting even worse. The ache and sharp pains were no longer segregated in her lower back, but were beginning to move into the lower part of her stomach. She did not feel like eating breakfast and when Ma Annie came in to see about her, Lorene told her what was going on. Ma Annie felt of Lorene's stomach and confirmed Lawton's question as of the night before; Lorene was starting labor.

Lorene's pains came and went throughout the next day, which was Sunday, but the terrible ache in her back and stomach did not subside. That night she rested even less than the night before. Monday brought sharper and more frequent pains along with the containing ache. Sometimes the pains were so fierce she would cry out. Lawton kept insisting he go for the doctor, but Ma Annie said it was not yet time. Around ten o'clock that night her water broke and the pain became almost unbearable. Lorene sent Lawton for her mama. She knew Ma Annie was giving her good advice as far as getting a baby into the world, but she just needed her mama and she knew her mama would want to be there, too. By nightfall that Monday, Lorene was in such agony that she began loosing consciousness. Duck wanted Lawton to go for Dr. Rollins, but Ma Annie, after examining Lorene, said she was not far enough along for the doctor to come. Well, Duck knew Dr. Rollins was awfully busy since he was the only doctor for miles around, and, she had enough youngens, herself, to know when the time was right, so she dropped the subject, but it was awfully hard to watch her daughter suffer so severely.

The next day, Lorene was in even more torment. With each contraction, which came from two to five minutes apart, she would writhe on the bed, her gown wet from perspiration, then lapse into a state of unconsciousness, yet according to Ma Annie, she was making very little progress, as far as dilating. Finally, Lawton put on his coat and hat, slammed out the door, got in the car and went for Dr. Rollins. The doctor was able to leave with him shortly after Lawton arrived, so they were back to Ma Annie's before noon. The doctor examined Lorene and shook his head, expressed his wonder as to why she was not dilating, and decided to give her quinine to increase the pains in hopes of aiding the dilating. The quinine only added to the intenseness of the contractions. By nightfall that Tuesday, Dr. Rollins told Ma Annie he could not understand why Lorene was having so much difficulty, unless it was because she was so small, while the baby appeared to be rather large. He also confirmed that the baby's head was in the birth canal, and had been for sometime, but, it appeared Lorene's pelvic bones just weren't expanding to allow the completion of birth.

Throughout that night, Lorene suffered, crying out in such agony that her mama had to leave the room. Finally, as dawn grayed on Wednesday, Dr. Rollins made the decision to use forceps to take the baby. At eight o'clock in the morning, little Virgil Higgins finally came into the world, giving his totally exhausted mother the rest her disheveled body so badly needed.

"He's a big fine boy, bet he'll tip the scale at over eight pounds," Lorene vaguely heard Dr. Rollins say as he was wrapping the baby in a blanket. She heard him lower his voice and say something to Lawton, but she could not understand what he said. She was alert enough though, to notice the look on the faces of those around her as the doctor handed the baby to her mama, who in turn, came bringing him around the bed for she and Lawton to see.

"Is...is he all right?" Lorene whispered weakly to Lawton, who had just sat down on the bed beside her. It was when Duck laid the tiny bundle between she and Lawton, that she knew why mama and Ma Annie's faces had held such a strange expression: Little Virgil's misshapen head and distorted facial features were more than Lorene could bear to look upon. What she saw when she viewed her first born was so devastating that she once again lost consciousness.

Days passed before Lorene was strong enough to stand. She was so weak from loss of blood and the days of suffering Ma Annie, Duck and Dora May had to tend the baby. Since the smell of food made her too nauseous to eat, she was not getting enough nourishment for her milk to "come down" so the baby could nurse. Ma Annie made a "sugar-teat", which was a clean, white cloth folded several times to form a narrow rectangle about as long and as big around as one's fore finger. It was soaked in sugar water and put in Virgil's mouth to keep him pacified.

It seemed Virgil cried constantly, even after Lorene's milk became plentiful. He was growing fast and looked healthy enough. His misshapen head was beginning to round out and his little face was getting smooth, but still he cried night and day. Before the end of his first month, Lorene noticed a thick liquid had started to run from his ears. This answered the question of why he cried continuously. He was suffering with earache. Ma Annie administered warmed sweet oil, the same as all other mother's did for children with earache, but it did not seem to give baby Virgil relief for any measurable amount of time, and the fluid kept draining from his ears. Ma Annie tried every home remedy she knew, from the warmed sweet oil, to placing a warm rag over his ears, to blowing smoke in his ears, but none seemed to have any healing and very little comforting effect. Finally, after six weeks of sleepless nights and days of bouncing, rocking and walking the floor with crying Virgil, they all decided it was time to take him to the doctor. Dr. Rollins, after giving Virgil a thorough examination, pronounced him as being a sound healthy baby, except for his ear disorder, which he thought would begin to clear up as he grew older. In the meantime, he prescribed some drops for his ears, along with another kind to give him orally, to help him rest. The drops did help some, but when they wore off, little Virgil would start crying again.

A week following the visit to the doctor, Lawton came home one afternoon announcing he had to appear in Federal Court in Paducah in early April, which was less than two months away. The sheriff had served the papers on Lawton while he was in town. Lorene and Ma Annie were very upset with the news, but they had known this time would come, so all they could do was calm down and make the most of the situation. By this time Lawton had become pretty adamant about the raid, for he had a fairly good idea as to who had snitched on him. He had no proof, therefore he couldn't talk about his feelings, but word had a way of getting around between the rivers when the misfortune of a raid transpired. Snitching was usually done by someone in the same "business", in an attempt to eliminate competition, and since there were several in the moonshinin' business besides himself, it could have been a number of people, but he felt pretty strongly he knew who the "snitcher" was.

Balmy southern breezes had pushed most of winter's chill from the air by early April. The dogwood and red bud trees added a bright splash of color to the maple, oak and walnut trees that were boasting of small green leaves that grew along the roadside as Lorene, Lawton and Ma Annie drove to Paducah, the day of Lawton's trial. Dora May had kept Virgil and was planning for she, Maxine and little Virgil to spend the day with Clara. Lorene could have enjoyed the picturesque country side as they sped along highway sixty eight that spring morning, but the circumstances that prompted the trip were bearing heavy on her mind. She already knew the consequences of Lawton getting caught moonshinin' could mean him spending up to two years in prison. This was not a pleasant reality for any young wife and mother to deal with. She could tell Ma Annie and Lawton were concerned also, but Lawton, not wanting Lorene and Ma Annie to worry, kept trying to reassure them things would work out. Lawton thought he would get by with paying a stout fine and be on his way home, considering this was his first offense.

Well, just before noon that day of the trial, the judge sentenced Lawton Higgins to one year and one day in the federal penitentiary in Marion Illinois. Lorene and Ma Annie went into hysterics right there in the court room and Lawton looked as though he was being sent to the gallows. Lorene had never before seen Lawton look so beaten. She thought he was going to break down when they led him away to be placed in the county jail in Paducah where he was to be lodged until there was a space available in the Federal prison.

Well, they say when a door closes, a window opens and Lorene certainly felt as the door of her young life had closed when the police took Lawton out of the court room. During the time of Lawton's incarceration in Paducah, Pearl and Jewel Lawrence, who lived in Paducah (Jewel being a cousin of Lawton's), got word of their misfortune and went to visit Lawton. Lorene and Ma Annie were at the jail visiting him at the same time, and Pearl and Jewel asked her to stay with them so she and baby Virgil could be near Lawton. Lorene accepted the offer with great gratitude and she and Virgil moved in with them. Lorene and Pearl cooked every day and took hot food to the jail for Lawton, for he had complained that the jail food was not fit for a hog to eat.

In less than a month after his incarceration in the Paducah jail, Lawton learned he was going to have to serve only a total of ninety days for his crime. This time would be spent there in the Paducah jail and he would not have to go to the Federal Prison. Now the end results of his shortened sentence were attributed to several factors. Number one, this was his first offense; number two, a minimal amount of illicit whiskey was found on his premises; number three, he was a model prisoner and last but not least; Ma Annie's ingenuity. She had made some important contacts, scraped up as much money as she could by depleting all of the back room's inventory and cleaning out all of their savings, and in so doing, hired the best defense lawyer in the country, Jack Fisher. It had taken some doing on Ma Annie's part, but her efforts had managed to get Lawton's time cut from the initial sentence of one year and a day in a the Federal Prison to the ninety days he was now serving in the Paducah county jail. Lawton was back to his old self once more, making plans, making promises and looking ahead to the end of his ninety day hitch.

Pearl and Jewel Lawrence were not only helpful in providing lodging for Lorene and baby Virgil in their home, they were instrumental in finding a specialist there in Paducah to examine Virgil. Lorene had prayed so diligently that the specialist could find the problem and provide a cure, but her heart sank the day of Virgil's appointment when the doctor looked at her and shook his head after the examination. What he told her was some of the saddest words Lorene would ever hear in her whole life. He explained to her that the bones in Virgil's ears were severally damaged, likely during birth. Upon questioning Lorene about his birth, and she explaining the whole ordeal, he concluded that the baby's head had laid in the birth canal so long and since her pelvic bones did not expand for such a long time, his head was pressurized to the extent it caused permanent damage to the bones in his ears and he would more than likely be deaf. Lorene's heart sank and a flood of tears over took her as she sat before the doctor holding little Virgil in her arms. She even wished her life and that of her child would just end there and then. She was surely being punished by the Lord for some unforgivable sin of which she knew not what, but the burden was just too much for her to bear.

Well, Lawton did his ninety days, then he and his family came home to Ma Annie's. Little had been done for Virgil, but according to the specialist, all was being done that could be. He had prescribed some new drops which did help some, for Virgil was not crying as much and some of the drainage had stopped, but Lorene knew in her heart and mind that she could not give in to all the doctor had said. Surely there would be a way to help her child. She simply could not believe her child would have no hearing, not until she had exhausted all of the medical avenues that could be pursued in the country at that time.

Chapter Five:

The Courtship

The air was humid. Gray clouds, seemingly heavy with moisture, hung in the western sky. Puffy mounds of thunder heads were pulling away from the darker, lower clouds, piling higher and higher, engulfing the sun and smothering it's rays. The leaves of the maples and oaks that stood in the front yard were beginning to stir and the breeze was a welcome recluse from the July heat. Lorene rocked Virgil in one of the high-back, rocking chairs on the front porch. He had spent most of the morning crying. She had tried to help Dora May with fixing lunch, but wound up spending most of the time walking the floor and bouncing Virgil. After lunch she administered some of the drops the specialist had prescribed and came out on the porch to try and get him to sleep. The drops began to take effect within several minutes, at which time, Lorene could feel little Virgil beginning to relax against her. His crying had stopped and his eyelids were beginning to droop with sleep. He was such a robust, healthy baby, except for the problem with his ears.

Lawton was so proud of little Virgil. He took him places to show him off. He was forever bragging how strong Virgil was, and how much he weighed. He would beam with pride when someone said he resembled Lawton. Lorene had to agree, he did look a lot like his daddy. When Ma Annie brought out Lawton's baby pictures, there was definitely a strong resemblance. Although, Virgil was only six month's of age, he was beginning to display determination and strong will, just like his daddy. Lorene prayed they would enable Virgil to overcome his ear condition, as they had helped his daddy survive polio when he was little. Lawton had lost all the muscles in his left leg from polio, leaving him with a very noticeable limp, but it had not kept him from doing most anything he set his mind to do.

Lorene leaned her head against the back of the chair and let relaxation over take her, also. These last six months of motherhood, especially with little Virgil's ear condition, had taken it's toll on Lorene's nerves. Watching the billowing clouds and enjoying the refreshing breeze on her face as she continued to rock her now sleeping child, she began to think of those care free days of she and Lawton's early acquaintance and courtship.

Lorene had seen Lawton a few times when they were growing up, since they lived in adjoining communities. She guessed that she first came to know the boy with a limp, Lawton Higgins from the Oak Ridge community, while attending one of the Mormon Conferences. Lorene's family were Mormon by faith, as were Lawton's. There were no Mormon churches between the rivers. Since the closest church was in Hopkinsville, some twenty miles away, the Mormon Elders would arrange for conference's to be held two or three times a year in the various communities in the land between the rivers. These conferences were usually held when the weather was favorable, allowing people from the various communities in the land between the rivers to attend. The conferences were similar to the Brusharbor and Protracted meetings of the various Protestant beliefs. Services would be held nightly for approximately two weeks, consisting of worship, study of the Mormon Bible, prayer and baptizing new "Saint's" into the faith. It was during one of these conferences, when Lorene was thirteen, that she was baptized in the Tennessee River by one of the Mormon Elders.

Lorene could remember seeing Lawton and his family during these services. In fact, she had even played with him, along with other children of the congregation, after the services, while they waited for their parents to finish visiting. But, the occasion that brought Lawton and Lorene together on a one on one basis was when Lorene was ten and Lawton was twelve.

That year, Fenton School was, once again, having a "Pie Supper." Now, a pie supper was a fund raising event put on at the beginning of the school term, while the weather was still nice. The young ladies in the community were expected to bring their own, special recipe pie in a fancy decorated box, to be auctioned off to the highest bidder. The proceeds would go for various, necessary, supplies for the school. Actually, a pie supper at a country school would sometimes be more than just a fund raiser. You see, the gentleman who bid the highest not only got the pie, but the young lady who baked the pie was expected to help the young gentleman eat it. It is a known fact that many long term relationships, including marriage, have been the results of these pie suppers sponsored by the various country schools.

This particular pie supper would be a special one for Lorene. It would be special in more way's than Lorene really anticipated. She was excited and calling it a special "Pie Supper," mainly, because, it was the first time she had been given permission to make a pie and take it to her school to be auctioned, just like the older girls. Lorene knew, because she was only ten, she would not have been permitted to enter her pie had not two other young ladies, with whom she went to school been permitted to enter their special pie recipes.

Now, Lorene was well aware that it was customary for the one who baked the pie to eat with whomever bought it, so, she was a little uneasy as to how this would work out. You see, Lorene already had a beau, Sidney Euen Rhodes, and she thought it would be nice if he could buy her pie. She didn't figure Sidney would have the money, though. She thought, surely, her daddy would make the final bid before he would let her share her pie with some unthought-of character she had never seen before. Well, little did Lorene know that the events that unfolded that pie supper night would pave the direction for her entire future. It was doubtful that twelve year old Lawton Higgins had any long term relationship ideas in his head when he made the highest bid on Lorene's chocolate pie, or did he? Yes, the same Lawton Higgins, the boy with the limp, from the Oak Ridge community, bought her pie and, for the sake of courtesy, she ate a piece with him, having no concern one way or the other while she watched him devour the remainder.

Well, after the pie supper event, Lorene went right on sparking Sidney Euen Rhodes, thinking nothing else of the dark-featured cripple boy, who bid the highest dollar on her pie. Sidney, was a tall, thin boy with brown hair and brown eyes. He and his parents lived a short distance from Lorene and she and Sidney saw each other, practically every day. Sidney's mother was good with tending the sick and was called quiet often to various homes in the community. One spring day she and Sidney came to Lorene's house to pick some turnip greens. That was the first time Lorene had been around Sidney's mother, very much, and they racked-up quite a conversation as they picked the turnip greens. Lorene liked her immediately, so, from then on, Mrs. Rhodes and Lorene were good friends. She felt as though Mrs. Rhodes liked and approved of her, which enabled Lorene to feel very much at ease around Sidney's mother. This fact, "un-be-knowance," to Lorene, be a total contrast to the relationship she would experience with her future mother-in-law.

Well, the years went by, and Lorene grew into a right pretty, young lady. She was thin, with dark hair and eyes and plenty of spirit, and she kept on sparking Sidney Rhodes. Why, it seemed just as natural as rain for Lorene to be sparking Sidney. When their schoolmates spoke of one, they spoke of both. It was a known fact, during those years, everyone thought Lorene and Sidney would someday marry. In all honesty, Lorene had thought of the subject a time or two herself, but she hadn't mentioned it to Sidney. It was, just customary, in those days, for a young couple who pleasured each others company for any given length of time, to marry and start a family as soon as they finished school; and school, for most, consisted of an eighth grade education.

So, as for Lorene and Sidney, school and sparking went on as usual, and other pie suppers transpired in the various communities. Lorene entered her special recipe chocolate pie in some of these. Most of the time, if he could scrape up a dollar or two, Sidney bid the highest and shared Lorene's pie. If his pockets were empty at the time of a particular pie supper, she would, either not enter her pie, or her daddy would place the highest bid. So, as one could see, Lorene and Sidney's bond of commitment was pretty concrete.

Now, during Lorene's fourteenth year, two things happened that totally changed the course of her young life. Sidney Rhode's father accepted a job in Colorado Springs, Colorado and immediately moved the family away from the Fenton School community. That move, needless to say, put to an end to Sidney and Lorene's long years of "Puppy Love." Life was very strange for Lorene after Sidney moved. In school, as well as the community, it had been "Lorene and Sidney" or "Sidney and Lorene", among the other kids, but now Sidney was gone. Yes, Lorene missed Sidney, even though, they corresponded, often, by mail.

In the fall of that same year, Fenton School once again had their annual pie supper. Lorene, reluctantly, baked her special recipe, chocolate pie to be auctioned off to the highest bidder. Although her heart was not in the venture, the school did need lumber for mending a portion of the floor, and she felt an obligation to do her part. Well, much too her surprise, the young man, Lawton Higgins, who had bought her first pie some five years earlier, just happened to be the one to place the highest bid that bought her pie, again. This time, they did not sit on the school steps to share her pie, but leaned against the front fender of Lawton's sleek, black, '27 Chevy Coupe. Yes, young Higgins had turned sixteen, learned to drive, and bought a new car, which he drove wherever he chose, without a drivers license....And, it was there, as Lawton, again, devoured the remainder of Lorene's chocolate pie, that he asked permission to drive her home. It was there she accepted, as she tried to suppress her excitement and not give way as being too anxious.

Lorene had never ridden in a car as new and nice as Lawton's Chevy coupe. In fact, he was the only boy at the pie supper with a car. Out of the corner of her eye, she could see the jealousy and envy of every girl at the pie supper when she crawled into Lawton's new automobile. As they started down the lane from the schoolhouse, Lorene couldn't help but wonder how he could afford such a nice car. Naturally, she did not speak her thoughts; neither would she let herself dwell on the answer that kept creeping into her mind. After all, gossip was all she could base her thoughts upon, and besides, daddy always said not to believe a thing you heard nor half of what you saw. She was too excited to let anything interfere with her enjoying this fine ride home, not even the look of concern in her daddy's eyes when he, somewhat reluctantly, gave his permission for Lawton to drive Lorene the short distance to the house.

Lawton had also changed in many other ways since their first meeting. He still had the limp, but had grown much taller. He was slender, yet muscled and his prior boyish, facial features had matured into a strong chin and high forehead. The lock of unruly dark hair still fell into his eyes, occasionally, and he still had a crooked grin, but his bib overalls and work shoes were several sizes larger. Despite the visible limp in his left leg, he carried himself with an air of confidence.

Lawton was, definitely, not at a loss for words as they sped along the dusty lane, the short distance to Lorene's house that pie supper night. He joked and told funny stories about himself and other boys from the Oak Ridge community that kept Lorene laughing all the way home. Yes, Lawton was very easy to be around so, when he let her out at her front yard, she readily told Lawton the ride home had been a very pleasurable one.

Well, that's how Lawton and Lorene's courtship began. As time went on, it was nothing for Lorene to be helping Duck cook or tend the youngens, and hear the sound of Lawton's car coming around the bend as he sped up the lane to pay her a visit. Lawton and Ed got along well, and Duck never insulted Lawton, but she held more of a distance from him. Duck tended to listen to community gossip more than Ed. People talked that Lawton was moonshinin'; they claimed that was how he afforded his fine new car. Sometimes Duck would drop a remark to Lorene, as to the perils which could come to moonshiner families, but Lorene would either ignore her or change the subject. She was too smitten by this somewhat reckless, yet winsome young man, whose Chevy coupe frequently came barreling up the lane in a cloud of dust.

The following months held new excitement and new experiences for Lorene. She and Lawton drove all over the Fenton and Oak Ridge communities, as well as frequent trips to Golden Pond. By spring, "Lawton and Lorene" had become as hot an item as "Lorene and Sidney" had been. Yes, Lorene and Sidney still corresponded, by mail, but her answers to Sidney's letters had become much less frequent. She, quite simply, had difficulty finding the time to write. Well, after a firm conversation from her mother, following four letters from Sidney, each begging her to explain why she had stopped writing, Lorene answered with the truth. She never heard from Sidney again.

Lawton had a friend named Riley Conner, who did not have a steady girl, so Lorene mentioned her close friend Zelphia Joyce to Riley. Riley asked Zelphia out and the four of them spent many pleasurable afternoons cruising the countryside in Lawton's coupe. Since the coupe only had one seat, someone had to sit double, so Lawton and Riley took turns driving, allowing the girls to sit on their fellow's lap. "Those were fun and carefree times," Lorene mused as she sat there rocking little Virgil. Little did she know, in another year she would be experiencing the measure of responsibility with which she was now wrestling. "I sometimes think I showed more sense at ten than I did at fifteen," she thought.

Now, it was confirmed to Lorene, long before they married, that Lawton was making moonshine, but that did not sway her thinking, nor change her feelings for Lawton. When she approached him with the subject, he laughed it off and informed her that more than half of the men between the rivers made moonshine, which she knew was true. He assured her, she shouldn't worry her pretty little head over the matter; after all, if he were depending on farming for a living, he would be hauling her around in the buckboard, instead of a new car. Well, Lorene pondered the situation concerning Lawton's means of livelihood, along with the hints of warning her mama kept dropping every time she had the chance. However, Lawton's theory and winning ways simply overruled. The September of her fifteenth year, and Lawton's seventeenth year, they had a small wedding in his mother's home.

Lorene chuckled to herself as she remembered that first dress Lawton bought for her to wear to their wedding. It was, of all colors from which to choose, black. She was so appalled at the thoughts of wearing a black dress to her own wedding that he took it back to the dry goods store. He, then, bought her a beautiful satin dress, wine in color. The tightly fitting, brocade bodice had a high collar and long fitted sleeves. The skirt was ankle length and straight. It was, truly, a beautiful garment. Her daddy declared, she was bound to be the prettiest bride he had ever seen, next to her mama, of course.

Ma Annie's house was filled with family and friends, of both the bride and groom, who came for the ceremony. Ma Annie, Duck, Dora May, and Clara had prepared a fine wedding supper which was served immediately following the ceremony. Food and drink abounded, freely. Everyone was in high spirits as they participated in the celebration. As the evening went on, there was much "conjolling" of the newly weds, along with the extending of well wishes.

The wedding guest's started leaving a little after sundown. Ed, Duck and the youngens were the last to leave. Duck brushed Lorene's cheek with a kiss, then started loading the youngens in the buckboard, but Ed lagged behind, momentarily, and called Lorene aside. He reached out to her and, at arms length, took her by the shoulders, and looked down at her. She saw tears in his eyes. He then pulled her close in a hug and said, "I'll sure miss you Renie..." His sentence trailed off as though he was going to say more, but, instead, he kissed her on the forehead, released her, then went to the buckboard, climbed on the seat beside her mama and snapped the reins. Tears flowed down Lorene's cheeks as she stood at the edge of the porch and waved good-bye until the buckboard faded into the twilight.

Well, Lorene and Lawton spent their honeymoon at the same place they would be living for the next eight years...in Ma Annie's house. Would Lorene ever remember that first night of their honeymoon! Ma Annie, whom by now had been a widow for several

Newlyweds pose with the '27 Chevy. Photo taken in 1928.

years, was seeing a man in Calloway County. He had attended the wedding, after which, they had arranged a short visit to his daughter's home. So, they left shortly after the wedding supper, allowing the newly weds some time to themselves. Well, sometime around midnight, Lorene and Lawton were awakened by a terrifying racket coming from the front of the house! It was the sounds of bells ringing, accompanied by numerous "hoops and hollers!" Needless to say, Lorene was scared to death at first, but, Lawton just calmly, climbed out of bed and began putting on his pants.

"Lord, Lawton what is goin' on?" Lorene asked terrified.

"Don't be afraid, we're just gettin' shivareed," he answered, heading for the front door, "just get up get your clothes on."

When Lorene finally got dressed and made her way to the front of the house, she saw the front yard was filled with people! After her eyes adjusted to the dim light of the half-dozen or so lanterns, she was able to recognize most of the intruders. They were young people of the community, most of which, had attended the wedding. Zelphia and several other girls came running to the porch, where Lorene stood, barefooted, watching the "going's on". They were excited and called for Lorene to join them. She left the porch, bare feet and all, to watch as several of the young men and boys put Lawton astride a rail, then head for the creek just below the barn. The girls and Lorene joined the chase! After being thoroughly dunked in the creek, he, dripping wet and laughing good naturally, crawled up the creek bank where Lorene stood, laughing also. He put his arm around her and they, along with the rest of crowd, gathered in the house. It was now Lorene's turn for participation in the shivaree. Her part in the initiation into martial bliss was to do the Charleston before each member of the shivareeing party, including her dripping wet groom. Well, eating, drinking and merry making were then carried on till daylight! It was a settled fact in the land between the rivers, in those days, that no bride and groom were properly wedded until they were "shivareed"!

"Yes, those were carefree days," Lorene mumbled to herself, and sat there on the porch watching the dark clouds, which by now had thickened. The rumble of thunder could be heard in the distance and the gentle breeze of earlier, had become a sharp wind, bending the boughs of the trees and rustling the chin high stalks of corn in the river bottom.

She rose from the chair carefully, so as not to arouse the sleeping Virgil, who was still cradled in her arms. She made her way into the dimness of the large stayin' room and proceeded to the adjoining room she and Lawton and little Virgil occupied. After laying him gently in his crib, she stood watching his steady breathing, which revealed, he was at peace, for the moment, from the constant discomfort he experienced when he was awake. How she wished for a doctor somewhere that could cure the malady from which her precious child suffered.

Lightening was making jagged streaks across the darkened sky and the thunder rolled with a tumultuous sound, in contrast to the low rumble, of moments ago. Lorene stood at the open front door, peering through the screen as large drops of rain began to fall on the dusty path that led across the front yard to the lane. The welcome scent of the coming rain filled the atmosphere, bringing to her mind a humorous story her mother told many times when Lorene was growing up.

Duck would begin, "It was a hot, dry day around the middle of July. We hadn't had a rain for the entire month; crops were a dryin' up, the river was gettin' low and Grandpa Birdsong and your daddy were beginnin' to worry we were in for a bad drought. You were a little over three months old at the time and we were livin' in the same little log cabin where you were born. Right after dinner I'd got you to sleep and put you in the middle of the feather bed so you wouldn't fall off, for you were beginnin' to roll around. Your daddy had gone with Grandpa Birdsong to talk to a man that lived a piece down the river, about some cedar trees to cut for fence posts, an' I had come in the house from gettin' the washin' off the clothes line, for it was a Monday and Monday is always washday...an' there was a cloud comin' up. I didn't want the clothes to get wet, so I brought the clothes in the door and put them on the eaten' table which set in front of the window. By that time it was a thunderin' up close and the wind was beginning to get up a right smart, an' you could smell the rain in the air as it begin to blow through the door. It was dark as night in the cabin as I went across the room, to see about you there on the bed. Well, Lord a'mercy! What I saw when I looked toward that bed just about caused me to have a heart attack! Laying there beside you on that feather bed was the biggest snake I had ever seen in my life! Well, I started a' screamin' and just froze in my tracks!!! I didn't know what in the world to do! I couldn't see good enough t' tell what kind of snake it was, but I don't know if I'd acted any different if I'd been able t' tell, for I'd always been scared to death of snakes, anyway. All I could think of was getting you off that bed and away from that snake, but I was so scared I couldn't move anything, 'cept my mouth to scream. Well, they say the good Lord looks out for his own and I do reckon he was lookin' out for you that day, and I reckon me a hollerin' at the top of my lungs might have helped out some too, for next thing I knew, that snake went slithering' off the side of the bed. Lord, I didn't take time to look where he went from there; I just ran to the bed, fast as I could, snatched you up and ran to the door. That's when I realized I couldn't take you outside for it was stormin', an' the wind was blowin' the rain across the front porch an' in the door, but I didn't think there was room in that cabin for me an' you an' that snake, too. I just didn't know what to do. Finally, with you still in my arms, I climbed up on the eaten' table. Well, by this time you were a'screemin', too. It was lightenin' and thunderin' and rainin' something fierce an I just huddled there on the table and cried along with you. Well, that's where your daddy found us when he got home. I wasn't about to get off that table 'till I knew, for sure, that snake wasn't there in the cabin, anywhere. Well, your daddy pretended to look around the room to please me. He said the snake was long gone, or that I'd probably scared it to death. And do you know, your daddy just laughed about the whole thing? He did; said it was likely a harmless chicken snake. It made me plum mad. No snake's harmless in my book. They may not be poison, but that don't keep a person whose scared to death of them, like myself, from hav-ing a stroke or a heart attack!" Then Duck would giggle and say, "Your daddy did search the room before we went to bed, though. To tell the truth, I don't think he relished the thought of goin' to bed with a snake any more than I did, even if it was a harmless chicken snake, as he called it. Well, we didn't find no snake, but we found a crack, between the logs, behind the headboard of the bed, and we figured that's where the snake got in, an' we hoped that's where he got back out. Your daddy made some putty out of mud and filled the crack, but it was some time before I could put you on the bed, or go to bed myself without looking under and behind the bed, and even through the covers. Lord have mercy, I still have nightmares about that snake!"

Rain was, now, coming down in torrents, as Lorene gazed through the storm toward the river. The lower limbs of the trees were almost touching the ground under the pressure of the rain and heavy wind, which was also, blowing the rain across the front porch and through the screened door. She feared the loud bolts of thunder would waken Virgil, so she closed the heavy, wooden door which made the room dark as night. She then, made her way across the room to light the coal oil lamp that set on the mantel. Soot began blowing from the open grate and onto the hearth and floor around her. Small twigs and dried blades of grass, followed by a tiny chimney sweep, fell on the hearth, it's wings and Downy feathers fluttering, as it rolled from the partial nest, while it's frantic chirps called out at Lorene's feet. She stared at the tiny bird whose eyes were still closed and it's legs not yet strong enough for it to stand. She could not imagine what to do with it. She couldn't throw it out into the storm, nor could she put it back up the chimney to be blown out again, so, she went to the kitchen and found an empty match box. Returning to the fireplace, she retrieved what she could of the twigs and dried grass, placed them in the box and put the poor little creature in, also. She slid the cover of the box almost closed, just leaving a crack for air and amazingly, once inside the covered box, the little chimney sweep hushed it's pitiful cheeps. When the thunderstorm subsided, she put it back up the chimney, on one of the rocks that protruded just above the firebox, in hopes it's mother would soon find it.

Soon after the thunderstorm was over, Lawton came driving up the lane. He had been to Hopkinsville, delivering a batch to a customer. Lorene hushed him as he bounded through the kitchen door, for Virgil was still sleeping.

"I've got some good news," he whispered, as he took off his hat and hung it on the peg beside the kitchen door. "I ran into a fellow in Hopkinsville who gave me the name of an ear specialist there in Hopkinsville, and I went and talked to him and he set us an appointment to bring Virgil for an examination, next Wednesday. He thinks he might can help him; here, I've got his card," he said, taking the card from his shirt pocket. "It says Wednesday, July twenty sixth at one o'clock. They say he's one of the best in the country!"

"Oh Lawton! Praise the Lord! Maybe he's just the one that can fix Virgil's ears," Lorene whispered excitedly, clasping her hands together.

Chapter Six:

Doris

Spring once more returned to the land between the rivers. Lorene and Lawton were still living with Ma Annie, despite the arguments they had concerning the matter. Lorene wanted so much to have a home of their own, but Lawton would evade the issue or use some excuse to keep from looking for a place. Little Virgil still suffered with the malady of his ears. Lorene and Lawton had taken him to specialists in Hopkinsville, Owensboro and Evansville in hopes they would hear some encouraging words as to the solution of his condition. To their dismay, every doctor had given them the same answer as the specialist in Paducah. Virgil would likely be deaf for his entire life. The infections were less frequent, therefore, allowing him to be free of most of the terrible pain he experienced the first several months of his life. He was a robust little fellow and he caught on fast, despite his handicap. He was spoiled, of course, demanding constant attention, and of course, he knew nothing of how to act without constant attention, for he had suffered so much of the time. It seemed, someone was having to bounce, rock or entertain him day and night. Lorene would not give up hope that a doctor, somewhere down the road, would discover a way to correct Virgil's problem. After all, Lorene knew from talk in the community that times were changing. There were modern conveniences such as indoor plumbing, electricity and faster running automobiles becoming prevalent, especially in the urban areas. There was talk of flying machines, something Lorene had her reservations about. She felt if the good Lord intended for people to fly, he would have given them wings. Most of these changes did not affect many people between the rivers. However, Lawton was talking about buying a new and faster running car. Lorene thought they needed a home of their own more than a new car. And, she was quick to express her opinion. You see, she and Ma Annie were having several spats about she and Lawton finding a place of their own. Of course, Ma Annie wanted Lawton right there in her clutches and Lorene knew she always would, but Lorene had set her mind on them having a place of their own and she was determined to have that dream until it actually took place.

The farmers between the rivers were once again stirring the soil, preparing it to receive the seeds of the various crops they planned to harvest come fall. Same as times past, gardens were being planted to provide fresh vegetables for the table and refill the jars emptied during the past winter. The old Rhode Island red hen was setting on a dozen or more brown eggs in the hen house and their jersey cow was due to calve any day. Yes, the bringing forth of new life and the awakening of the things of nature that went dormant in the fall to endure winter's harshness, was now depicting the miracle of spring.

Lawton and Jake were still making moonshine, and thriving. Lawton had hired a couple of boys from the neighboring community to help Jake at the still, while he made runs and drummed up new business. Lawton wasn't a man to dress up in "finery", but he did set aside his bib overalls for "everday" wear and began wearing matching khaki pants and shirts, which were becoming the fad dress for most men living between the rivers. Lawton always said he'd have to be hog tied before he would wear a tie, but he would put on his khaki's, make padding of an old towel, wrap it around his left leg where polio had deteriorated the muscles, then put a spit shine on the lace-up, high-top boots he always wore and feel as dressed up as any man in a "serge" suit and neck tie. He knew for sure, he was a lot more comfortable, too.

Lorene was still spending a lot of time watching and waiting for Lawton to return from a delivery, either out of state or the neighboring towns. To Lorene, it seemed he was gone practically all the time.

Now, the Prohibition Law, which prohibited the making or dispensing of any alcoholic beverage, legal or illegal, had been in effect since the early Twenties. Prohibition was still a major issue throughout the whole United States, but the Jones Law, which was passed in 1929 and provided fines up to ten thousand dollars or five years in prison for violators of the Prohibition Law, put the squeeze on many of the large brewing companies throughout the country. Since the main stream of enforcement of the Prohibition and Jones Laws was centered in the larger urban areas, this caused the demand for the making of illicit whiskey in the remote, rural areas throughout the country, including the land between the rivers, to skyrocket. Lawton, as well others in the moonshine business, were keeping busy day and night trying to meet the demand. Now Lawton, as well as the others, was not free of being discovered and prosecuted. Not by any means, for revenuers were a constant threat unless one was on the good side of the local law. It was imperative for a man in the "business" to watch his back at every turn.

While Lawton was making "runs," Jake and the boys Lawton had hired to man the still, in order to meet demand, were having to cut the aging process of the brew shorter than necessary to get the proper color of choice "shine." In order to reach the reddish tint most customers desired, Lawton gave Jake and the boys permission to add a little bead oil to the brew in the early stages of aging. Of course, the customers never knew this. This artificial coloring did nothing to the taste and, after all, the brew was still near eighty proof, and carried a suitable "wallop".

Lorene was forever hoping Lawton would find a legal occupation, and Lawton was sympathetic with her earnest feelings, but it seemed nothing she said could make him change their livelihood, not even the busting of their still late one night that May. Seeing as to how Jake and the boys were the ones at the still, Jake didn't mention that it was Lawton's still. He took the wrap thinking he would spend only a few days in the county jail in Paducah as Lawton had the year before, but to his surprise, seeing as to how this was his second offense, he didn't get off the hook so easily. Jake spent a year and a day in the Federal Penitentiary in Alabama. Of course, Lawton paid him well for his trouble and promised him his place in the "business" would still be waiting when he got out. Well, Jake wasn't the only one Lawton paid well to take the wrap for him down through the years. That was one of the luxuries of which the man in the driver's seat could boast.

Spring days rolled on into June that year, and after the raid things settled back into the normal pace, if one could call Lawton and Lorene's pace normal. Crops were in the ground, the days were getting longer and hotter and Lorene was beginning to notice she wasn't feeling well, some days. She didn't convey her feelings to anyone, but by the second week of July she was experiencing some nausea, especially in the mornings. One morning, in particular, when she entered the kitchen, the aroma of the middling Ma Annie was taking from the skillet was so strong she had to flee to the back yard and vomit. The next morning she wasn't quite as ill, but during the day she would have weak spells and when she got little Virgil down for his morning nap, she laid down with him. Dora May was the first to notice her malady, and confronted Lorene when she and Virgil got up from their nap a few days later.

"I guess it's just the heat or some sort of stomach complaint," was Lorene's reply to Dora May's questions.

"I don't think it is the heat or just a stomach complaint," Dora May answered shaking her head. "Sounds to me like your in the family way again."

"Oh, Lord have mercy, no! I can't be in the family way. I just can't be!" Lorene blurted out, hysterically. "Why, I'm still nursing Virgil, and I can't go through having another baby, and with Virgil's ears like they are. Another one might have the same problem. There is no way I can be having another baby!"

"You've been sleeping with your husband, haven't you?" Dora May asked.

"Well, yes, but..." Lorene stammered, her face becoming flushed as she fought back tears.

"Well, you've had one youngen, and you know what caused that, don't you, so?" Dora May continued

"Yes, but...but...Oh Lord, what'll Lawton say? What'll Ma Annie say? Oh Lord, I wish I could just die," Lorene "boo-hooed."

"Aw Lorene, don't take it so hard," Dora May said, trying to soothe the pitiful girl. "Lawton will just laugh and say maybe this one will be another fine boy and as for Mammy, well, she'll fuss... no, she'll rave, but there's nothing can be done about it if you are, so worrying and fretting won't change a thing."

"Oh, Lord Dora May, take Virgil, I'm gonna throw up," Lorene gasped, shoving Virgil into Dora May's arms then running for the back door.

Well, Dora May's diagnosis and Lorene's worst fears were being confirmed more and more as the long days of summer dragged on. She was sick every day, leaving her thin as a rail with her eyes sunk back in her head, and her emotional state was totally chaotic. She was so distraught, in spite of the understanding she received from Lawton, that she prayed to die. Her physical and mental state were so frail that Dora May and Maxine did most of the caring for Virgil, who was, by the end of the summer, learning to walk. Yes, Ma Annie did rave when she found out she was to be a grandmother again, but after a few days she calmed into a despondent attitude and only shook her head and smirked at Lorene when they were in each others presence. Lorene tried to ignore her for the sake of her own sanity. But, it was hard to do, for Ma Annie began hounding her about weaning Virgil. She declared it would stunt the baby if she didn't quit nursing Virgil. Lorene tried, but Virgil's constant crying kept getting the best of her and invariably she would break down and let him nurse. She tried to hide it from Ma Annie, but this effort was not very successful. There wasn't much went on in Ma Annie's household that she didn't know about.

The hazy days of summer gave way to cooler crisp mornings filled with vibrant colors of red, yellow and rust as fall pushed it's way into the land between the rivers. Lorene was still experiencing nausea every day. Her nerves, however, had calmed somewhat since she had resigned herself to the fact that she was going to have another baby, like it or not. If Ma Annie would just quit hounding her about weaning Virgil, things would be a lot more peaceful for Lorene.

Lorene was beginning to show by Thanksgiving, at which time, Ma Annie put on a large feast for the family. Dora May, Maxine, Clara and Hiram and their daughter Gelena, who lived just across the creek from Ma Annie's house, along with, Buina and her family who lived in Harden, all gathered in for the Thanksgiving meal. Now, Ma Annie was a good cook, no mistaking that. She could cook some of the best fried chicken that ever graced one's palate. That Thanksgiving, it so happened, Ma Annie's fine, fried chicken was the main item on the menu. The contents of the dinner table were dried beans, green beans, butter beans, mashed potatoes, candid yams, corn, turnips, turnip greens, dressed eggs, a large platter of fried country ham, complete with "red-eye" gravy, accompanied by hot biscuits, corn bread and a mold of fresh churned butter. There were jars of pickled beets, cucumber pickles, sweet and dill, along with sweet and hot relish. Buttermilk, sweet milk, and coffee, not to mention a jug of Lawton's "finest" brew, awaited consumption on the sideboard, along with, a three layered sorghum molasses cake, a bowl of fruit salad, a coconut cake and three chocolate pies.

Everyone was gathered around the long table at their designated spots, ready for Ma Annie to bring her heaping platter of fried chicken, to be placed in the center of the table. As she approached the group, carrying the savory, perfectly, browned chicken, she hushed the children, bowed her head and gave a quite lengthy thanks for the bounty before them. Then, she took the fork that was laying on the edge of the platter and began putting a piece of the steaming chicken parts on her children's plate. Clara got a thigh, Dora May, the back, Buina, a leg and Lawton was given the meaty, succulent breast. This ritual, of giving each of her children the piece Ma Annie wanted them to have, had been carried out since the children were small. As for Lorene's sentiments on the subject, she thought the whole thing was just right tacky, especially since they were now adults and others were present. Her daddy always said company was to be served first. Ma Annie then placed the platter of remaining fried chicken in center of the table for the rest to partake.

Thanksgiving gave way to Christmas, which dawned clear and cold. Lorene could have enjoyed watching Virgil's excitement as he discovered the many surprises under the tree much more, had she not been so plagued with the morning sickness. Of course, there were toys of all kinds, from a red wagon and a tricycle, to a toy train, trucks and cars, all to accelerate Virgil's confusion and excitement. Lawton and Ma Annie had barred no expense in making Virgil's second Christmas grand. "After all," Ma Annie said, "He's big enough now to really get up in the air about all of the toys!"

Mid January brought bitter cold and a heavy snow fall. The snow came down for three days and nights. High winds drifted the snow five feet high in some places, making the roads impassable. It was a major chore for Lawton to get to the barn to tend the stock and keep all the fires going in the house. Each morning, shoveling a path to both the wood shed and the barn was necessary, for the continuing snow during the night covered the path shoveled out the day before. Since there was little or no traffic, Ma Annie did not open the store for several days. With everyone having to be cooped up in the house, after the third day, tempers were short and cabin fever, especially for Lawton, had set in. He made up his mind that third night, snow or no snow, he was going to find a way to go to Golden Pond. Lorene had made the decision to busy herself. Ma Annie had a Singer, treadle sewing machine setting in the corner, next to the fireplace in the stayin' room, and Lorene decided to put the sewing skills she had previously learned from her mama into practice. It delighted Ma Annie and Dora May when Lorene told them she would start sewing them, along with little Maxine, some aprons, petticoats, bloomers and dresses, if they would furnish the material. They dug through trunks, dresser drawers and closets until they found printed, chicken feed sacks, a piece of plaid gingham and a yard or so of calico, which was enough to get Lorene started. Lorene dived into her new project with enthusiasm, for it helped take her mind off the morning sickness and the ever present fear of this baby having Virgil's malady. Lorene spent as much time as she could sitting at the old Singer sewing machine, treadling away as she produced garments for all the ladies in the house, including herself, and a good job of the sewing she did!....Ma Annie and Dora May were both amazed and pleased with the splendid job Lorene did on the garments. They were also glad to see the sparkle return to Lorene's eyes and a little color back in her cheeks. Ma Annie allowed, tho, a lot of the reason Lorene was feeling and looking better, was because she had finally weaned Virgil. She still declared that the baby Lorene was carrying would be stunted because she had waited so long to do so.

One sunshiny afternoon in early March Lorene and Dora May were sitting on the edge of the back porch, just enjoying the sunshine and talking, mostly about Virgil's handicap. During the run of conversation Lorene told Dora May about having typhoid fever when she was twelve. She could remember, very well, the terrible time she endured. The symptoms started with a head-ache and fever. She became so sick to her stomach, she could not eat, and red whelps broke out on her stomach. As the days went by, despite the doctoring of her mama and Aunt Rhodie and Grandma Birdsong, her condition grew worse and worse. Ed finally went to Cadiz for Doctor Rollins. He diagnosed her as having typhoid fever and told Ed and Duck her condition was very serious, and that typhoid fever was also very contagious. He explained that Lorene should be isolated from the other children and that family members who cared for her should use alcohol to wash their hands and scalding water to wash dishes and any clothes or bed clothes with which Lorene had come in contact. Dr. Rollins left a bottle of medicine which was the worst tasting medicine Lorene had ever tasted in her whole life. It tasted so bad, in fact, she refused to take it. Her stomach was so sensitive much of the time she would throw it back up, however, Dr. Rollins said it was imperative that she have the medication or she would have to be taken to the hospital. Lorene tried to swallow the horrible liquid, but there were times she had to be held down and force fed from a spoon. By the third week of her bout with typhoid fever, Lorene had lost almost all of her hair, along with her finger and toe nails. Due to the fever having been so high for so many days, in addition to her inability to take any measurable amount of nourishment, she was so weak she could hardly raise up from the bed. Lorene remembered it was weeks before she was able to run and play or tend the youngens.

She also remembered, shortly before she came down with the typhoid fever, that she had confronted Aunt Rhodie about the details of her Jewel's death from influenza when she was five. Lorene had always wondered if her mama hadn't wished it were she that died instead of Jewel, for Aunt Rhodie had explained that the morning Jewel died, while cradled in Duck's, arms that everyone else in the house was awakened with Duck screaming, "Why her, Lord? Why her?"

Tears were rolling down Lorene's cheeks when she finished telling her story to Dora May there on the sun-warmed back porch.

"Aw, Lorene," Dora May said patting Lorene's shoulder, "I don't think what your mama was screamin' that mornin' Jewel died had a thing in the world to do with you. She was likely in such pain and sadness, she meant, why did it have to be one of her children. She probably thought, "why couldn't it have been some little child who had no mama to love it."

Lorene managed a grin and said, "Mama finally tied an asafetida ball around my neck, under my clothes, when I was finally able to go to school after my spell of Typhoid fever. She told me to take it out and chew on it ever now and then, but the smell was bad enough, an even though lots of the kids at school wore one, I was getting big enough to be embarrassed."

"Aw, I never did believe them things kept away diseases," Dora May said, laughing. "The smell might keep puny people at a distance. Why, I always thought eaten' plenty of

Lawton and Lorene, holding Virgil and Doris, 1932.

onions would do more good. There was a little boy at Oak Ridge that carried onions in his overall pockets all the time, an' ate them just like apples. He smelled to high heaven, but come to think of it, he wasn't sick much."

Thin, low clouds parted enough to expose a full moon, at eleven o'clock, on that night of March twenty eighth. The fierce, west wind that whistled around the corners of Ma Annie's rambling old house, rattled the window panes, and mingled with the piercing cries of little Doris Higgins, following a sharp slap on the buttocks by her grandmother and deliverer, Ma Annie.

"It's a little girl!" Ma Annie announced, holding the tiny, trembling form, high in the lamp light, for the exhausted Lorene and the smiling papa, to see. "And ain't she a pretty little thing?"

And pretty she was. Lorene was able to enjoy Doris during her early infancy, for the delivery was a breeze compared to the agony she suffered with Virgil. In contrast to the eight pounds plus of Virgil, Doris weighed less than seven. Of course, Lorene had to stay in bed for nine days, but when Doris was brought to her side to nurse, she seemed to be a calm, happy baby, in contrast to little fretful, suffering Virgil. Doris thrived and seemed healthy, but she was tiny. Her frame was small, yet she was filling out nicely. It was a settled fact, she would not become a stocky, robust, baby like Virgil. Of course, Ma Annie was quick to place the blame for Doris' size on Lorene for not weaning Virgil soon enough, but Lorene learned to tune her out. Lorene didn't deny, it likely did contribute to Doris' size. However, she did what she felt she had to do, and since Doris seemed healthy enough, she could live with her decision.

The seasons came and went. Virgil and Doris thrived. There was still no improvement in Virgil's ear condition, other than fewer bouts with infection. Doris, on the other hand, had perfect hearing and was now talking and walking, doing all of the normal things of a typical three year old. She was still petite, but had plenty of meat on her tiny bones. She did, however, experience several bouts of throat and ear infections.

Now, Lawton went right on with the making of moonshine, long after Congress repealed the Prohibition and Jones laws, and Jake, who was out of prison was back in his old position, faithful as ever. Although, the entire nation was experiencing The Great Depression, it affected the moonshiners between the rivers very little, other than making the purchase of sugar difficult at times. It seemed people were still consuming alcoholic beverages, depression or no depression.

President Franklin Delanor Roosevelt was already putting into practice many of the promises he had made in his inaugural speech. He promised to bring the nation out of the terrible economic state in which it was suffering. He promised jobs for the unemployed and aide to farmers. By the late '30s, it seemed apparent he was following through with his promises and his statements for the average man, the "unforgotten man' as he stated, and some government aide was being passed on to the farmers of the area, for they had been hard hit by the Depression. But, Washington, the White House and President Roosevelt were a far piece from those in the moonshine business between the rivers, therefore, Lorene gave little thought to the messages sent out over the air waves as they were brought into Ma Annie's stayin' room, by means of the console, battery operated radio. Lawton, however, listened pretty attentively to the news daily. When Lorene would complain, because she liked to listen to music, he explained he was out in the world and needed to keep up with what was going on.

Ma Annie, whose store business had declined somewhat, for less money was in circulation among farm families in the communities, decided to close the store, making for more time for her to be in the house, which was now, too small for three families, for sure. Some days Lorene thought she would pull out her hair. More than ever, did she approach Lawton about finding them a place of their own. Lawton did promise her he would ask around about places for sale, which was more encouragement than she had gotten in the past.

Lawton and Lorene were still making periodic trips, with Virgil, to the specialist in Hopkinsville. On one occasion they took Doris, who had come down with another bout of sore throat and earache. The specialist, Dr. White, suggested that removing Virgil's tonsils might be of some benefit to his hearing, and he knew, for a fact, it would eliminate a lot of the throat and ear infections Doris was having. Well, after considerable discussion Lawton and Lorene decided to let Dr. White extract both Virgil and Doris' tonsils, in addition to Lawton's, also. Yes, Lawton had suffered throat and ear infections, periodically, since Virgil was born and he figured, what would work for the kids, would work for him too. So, Lorene and Ma Annie checked Lawton, Virgil and Doris into the hospital at Hopkinsville and Dr. White did a tonsillectomy on them all the same day. Well, needless to say, the patient who took the longest to recover and required the most attention was not Virgil or Doris. The tonsillectomy could be deemed as being successful in eliminating many of the infections, but it did nothing as far as improving Virgil's hearing.

Visits to Dr. White became less frequent as time passed. Each time they went

Doris and Virgil Higgins, August 4, 1935.

for Virgil's check up, they hoped for a breakthrough, which they did not receive. The year he was five they did not receive any encouragement as to a solution to his handicap but, Dr. White gave them, in depth, information concerning the Kentucky School for the Deaf in Danville. At first, Lorene refused to listen with any interest, as Dr. White conversed with them. Finally, as he continued, in depth, as to Virgil's condition, it began to dawn on Lorene that she was going to have to stop living on hopes that a breakthrough might come before Virgil was old enough to take care of himself. Dr. White was trying to help her see she could not rely on something that hadn't yet been discovered in the medical world. Yes, Virgil was able to speak a few legible words, but as hard as it was for Lorene to consent to the fact he could not hear. He was nearing school age and Lorene knew he must get an education, but she could not bear the thought of him being sent all of the way across the state. She and Lawton had hashed and re-hashed the situation and they finally decided, contrary to the advice of Dr. White, they would try sending him to the local public school before sending him to Danville. However, the year he turned six, Lorene could not bring herself to send him to the Oak Ridge school. She felt, due to his handicap, it would be too hard on him to adjust and compete with other children. She consoled herself that she would hold him out one more year. "Maybe he will be more ready in one more year," she thought. "Maybe we'll both be ready."

Chapter Seven:

Golden Pond

By the year 1930 many changes were beginning to take place. The country, under the leadership of President Roosevelt, was finally seeing a light at the end of the tunnel of the Great Depression. Factories, once again, had machines humming and people back at their jobs, just as the President had promised. Farmers were receiving Government aide for a new beginning in the industry, along with new hope in corn, grain and tobacco prices being on the rise. The President's "Good Neighbor" policy was paving the way for exports of raw materials, manufactured products and farm products to grace the shores of foreign soil. A new light was being shed on the critical banking industry. New banks were springing up across the country, and deposits were being made in banks, once insolvent, creating money now available for lending. "Happy days are here again," the Democratic campaign song, was being sung once again through out the country!

The large brewing companies of the Prohibition and Depression days, as well as new plants, in places such as Chicago and New York, were now doing a thriving business. This renewed outpour of liquor, however, had not hampered Lawton Higgins' moonshine business any, or at least not much. He and Jake were still turning out a good size quantity of some of the best quality "brew" of their time. Lawton would beam with pride when complimented on his fine moonshine, rare back and relate the old saying, "practice makes perfect!"

Lorene and the children were now going with Lawton to make deliveries, quite often. On one such occasion that Spring, Lawton loaded up the car, a '34 Studebaker four door sedan, tan in color (this being the fourth car he'd bought since they had married), and headed out for Paris, Tennessee. It was the rainy season, and flooding was common between the rivers. The forecast for that particular day, was for more rain by afternoon, with heavy flooding, possible.

Now, there was a large creek, just a few miles across the Tennessee state line, that was long over due for repair. Lawton had crossed this bridge many times and knew the heavy rain from the night before could have flooded the creek, road and creek bottoms, so he inquired of some truckers coming from Paris as they passed through Golden Pond, as to the condition of the bridge. They informed him the water was very high, with the bottoms flooded, but they had not flooded the road. Lorene had reservations about starting for Paris that morning, but Lawton assured her, since the sun was out and the rain wasn't due to start before noon, they would have plenty of time to make the trip safely. Well, Lorene consented and off they went, kids, moonshine and all.

Sure enough, the sun stayed out and there was no rain in sight as they sped along the winding road to Paris, Tennessee. The creek, which proposed a hazard to their travel, was very full of muddy, swirling water and the bridge creaked and groaned as they crossed, but they reached the opposite shore safely. It was a beautiful morning for the drive and Lorene and the children were enjoying the trip very much. Lawton even indulged them with a hamburger and a coke in a small restaurant on the outskirts of Paris.

Lawton made his delivery to an abandoned warehouse on the west side of the city and soon they were on their way home. As they were leaving the city Lawton pulled up in front of a small drug store and told Lorene and the children to wait, that he'd be right back. A few moments, much to their surprise, Lawton came to the car with four ice cream cones! It seemed they had no more than left the outskirts of the city, when, out of nowhere, a storm cloud rolled in and rain started coming down in sheets. It was such a blinding rain that Lawton pulled off on the side of the road and waited until it let up. Meanwhile, Lorene was worrying about the bridge near the state line. Well, to their relief, when they resumed their journey home and neared the large creek, the bridge was still intact, but the swift muddy water was, now, swirling just inches beneath them as they crossed. The bottom land on either side of the road was swollen and muddy water overflowed the road in places. Lorene held her breath as they proceeded across the bridge and through the muddy water swiftly running across the low spots in the road. She was relieved when the car eased out of the water and began climbing the steep hill just a few yards past the bridge. But, what they saw when they looked back was a sight frightening enough to make even the blackest sinner see that a higher power had a hand in getting them across safely. The bridge, which they had crossed only moments ago, was beginning to sway as it was being loosened from its trestles by the swirling, angry waters of the swollen creek! Virgil and Doris were frozen, eyes wide and mouths open as they viewed the sight on their knees looking out the back window of the car!

"Lord have mercy, Lawton! We just made it in time," Lorene whispered, breathing a heavy sigh of relief.

"Damned if we didn't," Lawton replied. Then he grinned and said, "I've always been told, though, an inch is as good as a mile!" He then jerked the Studebaker in second gear and they roared on over the hill.

Lorene just shook her head and silently gave thanks to God for His intervention.

Well, it seems Lorene soon forgot the perils of that stormy day in the early spring, for a few weeks later, Lawton again, loaded the Studebaker to make a delivery to Murray. This time there was a total of one hundred and ten gallons of choice "brew" in the trunk and back seat, which left no room for the children, but he insisted Lorene go along. He had designated Ma Annie to keep the children, and if Lawton wanted Ma Annie to do something, she'd drop all plans to do so. The children did not mind staying behind that particular day, for it was the day for the Huxter truck. The Huxter truck was a General Merchandise store on wheels. The driver and owner had everything from tonics, groceries, candy and sewing notions, to small tools, bib overalls and numerous sundry items. So, Virgil and Doris knew they would not miss out on a treat by staying with Ma Annie that day.

Lawton turned the Studebaker off the narrow lane leaving Ma Annie's house, onto the highway. Now, this was a bright sunshiny day and as he and Lorene sped along they were thoroughly enjoying the ride, thinking how nice it was to get out without the children once in awhile. They were just cruising along when, all of a sudden, they spotted a car coming behind them at a fast rate of speed! It was only seconds before it dawned on Lawton to whom the other car belonged...it was the law! Now, the '34 Studebaker wasn't the fastest running car Lawton ever owned in his lifetime, but, that day it did come awful close. Instantly, Lawton mashed the gas petal to the floor! All eight cylinders opened up in a flood of response to his command. The squalling of all four tires screamed, along with the roar of the motor, and in seconds no evidence was left of the tan Studebaker except, flying gravel, the smell of burned rubber, and a cloud of smoke!

"Hang on baby, you're in for a ride!" Lawton laughed and yelled at Lorene who sat stiff as a board, bracing herself with her palms flat against the dashboard.

"You're not thinkin' of out runnin' ttth...them are you?" Lorene yelled in a shaky voice, her eyes not leaving the road.

"Why, hell yes, I am! You think I'm gonna let them catch me with a hundred and ten gallons of moonshine in this car?" Lawton yelled back as they "fled" down the road. "Bout time I blowed the soot out of this ol' gal, anyway. Now you just hang on and be quiet, I gotta keep my mind on what I'm doin' here."

Lorene turned in the seat when they reached a long stretch in the road, only to see the pursuers in the distance. By now their red light was flashing and their sirens roaring. She glanced at the speedometer; they were doing eighty miles an hour! Glancing back out the front windshield she saw the toll station looming a short distance ahead of them. The next thing she knew they were barreling through the toll station, still doing eighty miles an hour! After they whizzed through, the attendant jumped out of the booth and started waving his arms in the air, holding, what Lorene thought, looked like a pistol. He jumped back into the booth with the speed of a ball being shot out of a cannon as the police car came to a screeching halt at the booth. A short distance beyond the toll station was a bridge and the law, who after squalling out of the toll station, was now gaining ground. Lawton glanced in the rear view mirror, let out an oath through clinched teeth and stomped the accelerator once more! The Studebaker was up to ninety miles an hour by the time they started across the bridge. A sharp curb just beyond the bridge enabled the law to lose sight of the Studebaker. Shortly beyond the curb, the road forked, each fork turning immediately into another sharp curb. Lawton veered to the left onto Highway 90, which led to Murray. When he left the curb and started down a straight stretch, he glanced in the rear view window and no sight of the law was behind them. He did not ease up on the gas until he was satisfied he had lost them. The law, obviously, thought Lawton was on his way to Paducah, for it was evident they turned off on Highway 68. Lawton finally slowed down a little, but his excitement was still high.

"Hot damn! I knew this ol' gal had it in her! Did you know she was doin' ninety miles an hour when we went over that bridge? Man, she's a runner ain't she? You alright Renie, honey?"

"Well, what do you think?" Lorene exploded! "I thought I was scared the other day when we almost got washed away in that flood, but right now my heart's beaten' so fast, I don't know if it ever will slow down. This is the last time I'll ever make a run with you, Lawton Higgins. You hear me, the last time! You may not care to get yourself killed, but I ain't quiet ready to die yet, and if the good Lord lets me get back home in one piece, I'll guarantee you one thing, you'll not catch me flying across the country with the law on my tail like I'm some kind of criminal again! Now, does that tell you if I'm alright or not, Lawton Higgins!"

But, she did. Yes, Lorene, along with the kids, did make several more trips with Lawton. That chase did, however, prompt Lorene to do one thing. She let Lawton's sister Clara teach her to drive, and it did cut down on the times she went with Lawton, for after getting her driver's license she didn't have to stay at home as much, and making a "run" with him wasn't her only way to go places. But it seemed Lawton liked having someone along with him and when Jake and the boys had to man the still, she and the children would go along, occasionally.

As time went on, Virgil's condition stayed, basically, the same. He would get very frustrated, at times, which made him hard to deal with. For example, one morning in early spring, he became so mad over Ma Annie trying to discipline him, he picked up a pet kitten and threw it in the fire, in the new heating stove Ma Annie had bought to replace the fireplace she had closed in the stayin' room. Well, Ma Annie quickly retrieved the kitten from the flames and, except for a few miner burns on it's feet and a few

Lorene's dream home, Golden Pond, Kentucky.

singed places on it's fur, it was alright. Virgil was so sorry for what he had done that nothing would do him but to help Ma Annie apply ointment to the kitten's feet. In the days to follow, he was very attentive to the kitten as it healed. Lorene still held to her dream of owning their own home, for she felt having so many bosses was adding to Virgil's frustration of being unable to communicate normally.

In late June, that same year, something happened that made Lorene's long years of dreaming come true. That sunshiny morning Lorene had walked the short distance to the mail box to purchase a stamp from the mail carrier. Mr. Forshee had been their mail carrier for as long as Lorene had lived at Ma Annie's and, he always conversed with any of the family who happened to be at the mailbox. In the run of conversation that day Lorene met him for a stamp, he commented that he would not be carrying the mail much longer. He went on to say, when he got a buyer for his house, which was on the outskirts of Golden Pond, he would be moving to Murray where his daughters were going to college. Well, Lorene hopped right on the opportunity to inquire about the house, and, before their conversation ended she told him, she and Lawton were interested and would like to take a look at the place. Well, that's how the ball got to rolling. She returned to Ma Annie's totally esthetic, but, decided she had better save her exciting news for Lawton; after all, if Ma Annie heard first, she might try to sway Lawton.

Lorene believed it was the longest afternoon in her whole life. She went over and over in her mind what she was going to say to him. Lawton finally came in around sundown, and she met him at the car before he even had time to turn the off the engine. She relayed her findings of the morning trip to the mailbox and, before dark when she followed him to the barn, still talking away, full of excitement, Lawton finally, consented to go look at the house.

Lorene broke the news to Ma Annie during supper. Ma Annie didn't say much, but Lorene could tell she was puffed up like a toad frog the rest of the night. This did not faze Lorene, though, she had dreamed of a place of their own for almost eight years now, and nothing was going to stand in her way. Her dream was just too close to coming true.

Lorene met Mr. Forshee at the mailbox the next day to tell him they were definitely interested, at which time, he set the following Saturday afternoon as the time for them to come and look at the house. Well, Lorene knew, already, the house would be suitable for her. Why, a hen house would suit her, if it meant moving out of Ma Annie's house into a place of their own.

Well, Saturday rolled around and Lawton and Lorene went to Golden Pond. Mr. and Mrs. Forshee's house, on the outskirts of Golden Pond, was totally perfect as far as Lorene was concerned. It was a two story frame structure painted white on the outside. There were four rooms downstairs and four upstairs. A full size basement was beneath.

There were long porches across the front and back. The house was in good repair; all it needed was for the Forshee's to move out and the Higgins to move in. Lorene asked for no changes at all.

There was a nice large yard, a good garden spot and a small fenced in area with a shed that would hold a cow. A cistern on the hill behind the house was their water supply and the main road through Golden Pond ran just beyond the front lawn. Oak and maple trees filled the yard, shading the front porch, while numerous, flowering shrubs rambled here and there among the trees. Lorene, so full of joy, could ask for nothing more than enough plunder to get by on. Lawton, in spite of his reluctance to leave Ma Annie, also liked the house. He was already figuring out the best place to store his moonshine for it to age.

Mr. Forshee was asking four thousand dollars for the place, and needed until the first of August before he would be able to move. That was agreeable with Lawton and Lorene. Lawton promised to bring him some "earnest" money on Monday, making the deal solid until he could get together the balance. At last, Lorene would have her dream house!! She was so excited she didn't sleep for a week! Ma Annie came down with a full-fledged case of the "muleygrubs" and did not try to hide it. She said over and over: "You may get Lawton to move over there, but I can guarantee you one thing, he won't stay."

"Well," Lorene would answer, "that's up to him. He can choose to live with you, or me and the kids, for I will be staying with my kids in my own home, whether he stays or not!"

Lorene began immediately getting together all of the cast away plunder she could find. She found various pieces here and there, and by the middle of July, she had accumulated enough to sparsely furnish at least six of the eight rooms. Ma Annie was still moping around, sometimes whimpering like a child, but Lorene kept a stiff upper lip. Lorene was not so cruel that she couldn't understand how the move would effect both Lawton and Ma Annie, but she was also mature enough to know it was time and past that she and Lawton took their family into a home of their own, and Ma Annie being down-in-the-mouth, was not going to have one bit of bearing on the action she and Lawton was to take. As the time grew closer, Ma Annie did come around, a little. She rode the twenty miles to Golden Pond with Lawton and Lorene one Sunday afternoon to have look at the place. The week following, she made the donation of some odd pieces of furniture, and told Lawton he could have the old jersey cow to put in the small field behind the garden. So, things were beginning to fall in place, after all. Lorene and Lawton were planning to move to their own home in the fall.

A terrible tragedy took place in Golden Pond a month before Lorene and Lawton moved. August first was primary election day, which was on a Saturday. It seems, the fire started when someone built a fire in an alleyway near the wooden structure, which was Futrell's General Merchandise. The wind was high that day and since there was not proper fire fighting equipment available, the people of the town and those who had come in from other communities to vote, could only watch as the flames swept through eleven of the fifteen buildings that made up the business district of Golden Pond. It was estimated the damage ranged from thirty to fifty thousand dollars. People worked with every resource possible to try and extinguish the flames, but soon realized their efforts were no match for the high winds and leaping flames that were sweeping quickly from building to building. It was then, they realized they should concentrate on keeping the sparks from setting other buildings on fire, so, both women and men wet quilts, blankets and any other large pieces of material they could find and spread them on roof tops. In about an hour and a half the fire was over. Several citizens declared it was definitely the hottest election Golden Pond ever had!

Very few of the merchants and owners of the burned buildings carried any insurance, but, before the tragic day ended, the merchants and towns people were, already making plans to start rebuilding.

When Lorene and Lawton received news of the fire, they went right over to view the damage and assure themselves that their house was not damaged. It was a sad sight to see as they slowly went up Highway 68, which was the main street through the town. The fire had done no harm anywhere close to their soon to be new home. Yes, Golden Pond, whose business section lay in almost complete rubble, was a discouraging sight that day in August, but it did not dampen Lorene's spirits in regard to making it's outskirts her home in a few weeks to come.

Well, Lorene and Lawton completed the move into their house in Golden Pond a week before school started. Doris was now of school age and Virgil two years beyond. Lorene knew in her heart that she must settle in her mind to enroll Virgil when she enrolled Doris. It had been one of the toughest decisions she had ever made, but it was either to give him a try in the Elementary School at Golden Pond, or send him away to Danville, to the State School for the Deaf. She and Lawton discussed the matter in depth, one more time, and when the school doors opened that first day, she enrolled them both. Virgil was excited, yet shy about being around so many other children. Doris fit right in and was thrilled with having so many little girls her age to play with.

Lorene was having the time of her life getting settled in her new home. The children were adjusting nicely to their new home, as for Lawton and the old jersey cow, well that was another story. The cow bawled night and day from home sickness, and Lawton, also suffering the pains of home sickness, made the twenty mile trip to Ma Annie's every single day. "Un-be-knowance" to Lorene at the time, it seems Lawton had been taking solace in conversing with the cow when he went to milk. Years later, he told Lorene he had promised the cow, they would try it one more week and if both he and the cow didn't get to feeling better about the move to Golden Pond, they would both just go back home to Ma Annie's.

Doris was adjusting well to first grade, but Virgil wasn't doing very well. The other children were really giving him a hard time, for children can be cruel. He would come home crying almost every day. Several of those first few days, someone from the school would have to walk him home before classes dismissed. Although his teacher tried very hard to relate to him, she had much difficulty trying to meet Virgil's needs, along with the needs of the twenty-odd others in her classroom. By the middle of the second week of intense frustration for Virgil, the teacher, the principal, and Lorene and Lawton as well, Lorene knew it was time to deal with what Dr. White, the Specialist in Hopkinsville, had spoken of since Virgil's first visit. Yes, the inevitable, was at hand. They had to enroll Virgil in The Kentucky School for the Deaf at Danville.

The main facility at the Kentucky School for the Deaf at Danville, was a large brick building on the outskirts of the city. Other buildings, along with the dormitories and a large play area were located behind the main structure. The facilities were surrounded by spacious, well kept, shaded grounds. The school's academic program included basic studies for the elementary grades, all of the required high school subjects, along with specialized training, in various trades, for the older students. All students were allowed to stay enrolled until the age of twenty.

That Indian summer Monday was undoubtedly the most difficult day Lorene had experienced in her entire life. Lorene and Lawton would be taking Virgil to a strange place and leaving him with people they didn't know. They had been informed that although the school provided a small facility for parents to occupy in the event of student illness, they did not advise the parents, when bringing the children for enrollment, to stay for a settling-in period. They were also advised, for the benefit of the child, to keep visits to a maximum of once a month. So, Lorene knew the thing she was having to do that day was one of the hardest things, if not the hardest, she would ever do in her life.

She, Lawton and Virgil reached the school a little before 8:00 a.m. and were directed, along with several others, to the classroom where Virgil would begin his studies. The room was large and airy, with tile floors and long windows across one side. Two large electric fans, hanging from the high ceiling on either side of a long florescent light, rotated the air that filtered through the windows. Some twenty small desks, the long teachers desk and one wall filled with shelves, made up the furnishings. A long blackboard hung on the wall behind the teachers desk. The atmosphere and surroundings were very similar to any city school classroom.

Virgil's teacher was Mattie Robinson, who Lorene and Lawton liked immediately, and it seemed Virgil did, also. Mrs. Robinson, after enrollment, took the children and parents for a tour of all of the facilities and grounds. Other faculty members were doing the same for the various classes.

Now, Lorene made it pretty well through the enrollment and tour. She and Lawton even made acquaintances with other parents, and had time to talk with, and share their experiences, with their children's handicap. Some of the children were not as handicapped as Virgil, while some were worse. Virgil and the children would play a little as

Golden Pond School.

1938: Doris' first grade school picture. Doris is first row, far right.

Lawton and Lorene conversed with the parents, but Virgil would return to their sides, often, and take the hand of one or the other.

Around three that afternoon, Mrs. Robinson asked Lawton to bring Virgil's things to his designated area in the dorm. Lorene thought her heart would totally break as she glanced at her watch, knowing the time for parting was near at hand. Tears welled as she tried to remain calm in front of Virgil, for she noticed the tears in his eyes, as well. When she and Mrs. Robinson gave him the opportunity to help put his things away, he flatly refused the offer, plopped down on the bed and hung his head, so Lorene and Lawton began putting his things in the locker assigned to him. Mrs. Robinson stood patiently beside the bed and commented on the many nice things Virgil had brought.

Other parents were doing the same throughout the room, as children, either clung to them or scurried about the dozen or so bunk beds that comprised the main furnishings of the large area.

Lawton and Lorene, bade their farewells to Virgil on the front lawn of the school around five o'clock that afternoon. Needless to say, it was an emotional and extremely painful experience. Virgil clung to his parents, sobbing uncontrollably, while Lorene did the same. At one point, Lorene thought she would simply have to bring Virgil back home with them, but Mrs. Robinson, in her unique and gentle manner, managed to persuade Virgil to come with her to the playground, where he could participate in a game of baseball. Lorene watched, her heart breaking as Mrs. Robinson started leading Virgil back toward the building. Virgil turned his tear stained face in their direction and barely waved his hand, just before they entered the double doors. Lawton, who had dampness on his cheeks also, put his arm around Lorene's shoulder and gently guided her to the parking lot and their car.

Chapter Eight:

More on Golden Pond

Autumn was loosing it's battle to ol' man winter as the north wind blew the brown and golden leaves from the trees, and, by mid October, frost had parched the few remaining sprigs of green vegetation in the town of Golden Pond. Wild geese were migrating to their winter homes, leaving behind only, the echo of their squawks as their perfect formation glided across the sky and out of sight. The merchants of Golden Pond were steadily rebuilding their businesses; their spirits high, overcoming the ravages of the devastating fire of only a few months, previously.

The Higgins family was now considered permanent residents of the Golden Pond community. Virgil was slowly adjusting to his new surroundings in the school at Danville, as was Lorene to the fact he was away. Little Doris was adapting well to her first year at the Golden Pond Elementary School, and Lawton, well, he still made daily visits back to Ma Annie's and yes, he was still in the moonshine business. The cow? Well, she had finally quit bawling.

Lorene was enjoying her new home, thoroughly, despite her loneliness and concern for Virgil. She had fixed the house up to be quite attractive and comfortable. She was proud of the freedom she felt in her own home, and was also enjoying the two modern conveniences she now had. A hand pump in the kitchen brought water, from the cistern on the hill, to her fingertips, while the generator in the basement, better known as a "dynamo", gave instant lighting, without striking a match, to the bulb which was on the end of a cord, suspended from the tall ceiling of each room.

Lawton would beam with pride when neighbors or family would drop in and compliment the neatness of the yard and the attractiveness of the house. Lawton, before they moved in, had carefully devised a plan as to where he would store and conceal his moonshine. There was a large basement, but, Lawton knew his fine "brew" would not age properly there because of the moisture and darkness. So, he came up with, what he thought would be, a "fool-proof" set up. There were four gables in the roof, under which were the four upstairs rooms. On the gable end of the four rooms, where the roof sloped, were closets, and against the back wall of each closet was a small door that opened into more space, enough room to accommodate a sizable amount of moonshine. Yes, the storage space behind the closets would be the perfect place to store his kegs. Lawton convinced Lorene that since they had not lived at their new home long enough to collect an abundance of surplus "plunder," he was definitely going to have to use the space. Well, Lorene knew she had no choice. Lawton had already set his head to use the space behind the closets to store the product of their livelihood. So, after getting their furniture all moved and arranged in their new house, Lawton set to work, moving his "brew" from Ma Annie's. He and Shaw carried keg after keg of moonshine up the stairs while, Lorene watched in dismay, for she had sworn if they ever had a place of their own, no moonshine would ever be stored there. She hadn't forgotten the horrible fright she experienced during the raid at Ma Annie's, where the back room was full of jugs and kegs. Well, for Lawton, this new idea seemed to work very well. The heat generated by the roof penetrated through to the attic, and helped the aging process to do it's job of mellowing and enhancing the "brew" to it's finest quality.

Well, it seems for some folks even the most perfectly planned ideas sometimes have flaws, and this was the case for Lawton's moonshine storage. He began to thinking that in the event of a raid, the upstairs closets would be, along with the basement, the two most obvious places for the Feds to look. The small doors in the back walls of the closets, would be pretty easy for a revenue man to notice when he moved the garments hanging in the closet, and he felt he had to come up with a way to better, conceal his brew. Well, Lawton got a tip, from a reliable source, that he was on the list for a visit from revenuers, likely within the next two weeks, and he began to get real nervous. So, once again, Lawton's brain set in motion. He came up with the idea of having Lorene hang wall paper on the back wall of the closets to conceal the small doors that led to the extra attic space behind them. This would leave the impression, to anyone who checked out the closets, that only a solid wall was behind the clothing and other items stored there. So, Lorene papered; and papered she did, every time more kegs and jugs were added or when some were taken out. Yes, Lorene's papering job was an ongoing process.

Now, since the days of Prohibition had passed, it seemed that more and more revenuers were infiltrating the land between the rivers. The large brewing companies were now free to produce legal liquor again, and barrel after barrel of whiskey, beer and ale of all sorts were being rolled onto the market every day. Liquor stores, bars, pubs and night-clubs in the cities, were filled to capacity every night, and it was evident, the demand for revenuers in those areas had declined. So, it just made sense for the government to start sending more of their employees to the remote, rural areas throughout the country to stamp out the making and selling of illicit liquor.

Lawton became very angered every time he heard of a still being busted or a house or outbuilding being raided. It seemed, news of the like was passed on every day. Lawton also came home with a new story about someone in the "business" getting "busted" every night; some near by, some out of town, and some out of state. Lorene was so tired of hearing about it, she'd be glad when the Feds cleaned out the whole lot of moonshiners. Word was, the Feds were picking their most rugged, well trained and fearless men to send to the remote, rural areas of Indiana, Tennessee and Kentucky, for the purpose of sniffing out any illicit whiskey operations.

One night Lawton came home with a story of a veteran moonshiner who had witnessed the destruction of three stills, within a two mile radius, getting busted in one night and hundreds of gallons of mash and moonshine being poured out, the old moonshiner's included.

Lawton quoted the old timer as saying, "Why, we'us jest a' gittin' ready t' run er' thru' fer t'secon' trip, me n' my two boys, it us' pert nigh dark, I reckon, fer Alvin, that's m' oldest un,' had done chunked the fire up, so we'uns c'd see better, an' I wus'a throwin' a little onto th' fire t' see ifn' it us' bout' rite. My youngest un,' Oscar, had jest set th' water bucket down, fer, he'd jest come from' th' sprang. All's goin' as usual, ye know? Jest like we allers' done, when all of a sudden this here feller, bigger n'a giant come like a streak uf lightenin' outta' th' bushes. He's on us for we knowd' what us' happenin, 'course, it skeered us s' bad we all lit out towards th' branch, an fore we could spread out, nes' thang we knowd,' there us' nother un' after us, yep, two uf' em' suckers. Th' othern' warn't big as th' first un,' an' not as fast, but he still knowed how t' travel. Well, bout' then we started headin' in different directions, goin' fast as our legs ud' carry us. We us' a runnin' thru' saw briars, bushes head tall. We warn't a'stoppin' fer nothin' 'till I hap-pened' t' stumble over a log an' roll off in t' sprang branch. Thought m' goose us' cooked then, fer shore, but since it us' pert nigh dark, reckon th' second feller, one closest hin' me, he us' sevral' yard back, reckon he didn't see me fall, fer he jest kept a'runnin,'so I jest laid thar' an' didn't move er' nothin; skeeriest thang ever t' happen t' a feller. Well, now I ain't a lyin' t' ye...that biggun' wus t' fastest movin' feller I ever seen! Well, since I'd done fell in th' sprang branch, I warn't in on the rest uf' it, but them two revenuers rum em' boys uf' mine fer over two miles afor' they caught up t' em,' an' I'm tellin' ye my boys can run! But, them revenuers was runners too. That biggun' was a runner fer shore! It us' slap dab dark b'then. Now, that ain't all uf' t'story; them Feds tole' m' boys when they took em' in, that whilst' they us' a runnin' they spied ol' man Hopson's "set up" down in th' holler, Clem Bradshaw's "set up" up n' th' bluffs and th' Rucker boys still down n' t' crick' bottom. Reckon my boys plum run en' right t'ward them other feller's "set up's", course, they didn't aim to, it us' cause they us' s' skeered.....Well, them Feds turned m' boys over t' some other'ns out on t' highway, an' went back an' they all got their "set up's" busted up an' their mash poured out, same as ourn'. All done fore' midnight. How they us' able t' spot all em' stills an' it purt ni' dark an' em' runnin' like antelopes, shore beats me..."

Now, if one doesn't think a story like that can make the hair on a moonshiner's neck stand straight up, well, one just aught to be in Lawton Higgin's shoes!

Lawton, as well as every other moonshiner in all of the hills and hollers of the Tri-state area, were soon, using every skill thought of to hide their "stills". Lawton even heard of some in the hills of the Eastern part of the state that buried their mash in barrels till it was ready to "run," then they would set their "stills" in as remote a place as they could find, many times, miles from their homes. Many, put up strings of barbed wire, head high, to discourage intruders. Others built barricades of briars or logs, while, still others, dug deep trenches around the site. Many of the moonshiners were now carrying guns, and all of them had at least one good watch dog they took with them to the "still", every day and night, to alert them of a strangers presence in the woods. Some even banded together by taking turns watching at a steak-out, on a high hill or in a tall tree located a safe distance from their "stills". It seemed, an out and out war was going on between the Feds. and the moonshiners, everywhere! Sure as day, moonshinin' was a lot more than a hobby to the wiry men of the hills and hollers. It was dead-serious business to them, for it was their livelihood. And, most revenue men were sympathetic to that fact, to a degree. One young moonshiner in the hills of Kentucky, who had a wife and a yard full of youngens, was caught red handed, for the third time, while he was working at his still, which was in a deep gully a few hundred yard yards from his house. He gave the two revenuers no trouble as they arrested him. The judge informed him, since this was his third offense, he would have to go to jail for a year and a day. The young man simply nodded his head in agreement, then told the judge his wife was due to give birth to their sixth youngen any time and he would like to wait till it came. The judge granted him permission wait to start his sentence until the new baby was a week old. Well, two weeks and a day after the young man's arrest, he came walking into the local police station, ready to begin his sentence, beaming with pride, for his wife had given birth to twin boys the week before. Many of the revenuers who were sent to the remote areas of Kentucky, Tennessee and Indiana, were sympathetic with the men in the moonshine business, mainly, because they were from a rural environment, very much like the moonshiners in Kentucky, Tennessee and Indiana. The government, as a rule, used this particular breed, who were from remote, rural areas, for they were familiar with the environment, as well as being in better physical condition than the revenuers from the city. Some of the revenuers were acquainted with, and some, even akin to some of the moonshiners.

The violator was usually granted permission to tell his family good-bye, or just go to the house to get cleaned up before they left for the jail. Permission was granted, in most cases, without any complications.

Yes, many stories, about stills being busted and men taken to jail were the constant "talk" of all of the moonshiners in Lawton's neck of the woods.

Lorene knew Lawton was worried and so was she. Deep down inside, she prayed, as she had for years, that something would scare Lawton enough to make him give up moonshinin' and seek a legal livelihood, but, she knew, also, deep down inside, that it would have to get closer to home, before Lawton Higgins got out of the moonshinin' business.

The red ball of sun was now half hidden behind the tree tops, as Lorene stood watching Ed's old pickup go out of sight, around the bend. He had stopped by to pick up little Doris to spend the night, and the next day, with he and Duck and Reba Nell and George Glenn, Lorene's brother and sister still at home. Actually, George Glenn was only a month older than Doris.

Lorene and her daddy had had a good visit; he sat at the kitchen table while she finished supper. She followed her daddy and Doris out on the front porch to wave good-bye. Little Doris had chosen to stay with Ed and Duck, rather than go with Lorene and Lawton to Danville the next day to visit with Virgil and at the School for the Deaf. It upset her to leave Virgil, so Doris didn't go every trip.

The crisp, fall air was rustling the leaves that had fallen from the many trees in the yard, it's nip causing Lorene to pull her sweater tighter about her as she sat down on the edge of the long porch. She placed her feet on the top step, as she awaited Lawton's return from a "run" to Owensboro and let her thoughts, same as many times before, drift to her childhood days. It must have been the "nip" in the air that made her think of Christmas time at home.

Now, Christmas time in Lorene's younger days was definitely a contrast to that of her own children. There was no Ma Annie nor the "good" money, if one could call it "good", Lorene thought, coming in from the moonshinin' business to shower Ed Young's brood of youngens with lavish gifts and toys. However, Lorene never remembered a time that she wasn't filled with anticipation and joy as she emptied her stocking on Christmas morning. The days leading up to Christmas in Lorene's childhood days was a time of accelerated excitement and joy for the entire community! The older boys at Fenton School would go to the woods and cut a cedar tree, while the younger students supplied the handmade decorations, as they prepared and decorated for the play they would be putting on for the parents on the last day of school before Christmas vacation. Each of the students, from grades one through eight, would have a part. The script was written by the older students, along with the assistance of the teacher. Although, the lines were simple and the props even more so, the true meaning of Christmas, expressed through the innocent lips of the children, either in verse or song, filled hearts with the joy of the season, both, to those performing and those observing. When the program was over, the teacher would pass out a peppermint candy cane and a pencil to each student. The parents would clap and clap and beam with pride as their son or daughter displayed his or her talent before them.

Lorene could remember her mama and Aunt Rhodie sewing shirts, dresses, underwear and rag dolls for days to give to the less fortunate children in the community so they would not be left out come Christmas morning. Uncle Joe and Ed, at night before the fire place, would whittle wooden toys and make sling shots to give to the unfortunate children, along with the clothing. Most Christmas mornings, some of the articles being manufactured at the hands of mama and daddy, Uncle Joe and Aunt Rhodie, could also, be found in the stockings of the Turner children.

Some of the things Lorene would always remember about those days leading up to Christmas were being allowed to feed the hen or turkey that had been put in a coop to fatten for Christmas Day dinner and the first hog killing, which took place a week or so before Christmas, for the weather had usually turned cold enough to keep the meat from spoiling. The fresh pork, ranging from sausage to ribs and backbone that was on the table to go with hot biscuits and gravy was a year long anticipation! The sights and smells in the kitchen were enough to keep the spirits high and the mouth watering! The pungent aroma of spices in the ginger bread cookies, tea cakes, fruit cakes, fruit pies and eggnog were almost too much for the children to resist as they darted in and out of the cozy kitchen where Duck and Aunt Rhodie diligently worked. Sometimes hands got smacked or ears pinched as the temptation to snitch a cookie became irresistible. Then sometimes, if behavior was well, a plate of the less perfectly round cookies would be passed to the children to sample. A very special treat was getting to sample the molasses taffy, hickory nut fudge and walnut divinity as it was placed on the sideboard to cool.

A few days before Christmas Eve, Ed, Lorene and Shaw would make a trip to the woods for the tree. They would choose the fullest, greenest and biggest tree to fill the corner of the stayin' room next the fireplace. Every family member, as time permitted, would make decoration for the tree. Duck and Aunt Rhodie made bells, angels, balls, Santa's boots and animals from bright colored fabric and stuffed them with cotton to hang on the tree. Lorene and Viona Katherine made strings of popcorn and cut angels from white paper, while Shaw would help guy string red berries to drape on the tree. Uncle Joe fashioned a large star out of a thin plank and painted it red, which was used year after year to adorn the top of the tree. Lorene could remember how beautiful it would look! Aunt Rhodie would place two red candles on the mantel on either side of pine boughs, tied with a piece of red material and their glow mingled with the firelight made the tree look so lovely.

All of the children would hang their stockings, on nails under the mantel, and listen from their beds, as the clock would slowly tick by the minutes, until their eyes would grow heavy with sleep. They always awoke early on Christmas morning, and scurried to the fireplace to examine the contents of their stockings. There was always fruit, nuts, peppermint candy and a small toy. There were newly, sewn clothes and sometimes new shoes and new coats under the tree! The excitement over these meager, and, even necessary items was just as great as the mounds of store bought toys Lorene's children found under the tree on these more modern day Christmas mornings, maybe even more so.

Of course, relatives and friends congregated for the Christmas Day dinner, which was so bountiful it spilled from the stove top to the long table and on to the sideboard. It was plain, home grown, home cooked food, but it was consumed in an atmosphere of enjoyment, satisfaction and thankfulness.

Lorene chuckled as she remembered the Christmas the younger children received tops from Santa. She and Shaw, who were around eight and eleven years old, retrieved the tops, once the younger ones had laid them aside and began pitching them back and forth to each other in the stayin' room. Now, Ed had called them down once, but they continued, unheeding. What great fun they were having, until Lorene missed a catch, allowing the top thrown by Shaw to go crashing into the chimney of the coal oil lamp that sat on the mantel. Ed started quickly across the room to administer some physical discipline, which he rarely used. This excited Shaw, who was holding the other top. He made a run for the front door, threw the top into the air, and of all places for it to land, it crashed into the other lamp that set on the table beside the door. Needless to say, that chimney also crashed into a thousand pieces. By this time Ed, who was quicker than lightening when he got riled, grabbed both Shaw and Lorene at the same time, and sat Shaw in a chair. Shaw knew not to move. Still holding on to Lorene, he picked up a small cane pole that was leaning against the wall next to the door, bent her over his knee and thrashed her soundly, for the first time in her life. He then did the same for Shaw. That was the only time Ed ever spanked Lorene in her whole life. Later, he told Lorene the spanking hurt him more than it did her. Well, at the time, she doubted his statement. However, as the years passed, knowing her daddy so well, she knew he was telling the truth!

Stars were peeking through night's curtain of blue, and the slice of a moon hung high in the autumn sky before Lawton's green Pontiac flashed it's head lights in the drive way. Lorene had been sitting in the stayin' room for some time, listening to the radio and hemming a dress for Doris. She would have to warm-up supper, she thought, as Lawton came in the door.

"You would not believe what a day I've had," he said, disgustingly, throwing his hat on a chair.

"What happened?" Lorene asked, laying her sewing aside and rising from the couch.

"People in Owensboro are scared to death of the revenuers!" he answered, stalking toward the kitchen. "I didn't know if I was goin' to be able to get the car unloaded or not. They was scared to death they'd be found out. Half the men in the "business" up there have been raided!"

Lorene followed him to the kitchen and headed for the stove to warm the food, still in the pans, that she had cooked some three hours earlier.

"There's men in jail that's been moonshinin' for forty years and never been caught before," Lawton went on, leaning over the sink and splashing water on his face. "Women and kids without food and banks about to foreclose on home mortgages. It's one sad situation, it is."

"Well, Lawton, this aught to be a warning to you..." Lorene started to say, but he cut her off short.

"Now, don't start in on me. I ain't in no mood to hear the get a legal job bit," Lawton said, turning his head sideways and glaring at her as he dried his hands. "I've been makin' moonshine, and blamed good moonshine, since I was fifteen years old, and I'll keep on making it till I get run out or sent up. So you're wasting your breath to start in on me and you know it."

"Lawton, I'm just scared, not just for you, but me and the kids, as well," Lorene started, determined to have her say. "What in the world would me an' the kids do if you got caught? There is no money in the world worth it, Lawton; no money in the world! Them Feds are ever' where."

"Now, Renie, just simmer down," Lawton said, sitting down at the table. "I've got it all figured out. I won't take on any new customers, right now. I've got plenty of regulars for us to get by on. They know my stuff, an' they want it, an' I'll deliver to them just as always. I've fixed a few things with some people today, and I've got people I can trust to keep me informed about what's goin' on, and where. So you can just quit your worrin'".

Well, it was pretty clear to Lorene that what he "fixed" today, involved getting on the good side of some law men, and that burned her up even more. That also painted a pretty clear picture, of the fact, that the new living room suit he had promised her out of the proceeds of this "run," were in the pockets of some law man. Her portion of the "proceeds had been spent on the expensive insurance that, hopefully, would keep the law away from Lawton's still in Ma Annie's woods. She was furious! He had promised her a new living suite when she began to get their plunder together for them to move to Golden Pond, but, where did the money go that was to buy the living room suite? They were riding it and Lawton was hauling moonshine in it. Yep, Lawton had bought a new car; the third new car this year. Just the thought of him paying off the law with money he had promised her made her blood boil! Furious as she was though, she did not say another word. She just brought the food from the stove, slammed it down on the table, and stomped out of the room.

She heard the scrape of the chair against the floor as Lawton slammed back from the table, but she did not turn around. She just kept walking through the living room and out the front door onto the porch.

"Now Lorene, you straighten yourself up and listen to reason, "he said, his voice raising with each step he took closer to the front porch.

"I've been listening to reason for eight years now. You listen to reason for a change!" She shouted back at him as she whirled around to face him, her eyes blazing.

"Now, I'm not goin' to listen to anything from you, a woman ain't got no sense about these matters; men are supposed to do the decidin' on things like this. 'Sides, a woman ain't nothing but a brawlin' hussy that'll talk to her man like you are!" he yelled back as stepped out onto the porch and slammed the screen door behind him.

"And a man who'll put a woman through what your puttin' me through, ain't nothing but a s__of- a- b____h!" She yelled back.

Lorene clasped her hand over her mouth no sooner than the words had left, for Lawton always said he'd kill anybody who called him that name. She could see fire dancing in his eyes, in the dimness of the light from the window, as he stood frozen, glaring at her. She stood, rigid, inches away from him. Finally he spoke, his voice low, through clinched teeth.

"Did you mean what you called me for me, or my mammy?"

"BOTH!" she yelled, staring right back at him. Then she lowered her voice, still looking him right in the eye, and said, "Now, move out of the door. I'm goin' to bed."

"I can't believe you called me a s__of- a- b___h," he said, in a whisper as he stepped aside to let her storm past.

She did not answer, but threw him a glare, cold as the frigid wind of the North Pole, then stomped passed him. She stormed through the living room and into the bedroom, where she began getting ready for bed. She happened to notice, as she glanced out the window while turning down the cover on the bed, the neighbors across the road were staring out their front window in the direction of the Higgins residence.

"So what, let em' look!" she mumbled to herself. "Let the whole dad blasted, world look! I don't care if they heard every word I said. I'm sick of this moonshinin' business. Sick and tired of it!" She then, jerked one of the two pillows off the bed, and threw it into the living room.

Well, needless to say, the atmosphere was pretty strained for the next several days. Lorene and Lawton hardly spoke a word as they made the long trip to Danville the next day. The friction between them was, definitely, thick enough to slice.

Mrs. Robertson had given them a good report concerning Virgil. She said, aside from the normal adjustment of being away from home and interacting with his classmates, that Virgil seemed to be doing well.

Virgil was so glad to see them! They had a joyous day visiting with him. He showed them his school work, and from time to time, he brought his new friends around for them to meet. The day sped by fast, and as the afternoon passed, Lorene's heart began to sink, for she knew that their departure would be, equally, as painful as the first. And it was; Virgil clung to Lorene, with sobs racking his body. Although he was unable to, verbally, relate his wishes, the sad and pitiful look in his tearful eyes struck straight to Lorene's heart, causing pain as fierce as it were a dagger. Lawton, who was in no better shape than she, had to literally prize them apart. With the help of Mrs. Robertson, they managed to get Virgil headed in the direction of the main building. As they disappeared from sight, Lawton, once again, placed his arm around Lorene's shoulder, and gently guided her to the car, a gesture which, incidentally, broke some of the friction, but she just could not warm up to him a hundred percent. Her frustration and fears would simply not allow it.

Chapter Nine:

From One Extreme to Another

❝It's the law, that's who it is!" Lawton replied, his eyes wide, as he turned from the window to answer Lorene's question as to who had stopped in front of their house.

"Oh Lord, Lawton what are we gonna do? I'm glad the kids aren't here," Lorene answered, ringing her hands and walking toward the kitchen.

"We ain't gonna do anything cept' act natural. Now get back in here. They're almost to the porch, there's two of em. One's the sheriff. Other one, I don't know, but for sure, he's a revenue man," Lawton said, then let out an oath, quiet as a whisper, as he started across the room toward the front door.

"Howdy," he said, in that good-natured manner of his. "What brings you out here, Sheriff?"

"I'd say you know, dad-burned well what brings us out here, Lawton. I've got a warrant here to search th' place," the sheriff answered, without slowing down, as he came across the porch, followed by the middle aged man accompanying him.

"This here's Robert Evers with the Federal Government, in case you hadn't already guessed, and there's three more like m' in that car, pulling up now, an in case you're thinkin' of high tailing it out of here, there's another car with two more revenue men in it, between your garden and the shed. We've been informed there's a possibility you've been dealing in the making and selling of illicit whiskey, and we're here to do the job of finding out, for sure. We've just busted up a still over at Oak Ridge, and your daddy-in-law and brother-in-law are in custody now. Your brother-in-law claims it belongs to him, but we have reason to believe you've got a hand in it. We found a small amount of mash ready to run, an' both your in-laws at the sight, fixin' to start the cooker," The sheriff went on, as he pulled the warrant from his pocket and handed it to Lawton.

"That was the last batch till spring," Lorene thought, as a rage of panic rose within her. She clasped her hands over her mouth to keep from crying out. "Oh, Lord, daddy and Shaw are in this deep as Lawton, maybe even deeper. Oh Lord, please, don't let them catch-on to the paper in the closets!"

"Well, Sheriff, Mr. Evers, you're more than welcome to search the place, but I'm afraid you won't find nothing illegal around here," Lawton said, real friendly like, as the two men paused to get their bearings as to where to start. Two of the three revenuers, from the other car, out front, were now casting long shadows across the yard as they made their way to the front porch.

Lorene was frozen in her tracks, as she stood in the doorway between the living room and the kitchen. Her thoughts were racing, back and forth, from worrying about Ed and Shaw being caught at the still, to what the revenuers might find up stairs. Her heart was pounding so hard she was afraid it was visible through the thin material of her cotton dress, and she felt like she was going to collapse, any second. She glanced at Lawton, who was watching from across the room, while the sheriff and the revenue man, Evers, proceeded through the rooms downstairs. They were opening closet doors, cabinets, and poking through any space big enough to hide a keg or jug. By this time the other two men had entered the house and were heading up the stairs. Lorene tried to swallow, but her saliva glands would not cooperate. Instead, a faint choking sound came out as the two men started to ascend the stairs. Lawton, was obviously the only one to hear her panicky sound, for the intruders were stomping around and slamming doors. Lawton threw her a warning glance, which was telling her to get hold of herself. She managed to draw a long breath, which helped ease her tension somewhat, but the churning in her stomach did not subside.

Now, Lorene knew they wouldn't find anything downstairs, but upstairs was a different story. The space behind the closets were filled, to capacity, with ten gallon charred, kegs of Lawton's finest "brew". The last keg, having been placed there only a few days earlier. Lorene prayed her wall paper job would conceal the products of their livelihood. Soon, the revenuers were banging on the ceilings and walls, in search of any concealed hideaway.

"Oh Dear Lord sweet Jesus, Lorene silently, yet earnestly, prayed, "I know you ain't proud of what Lawton does for a livin', an' I ain't either, but, if you'd just have mercy on us, one more time, and not let Daddy and Shaw go to jail, an' keep these lawmen from finding the kegs, I'll do everything in my power to try and get Lawton to get out of this awful, moonshinin' business. I promise I will."

By this time, the Sheriff and Evers had completed their search downstairs. The Sheriff asked Lawton, as he came back into the living room, where the entrance was to the basement. Lawton told him, acting as cool as a cucumber, but Lorene could see the muscle in his jaw flinching, and she knew he was as scared as she or madder than all get out; likely, a combination of both.

"It's clean up here!" one of the revenuers yelled from upstairs, as the Sheriff and Evers started to leave the living room. "Where to from here, Sheriff?"

"We're checking out the basement. You all help em' out back, check the out buildings," the sheriff answered.

Lorene breathed a sigh of relief, as the two descended the stairs, and headed toward the kitchen. She stepped out of the way, to let them pass. They both nodded as they went by her.

"Thank you, sweet Jesus," she breathed.

By this time, Lawton had crossed the living room, and was following them. Lorene stayed put. Lawton's face was still, stone cold, but he gave her a wink as he walked past her. She didn't know whether she wanted to hug him or kill him, but she strongly thought the latter better described her feelings. Did he care if Ed and Shaw got caught? Did he care if Shaw took the blame? At this moment, she truly believed, the only thing he cared about was that the Sheriff and the revenuers had not found the kegs upstairs.

The search, which only took some twenty minutes, seemed to Lorene hours long, and only when the last revenue man had slammed the car door and started the motor could she breath normally. She was so weak in the knees that she had to sit, and her hands were still trembling something fierce when Lawton stomped back into the house, at which time he went off!

He began rolling oaths and names out of his mouth that no sailor, in the history of cussing sailors, could match, as he stomped, back and forth, across the kitchen floor. Along with the swearing and name calling, came the pounding of his fists on the table, and the slamming of cabinet doors that had been left ajar by the revenuers. Lorene gritted her teeth and clinched her hands into fists to keep from tearing, verbally, into him. Finally, he calmed down enough to pick up his hat from the chair, across from the couch, where she was sitting and say, with a sly grin, sounding more like his old self. "Well, Renie baby, we fooled the s—s-of-b_____s one more time didn't we?"

Lorene was furious, but didn't say a word. He, then, put on his hat, and started for the front door. Lorene knew where he was headed, and it didn't bother her any that he didn't ask her to come along. Yes, Ma Annie would hear the whole story, and maybe even a little bit more, and when he'd finished, she would pat him on the back and tell him how proud she was that he had outsmarted the local law and the Federal Government.

"Wait, Lawton! Wait!" Lorene yelled, jumping from the couch. "We've got to go to Mamas! We've got to see about Daddy and Shaw! Wait!"

"Oh Lord, where is all this to stop?" Lorene mumbled aloud as she ran after Lawton, who was heading across the front yard toward the car.

"I've just got to figure out some way to get him to give up this moonshinin'. I've just got to!"

They made the rounds. First to Ed and Duck's. Duck was crying and having a raving fit, while Ed and Shaw were still at the county jail. Lorene joined her mother in her despair, for she, too, was worried about her daddy and Shaw. Lawton tried to console Duck by telling her he would get them out of all this mess. He told her he thought he could raise bond, and on and on he went about how he sure hated it they got caught, and that he was getting out of the moonshinin' business, allowing it had just got too risky. Well, Duck simmered down some, but she knew Lawton all too well to be consoled, very much, by his talk.

They stayed for a couple of hours with Duck and the youngens. Lawton did up the night work, while Reba Nell and Lorene washed the supper dishes. Lorene and Lawton then headed for Oak Ridge and Ma Annie's. Lorene was still crying when they got there and Little Doris, who was spending the weekend with Ma Annie, also became upset. Lorene tried to assure her everything would be alright. Now, Ma Annie was sympathetic toward Lorene's feelings to a point, but when the subject of Ma Annie getting Lawton off the hook the time he did only ninety days in the county jail in Paducah, when he was actually sentenced to one hundred and one, was mentioned, her cold reply cut Lorene to the core. Ma Annie made the comment that the place she lived on was hers, and that she'd not put it up as collateral for anybody's bond that wasn't Lawton's. And, sure enough, when she thought Lorene was out of earshot, she patted Lawton on the back and bragged on him for outsmarting the sheriff and revenue men, just as Lorene knew she would. The whole situation just drove the knife a little deeper in Lorene's heart against Lawton's actions and his mama condoning them.

It was well into the night before Lawton and Lorene returned to Golden Pond. Lorene said nothing all the way home, but silent tears spilled down her cheeks. Lawton made a feeble attempt to console her, but when she turned her head and glared at him in the dimness of the car, he caught the look on her face and immediately shut up.

Lawton did follow through with his promise, as far as getting bond for Ed. He didn't get it from Ma Annie though, "nawsiree." He went to a "friend" in Golden Pond, who had financed his bond a few times previously. Shaw, however, was sentenced to sixty days in the Federal Correctional Facility at Ashland.

Well, the old saying, "nothing ever stays the same," proved to be a true proverb in Lorene's life, once again. Soon after the raid and Lawton's narrow escape, things did take a different turn. It couldn't exactly be described as, "for the better," however, Lawton did finally start to seriously consider giving up moonshinin.' Ed and Shaw declared they had learned their lesson. Ed even made the comment that he would grub with the chickens before he would ever mix one more barrel of mash. Lorene knew in her mind that it wasn't because of her pleas, nor her tears, nor her throwing frustrated and scared fits that caused Lawton to change his perspective of the moonshinin' industry. One thing, and only one thing, contributed to his change of heart and mind: the odds were very high that, sooner or later, he was going to get caught and wind up in prison. The Feds were now thicker than fleas on a dogs back in the land between the rivers, and reckless, hard headed and "dyed-in-the-wool" as he might be, Lawton Higgins was no fool. You didn't see the Feds until it was too late, but they were out there, and Lawton knew it. The woods and hills and hollers were crawling with them, and they were dead serious about stamping out the making and selling of illicit whiskey in the land between the rivers, as well as every place else where it's practice was being carried on through out the country. It was fast becoming an all out war. Lawton was finally realizing he could no longer afford to pay off enough people to keep them away from his still.

The weeks that followed Lawton was gone much of the time. When Lorene confronted him as to his "whereabouts," he would tell her he was working on some business deals. It was nothing to see a strange car pull up in front of the house, and Lawton go outside and sit in the car and talk with two, three and maybe four men, never asking them to come inside. When Lorene would inquire about the details, he would answer her sternly, "You'll know what is goin' on when I think the time is right to tell you." Then he'd go on to say, "now, you want me out of the moonshinin' business, don't you?" When she'd nod in agreement, he'd then say, "then trust me and quit your naggin'." Well, this sort of situation continued till late in the fall. Now, Lawton had almost depleted the supply of kegs in the attic closets by making various "runs" to Murray, Owensboro, and Louisville, as well as Paris, Tennessee. Lorene guessed that was where he had come in contact with these strangers who would stop in front of their house from time to time.

The first frost came to Golden Pond in mid October, that fall of 1940. The garden "stuff" had been harvested. The apples and peaches were dried, and the jars of jam, jellies and preserves, were now added to the colorful arrangement of green beans, corn and tomatoes that were already on the shelves of the closet, next to the grate, in the living room.

How Lorene loved her home here on the outskirts of Golden Pond! This was her recluse from all of the rest of world. It was where she found comfort in her concern for Virgil's deafness and estrangement. This place helped her cope with her hate for Lawton's profession. The rambling old house in Golden Pond and Little Doris made up Lorene's "haven". She threw herself into the housework, sewing, yard work and garden; working diligently, many days, until she was totally exhausted. She was now, not only sewing for her family and Lawton's, but for neighbors, and making a little money for it too. She truly believed, had they still been living with Ma Annie during this trying time, she would have totally been out of her mind by now.

That crisp Halloween morning found Lorene engrossed in a complete, fall house cleaning. It was a Monday, Little Doris was at school, Lawton had been gone since sun-up and Lorene was hanging the last of the laundry on the clothes line, when a strange vehicle stopped in front of the house. She went around the house and a tall, rather nice looking middle aged man, dressed in khakis, and wearing a straw hat met her about half way across the front yard. He didn't give his name, but asked for Lawton. Lorene told him Lawton wasn't home, but didn't offer any other information, besides, Lawton hadn't told her where he was going anyway, which wasn't unusual as of the last few weeks since the raid. Well, the stranger didn't make any attempt to go back to his car, but pulled a cigarette from a pack in his shirt pocket and lit it up. Then, he took out the pack and offered Lorene one. She shook her head, thinking any minute he would go to his car, but he didn't. He just stood there, a few feet away, looking at her. Lorene began feeling very uncomfortable. She knew her hair was a mess, for she hadn't even combed it earlier, and she was wearing an old, faded dress and sweater, with the worst looking pair of shoes she had. She finally opened her mouth to speak, but the stranger spoke first, "Lawton's got an awful pretty wife to be leaving here by herself while he's out galivantin' around."

Lorene could feel the muscles tighten in her neck and the flush coming over her face. "Don't guess you know where he is or when he'll be back?" the man asked her. Then before she could answer he added, "Reckon it would be fittin' for me to wait for him? Me an him's got some pretty important business to discuss. Naw, I don't guess it would be fittin' for me to wait, huh?" He went on, but made no attempt to leave.

She hesitated in giving an answer, for she couldn't figure out what this man was up to. She only knew she didn't like him, he was making her feel uncomfortable, and she wanted him to leave.

"I've got work to do, and you just need to make it another time to see Lawton," she finally said bluntly, then turned around and started back around the house without looking back. She breathed a sigh of relief when she heard the car start up.

Lawton got home, from wherever, about dark and she told him of her encounter with the stranger. He fussed at her for not finding out who he was and where he was from. It seemed Lawton was pretty curious about he man, maybe even nervous, for he questioned her a couple more times about him that night. He finally asked what kind of vehicle he was driving and when Lorene said it looked like a late model, dark blue Ford, Lawton became at ease. Well, Lorene had, by now, stood about as much of Lawton's mysterious behavior as she could. She thought it was about time she found out what was going on in Lawton's business world. She was already tired of strange people pulling up in front of the house and Lawton not asking them in, and his going off everyday, and not telling her where he was going, or when he'd be home, really was wearing her nerves thin.

"Now, Lawton don't you think it's about time you told me what's going on, here?" she asked as they got ready for bed. "I'm uneasy, and yes, down right scared of these strange men that are coming around here, especially the one that came here today. Now I want to know, what the devil is goin' on?"

"Well, I've been making a lot of business contacts about makin' us a livin' at something different," he started, "an' these people I'm dealin' with, now, they ain't bad people or nothin,' they just don't want people meddlin'. They don't want things talked; you know...business?"

"No I don't know!" Lorene exploded. "What sort of business? What, in the name of God, are you gettin' into now, Lawton? Some of these men look like mobsters!"

"Well, they ain't mobsters. They're just business men, that's all. An' you needn't get yourself so riled up about it. You want me out of moonshinin', don't you?"

"Yes, but..."

"Alright, then hush up about it. These men ain't gonna' harm you an' I don't want you gettin' smart with em' either," he said, sharply.

"Then I guess you just expect me to invite some strange man I've never laid eyes on before, who is lookin' me up an' down like I'm some kind of trollop, to come in our house, an' wait till you come home, from wherever, at whatever time!" Lorene shouted.

"Aw th' Devil and Tom Walker, Lorene! I'm sick an' tired of trying to reason with you! You're worse than some kid. You won't trust me. You keep naggin' an' naggin' an' all I'm doin' is tryin' to make a decent livin' as best as I know how, for you and the kids. An' what's the thanks I get? A frigid woman that rakes me over the coals the minute I walk in the door. I'm sick of it Lorene. I'm goin' through a lot of pressure here, with this thing, an' all you want to do is add to it!" Lawton shouted back as he plopped down on the couch.

"Alright Lawton," Lorene began in a low, steady voice. "I won't ask no more questions, even if I do think your gittin' into somethin' that ain't exactly right, but I'll tell you one thing straight out. The next time a strange car pulls up, and an' you're not here, and a strange man starts across my yard, I'll sure as hell meet him with something besides a smile. I'll be meetin' him with that double barrel shotgun! So, I suggest you let your fine "business men" know when it's safe for them to be comin' around here."

Well, that following Friday, the mystery was solved for Lorene. Lawton was up and gone before sun-up. Lorene got Doris off to school, straightened the house, and started sewing for one of their old neighbors in the Fenton Community. She had only been at the sewing machine for and hour or so, when she heard Lawton pull up. Thinking nothing of it, she continued sewing. Soon, she heard their '40 Olds coming across the yard toward the back of the house. She got up from the sewing machine, which was in their bedroom, came through the living room, and was entering the kitchen, just as Lawton was coming through the back door with Jake behind him, each carrying two cases of beer. Lorene just stood in the doorway staring. "Move out of the way, honey," Lawton said, sweetly, as he proceeded across the kitchen. "Gotta get this stuff up to the attic."

"I will swear to my time! Out of the frying pan, into the fire!" Lorene said, shaking her head, for she knew, exactly, what was now going on.

Well, that was the beginning of Lawton's career in another facet of the liquor business. He had gone from moonshinin' to bootlegging. He and Jake filled two of the closets with cases and six packs of beer, whatever the customer could want: Papst Blue Ribbon, Falls City, Sterling, Schlitz or Falstaff... it was all there in the closets of the attic bedrooms, filling the space previously occupied by the kegs of moonshine.

That night, early on, the '40 Olds made it's way, once again, up the driveway, through the yard, and to the back porch. Jake and Lawton unloaded and stored, in the other closets, cases of Kentucky Bourbon, red and white wines, brandy, gin, vodka and eighty, ninety and one hundred proof whiskey, from Old Crow to Jack Daniel's. Lorene was too flabbergasted to put up a fight.

Well, Lawton was staying closer to home now. Lorene didn't know, if it was because he had completed his, "business

Lawton and Shaw with two that didn't get away.

dealings," as far as establishing his suppliers, or if he was afraid she was going to run off his customer clientele, with the shotgun. Anyway, business started. Some of the clientele were his old moonshine customers, and some were people Lorene had never seen before. This time Lawton didn't deliver to the customers, they came to him; sun-up till bedtime were the "business" hours.

Yes, Lawton was out of the moonshinin' business, and Lorene was glad of it, but it seemed anytime a ray of sunshine started to shine on Lorene, a cloud would manage to smother it. You see, this new livelihood, which did seem to be a little less risky as far as the law, was, more and more, requiring Lorene's assistance. Since Lawton's customer clientele was in the establishing stage, there wasn't a lot of money coming in. True, he had a good number of customers to start with, and more were coming on a regular basis, but word hadn't gotten around, everywhere that first month or two. So, Lawton decided he would try his hand at commercial fishing with Ed, Shaw and Guy. Now, Guy was in the process of getting a job with the state police, which later did transpire, much to Lawton's advantage, so much so, it contributed to Lawton's bootlegging business for thirty years, but while he waited for the state police job to come through, Guy was in the fishing business.

Although Lorene was glad to see her husband doing at least one legal thing, starting his fishing career put her, center stage, in the bootlegging limelight, a spot she totally detested. When customers came, while Lawton was away fishing in the Tennessee River with Ed, Guy and Shaw, it fell to Lorene to take care of them. She was polite, which most of the time wasn't a problem, but when caught in one of those rare occasions, when her politeness was taken for granted, especially by some of the few who came half-tanked to purchase more, and tried to loiter, she learned real fast when and how to draw the line, customer or no customer!

Well, time went on, and the business was growing, and true, more money was beginning to come in. However, Lorene and Lawton staged one of the major battles of their married life that following summer. Now, Lorene might not have been the most educated or smartest young woman in Trigg County, but, there was one thing for sure, she wasn't the dumbest nor the greenest either. Lorene knew she didn't have to be a college graduate to figure out that Lawton was letting part of his money get away, somewhere. This had been going on for most of the summer. His playing innocent of always letting Lorene know where every penny went, was not bought by Lorene at this particular time, and she confronted him with the subject one night. Lorene knew pretty well, through her experience of taking care of the bulk of customers in the daytime, the amount of money that came in from the liquor sales, and she knew, within a pretty close range, what he was making from the commercial fishing, so she pinned him down. After about thirty minutes of discussion, which she managed to dominate, she had him backed so far in the corner, Lawton had no choice but to admit to the little poker game in which he was engaged, two or three times a week. He even informed her of the meeting place and the dozen or so men and boys, including himself, who participated. The spot was less than a half mile from their house, in an old creek bed. Well, that explained the money situation. It also explained why some nights Lawton would come home in such a cantankerous mood, the good Lord himself couldn't stand to be around him. Evidently, on those nights he had all but a winning hand. Well, needless to say, when she heard this, Lorene cut loose on him full force! And, as usual, he defended himself to the hilt, even throwing in that the main reason for his participating in the poker game was because it was advantageous to his bootlegging business; "it drew customers," he said. When she asked him where they played when the creek filled up from rain, he just answered, nonchalantly, "we just meet up the holler."

At his point Lorene simply threw up her hands in disgust and bewilderment, and went to bed.

That night was certainly a pretty big showdown between Lorene and Lawton, but it was nothing compared to one that occurred just before school started that Fall. Lorene and Doris had gone to Ma Annie's to pick some apples, leaving Lawton and Virgil, who was winding up his summer vacation from the Danville school, at home. After some two hours, Lorene and Doris returned home with a bushel of apples, only to find Lawton and Virgil gone. They had gone fishing pretty often during the summer, so, Lorene figured that was where they were that particular afternoon. Well, Lorene didn't think too much about their absence until near sundown, when one of their regular customers pulled up to purchase a case of beer. Lorene was carrying on the usual conversation with him, as he made his purchase, and as he was paying her, he made the comment that he believed Lawton had more pocket money than any man he knew, for he'd sure pulled out a fist full of bills to bet on, what he thought was a "pat" hand, down at the creek just a few minutes ago. Well, Lorene kept her cool until the regular got in his car and left. Then, she grabbed Doris, piled her in the car and flew out of the driveway, heading for the dirt road that led to the dried-up, creek bed. She could feel the heat steaming from her face, as her anger rose to the boiling point!

"The very idea of him taking Virgil down there with that bunch of no good drunks to play poker!" she mouthed aloud. "One of these days your daddy's gonna push me too far, and I'm gonna hide these car keys, board up every door on the house, and he can find him another place to stay. I'm sick and tired of his nonsense, and I've had enough!" She stormed as they bounced over the bumpy road. Little Doris began to whimper, "don't be mean to daddy."

"Hush up your whining, I'm not mean to daddy. He's the one mean to me, and to Virgil, taking him down there in that mess of, no-account drunks!" she stormed on.

Now, Lorene had never been to the exact spot where the poker playing took place, but she chugged along the rutted road, till she found it. First, she saw three vehicles, two of which she recognized, parked in the bottom, a few feet from the creek. She pulled the car up close enough to see down in the creek. Sure enough, there was Lawton and Virgil, along with several others she recognized, down in the dried-up creek bed, under the shade of a huge oak tree that stood on the bank. They all looked up, surprised, when she drove up. By the time she got out of the car, Virgil was running toward her, with Lawton close behind. Lawton opened his mouth to speak, likely hoping to keep down a scene, but his effort was to no avail. Lorene had already cut loose.

"Lawton Higgins, I cannot believe you have brought Virgil down here with this bunch of, no good, scum buckets! What, in the name of sense, do you mean? It is bad enough for you to throw away money we don't have, but for you to bring your own son down here is as low as you can get! Have you no conscious? Teaching your son the devil's game! That's all you are doing, teaching him to play poker and throw his money away, just like you! I will NEVER forgive you for this, an' don't think for one minute you will just be able to walk in the front door and everything will be alright! I've got news for you, as far as I'm concerned you can just hitch a ride with one of your drinking, poker playing, low-life here, and keep goin' for all I care! I'm sick and tired of this mess, and I cannot believe you would bring your only son down here to see just what you are up to while I am at the house doing your job!!"

Lawton didn't say a word, but if looks could kill, Lorene would have been a dead young woman. Fire was blazing from his eyes, and his face was red as blood, and Lorene knew it wasn't just from the heat. She had humiliated him in front of his peers and customers, but she was too mad to care. She piled Virgil in the front seat next to Doris, who by now was crying, loudly. Virgil looked bewildered, and for a moment Lorene thought she he was going to refuse to get him in the car. Finally, he did. She slammed the door after him, stomped around the car, got behind the wheel, started the motor, jerked it in gear and tore out of the bottom. Hot tears were streaming down her face as she barreled down the rutted road, while Lawton stood, with fists clinched, in the cloud of dust she left behind.

Evidently, her little escapade broke up the poker game, for she and the kids hadn't much more than gotten in the house, when one of the vehicles from the creek pulled up in front of the house and let Lawton out, while another passed, as Lawton came across the yard.

Well, needless to say, the fireworks began all over again, and lasted until Lawton stomped out of the house to do up the night work. Virgil at his heels. Virgil might not have been, but a lad of a boy, and unable to verbally communicate his opinion, but his actions obviously displayed whose side he was on. It was evident, he thought his mama had come down rather hard on his daddy. That went for Doris also, but Lorene didn't care. Someday they would see why she was so distraught. Someday they would realize she just didn't want Virgil to follow his daddy in the moonshinin' and bootlegging business, and throwing away his money on poker games. She planned to do everything within her might to see that Virgil had a respectable, law abiding livelihood when he grew up, regardless of the cost.

Chapter Ten:

Life Goes On

G olden Pond, once again, became a thriving town within five years after the devastating fire, in 1937. Lawton and Lorene were happy with their home. Lawton continued as an "entrepreneur" in the liquor business, while Lorene continued to tend the house, along with Little Doris and Virgil, when he was home for the summer. She also did a lot of the garden and yard work, and it seemed she was taking on more and more seamstress work from people in Golden Pond, as well as surrounding communities.

In late spring that year the state allocated funds for the paving of Highway 68, which was the main road through Golden Pond and the road, on which, Lawton and Lorene lived. Numerous kinds of equipment were brought-in and droves of men made up the construction crews that were to complete the job. Some of them lived quite a distance away, and it wasn't long until the Golden Pond Hotel was filled to capacity, leaving several of the men looking for temporary lodging near the job site. Well, Lorene's mind set to motion as soon as she got word of this. The four rooms upstairs were not in use except when they had company, for there were enough rooms downstairs to accommodate she Lawton and the children. There were furnishings in three of the attic rooms, and Lorene knew she could get temporarily use another double bed from her mama to set up in the fourth room. There was an army surplus store on the outskirts of Hopkinsville, and if cots could be purchased for the basement, why not rent that extra space to these construction workers and bring in a little extra money? Along with a place to sleep for the workers, she would furnish breakfast and supper for those who enjoyed "country cookin'" and was willing to pay a little more. She presented her idea to Lawton, who agreed, and they set a price. He even talked to the men himself, that following Monday, when they came to begin the project. They were very glad to pay what Lorene was asking for the rooms and two meals a day. The price was a dollar a day, per person.

Now, Lorene had been cooking since she couldn't remember when. It wasn't a problem for her to put a five course meal on the table for her family, nor for occasional company. But, that next Monday morning, when eleven construction workers, ranging in ages from sixteen to forty, came to her back door to pay their first weeks room and board, Lorene knew she had her work cut out for her. It was certainly a time to give thanks for a bountiful garden.

Lorene finished getting her "washin" on the line that Monday morning, then headed for the garden. She managed pick about a peck of the tender green beans which were just coming in, along with a couple of dozen ears of early sweet corn. Lawton had dug several hills of the potatoes the Saturday before, and there was still plenty of green onions, radishes and leaf lettuce, which they had been having for several days, now.

Lorene, after bringing the garden "stuff" into the kitchen, put the tea-kettle on the hottest, burner of the stove, and headed for the chicken yard. This was a small, fenced in area adjacent to the garden that contained some fifty chickens of various breeds and sizes, along with a good size building, partitioned in two sections. One section had wooden boxes built, some three feet from the ground, all of the way around the walls, which were filled with straw. This was the laying and setting area for the hens. The other section had long poles which extended the length of the room. This was the roosting area for all of the chickens.

Lorene entered the gate of the chicken yard with a small pail of corn. The chickens flocked around her clucking and squawking as she threw handfuls of corn before them. Glancing quickly over the colorful flock that was hungrily pecking at the corn, she spied a plump, young red hen, and quickly seized her, then headed for the gate. The hen flounced and squawked, as Lorene made her way to the back yard, where she proceeded to perform the execution by "wringing" her neck. When this fatal gesture was completed, which only took one twist by Lorene's experienced hand, she dropped the hen to the ground where it flounced about for a few seconds, then laid still. Lorene went into the kitchen and brought a pail and the tea-kettle of boiling water, out to the back yard. There she completed the task of preparing the hen for the large pot where it would be accompanied with dumplings, when it had cooked until tender.

Lorene began preparing the remainder of supper around four o'clock that afternoon. It consisted of a stove top filled with cooked vegetables, along with the chicken and dumplings, a large platter of the fresh raw vegetables, cornbread and a three layer coconut cake. Well, there was not a picky eater in the whole bunch, for only a few green beans were left in the bowl when the eleven hungry men and her family finished eating.

The day ended with a balmy southern breeze stirring the trees in the front yard. Lawton and the children, along with the construction workers, retired to the front porch, while Lorene cleaned up the kitchen. The kitchen was hot, and she kept pushing the long strands of dark, hair back from her face as she placed the dishes in the cabinet. When she finally closed the cabinet door, she went to the wash basin and splashed cold water on her face, dried it with a towel, and went out on the back porch to cool. She sat on the edge of the porch, resting her feet on the top step, enjoying the recluse from the hot kitchen. She could hear the monotones and occasional laughter of the men on the front porch. She was sure Lawton was entertaining his new audience to the fullest with some of his favorite moonshinin' tales.

Lightening bugs could be seen, here and there, as they darted through the gathering, twilight, beneath the trees, as Lorene sat there on the edge of the porch. The sound of a whippoorwill, in the woods behind the barn, sang out it's call, either to it's mate, or maybe, just in harmony with the katydids and crickets, whose voices were beginning to fill the early, summer evening air. Lorene's mind once again began to drift back to the days of her childhood.

Now Lorene, in her early, childhood days, could not even, boast of a battery radio for entertainment. There were some folks in the community who had one, but not Ed and Duck. However, the Turner's knew how to create their own entertainment from time to time. Both of her parents could play a banjo and guitar. Lorene remembered one summer, in particular, when she was around eight years old, that her great Uncle Warner would come over with his fiddle. Ed and Duck would bring the banjo and guitar out on the front porch, and they would all make music till bedtime. Sometimes, on a Saturday night, several of the neighbors would come over to sit on the porch and take in the entertainment. Some would even join in by singing some of their favorite songs. "Barbara Allen, Red River Valley and On Top of Old Smoky" were among the songs they would sing, while, intermittently, Uncle Warner would liven up the session with "Turkey In The Straw and Fire On The Mountain." Lorene, Shaw, Viona and Guy would have a fun time playing with the neighboring children and listening to the music. She smiled to herself as she thought about those care free, times.

Now, Ma Annie could play an organ, and play pretty well. In fact, she even played occasionally at the Mormon conferences. Well, one particular time she played at Hopewell Baptist Church, which was located across the road from the Fenton School. They were holding their annual protracted meeting that fall, and as always, Ma Annie attended. Now, Hopewell was a right smart piece from Oak Ridge, a far piece to walk, that is, so Lawton had brought Ma Annie to the church on his way to Golden Pond to pick up Lorene and the children. Well, it seems Lawton had dropped her off early, and for the want of something to until service time, Ma Annie started playing the organ. Now, there really wasn't anything wrong with Ma Annie playing the organ. No, the Baptist congregation wouldn't have opposed that at all, had they been sitting right there in the pews, listening; not if she had been playing some Bap-

Lawton's mother Ma Annie.

tist or other Protestant hymn. However, Ma Annie began sounding out the cords of one of her favorite Mormon hymns, "Oh My Father."

Well, luckily, for Ma Annie, Lawton, Lorene and the children just happened to be next to arrive at the church. When Lawton turned the motor of the car off, they heard the music coming from the church, and they didn't recognize the song until they had gotten out of the car and were walking toward the building.

Lorene and Lawton glanced at each other in wide-eyed amazement at hearing a Mormon song playing in the Hopewell Baptist Church. Little Doris, who had run ahead of Lawton, Lorene and Virgil, was looking in the door and yelled back, "It's Ma Annie! It's Ma Annie playin' the organ!"

"Oh My Lord!" Lorene shouted as she started looking around to see if any of the congregation was in sight. "Mammy, Mammy, you'd better stop playing "Oh My Father" in this Baptist church or you'll get us all thrown out," Lorene yelled, quickening her stride, across the church yard.

Lorene stood, mouth open, in the door of the church. She looked from Ma Annie, to several families who were now coming up the road in the gathering twilight. Lawton was chuckling, but Lorene was wringing her hands in exasperation. Well, in a few moments time, the pastor and evangelist were leading a crowd toward the front door of the church. It was then, Ma Annie sounded the last cord, of the last verse of "Oh My Father." Whether anyone recognized the rendition Ma Annie had just rendered on the organ in the Oak Ridge Baptist Church, was never revealed. However, at the end of the service, when the congregation was shaking hands with the pastor and evangelist, the pastor did comment, "Why, Mrs. Higgins, I didn't know you played the organ." Ma Annie raised her eyebrows, tilted her chin and said, demurely, "I play a little bit." She then pranced on out of the church. Lorene and Lawton, who were behind her, threw each other knowing glances. Well, bound for Lawton. He was having the time of his life with the whole situation, for, he chuckled, and said: "She does play right, purty, now, don't she Pastor?"

The sound of the screen door slamming, jolted Lorene back to her senses. She turned from her position, on the edge of the porch, to see little Doris standing, in the door way, rubbing her eyes.

"I'm sleepy, mama," she whined, in her tired little voice.

Lorene rose from the edge of the porch, ushered Doris into the house, and glanced at the clock on the mantel in the living room.

"I'll bet you are sleepy, it's nine o'clock, and mama needs to get to bed too. I've got to get up at four in the morning in order to fix breakfast for all them workin' men. Come on, you can sleep with me til' daddy comes to bed," Lorene said, leading Doris to the bedroom.

Well, four o'clock came very early, that next day and after fixing a country breakfast for the eleven hungry men, as well, as her own family, Lorene made up her mind to recruit some help. Now, Lawton was of no help at all in the kitchen. He did go to the grocery store and lay in the groceries, most of the time, and he helped some, by bringing in the garden stuff, outside of that, Lawton was out about his own business during the day.

Well, around noon the next day, Lawton came wheeling in the driveway, with his cousin Clotis, to assist Lorene, in her cooking for the construction crew. Clotis was separated from her husband at the time, and needed a job and a place to stay. Lorene was, more than glad, to have her stay with them. That same day Lawton came bringing in two country hams, which he had purchased for twenty five cents a pound. The men from the construction crew sure knew how to put away country ham, "red eye" gravy, hot biscuits and eggs, along with sorghum molasses and fresh churned butter.

Spring slipped into summer, and the men of the construction crew, sleeping upstairs, were beginning to complain about the heat. One night, Lorene thought two of the younger men were going to fight over who was sleeping in the basement where it was cool. They finally agreed to take turns. All in all, though, considering there were sixteen people living under the same roof that summer, Lorene had to agree everyone got along very well. Ma Annie had to put her two cents worth in about Clotis being in the house with eleven men, though. Lorene let her know right quick that she wasn't having anything immoral going on in her house, and since Clotis was, three times seven, what she did away from the house was of her own doin'. Incidentally, Clotis did start seeing one of the single men in the construction crew.

Well, in repeating the old "adage" once again, "Nothing ever stays the same," was true of life in Golden Pond and the land between the rivers. Times were getting even harder for the average moonshiner. That is, what was left of them. Lawton had said more times than one, in the last couple of years, he was glad he was out of the moonshinin' business. He was still telling "hair-raising" stories about people in the "business" both near and far, that were having to resort to drastic measures to transport their "goods." Yes, Lawton still kept in touch with those left in the "business".

One such story was of a fellow over on the ridge near the Cumberland who worked and drove a truck for a feed company, and moonshined on the side. He would put a jug of his illicit grog in the middle of each, hundred pound sack of feed and transport it to Indiana, twice a week. This set-up worked for some time, until, an observant, government man, took notice of a couple of peculiar bulges in a sack of the feed while the truck was parked, unoccupied, on the main street of the town, to which, the deliveries were being made. Upon investigating more closely, it was discovered, that every sack on the truck contained a gallon jug of moonshine. Lawton told the story of another sneaky transporter who owned a small grocery store near the Cumberland. He slipped a quantity of moonshine into his store in molasses buckets, which was passed on to the consumer from a side door, by his twelve year old son.

It seemed, out of desperation some moonshiner's were converting the back seats of their sedans or coupes into a single tank which could hold up to two hundred and fifty gallons. They would fill the tank, then use whatever method available to camouflage their load as they carried their "wares" to other towns or states. Yes, times were hard for the moonshiner and from the number of "Feds" turning up in the woods, hills and hollers, it was risky business to be in the moonshinin' profession. Lawton often spoke of the moonshinin' "business" as soon be a thing of the past, maybe even a lost art.

Other changes were taking place in the land between the rivers, as well as throughout the country. It seemed like the government couldn't be content with the new prosperity the country was now able to enjoy since the depression days of only a few years prior. There was talk that the United States was likely to become involved in the war that was going on "overseas."

Now, Lorene didn't have a lot of time to listen to the radio and she definitely preferred music to the news, but Lawton hardly ever missed the evening news. Whether it was because Lorene was maturing and her interests were becoming broader or the fact that Shaw and Guy were of draft age, she found herself listening more intently to the evening news along with Lawton. Then, too she absorbed a lot from the conversations of Lawton, her dad and the road construction crew. The radio commentator spoke a lot of "The allied big three," Britain's Winston Churchill, President F.D. Roosevelt and Russia's leader, Joseph Stalin. Such places as Germany, Italy, Japan, Great Britain, Asia and France were already participating in war fare. The commentators explained that Adolph Hitler of Germany was a powerful figure and boasted of a well-balanced armed force. It seemed Hitler and Benito Mussolini of Italy, along with their well trained and well organized armies were aiming for a great world empire. Now, Lorene didn't understand the total extent of or the intricate details of the war "overseas," but the news stated Canada had declared war on Germany. She did know, however, Canada was getting pretty close to home. The news also stated that the United States, which previously chose to stay uninvolved, had now shifted it's policy from neutrality to preparedness. Lawton said a draft seemed inevitable. Her worries were not for Lawton going "overseas" to combat, for he could never pass the physical examination because of his crippled leg from Polio, but she knew Shaw and Guy would be prime candidates.

President Roosevelt had already called upon the United States to be "the great arsenal of democracy," which as Lawton explained, meant to supply war materials to the Allies through sale, loan or lease. In Roosevelt's last speech to the nation, over the airwaves, he stated the fact, that he planned to triple the number of military men in the U.S. armed forces, along with adding thousands of airplanes and war ships to the U.S. fighter vessels. All of this overwhelmed and frightened Lorene.

The fall, following the paving of Highway 68, the war "over seas" raged on and other changes took place in Lorene's world, as well. Ma Annie decided to buy the old Golden Pond Bank building which had incurred some damage in the thirty seven fire. The bank had constructed a new building and except for the Masonic Lodge meetings which were held once a month in the second story of the old bank building, it sat empty and for sale. So, Ma Annie hired carpenters to renovate the small amount of damage and convert the commercial building into a dwelling. So in late November, she moved in. Lorene knew the main reason for her decision was because Lawton's visits back to Oak Ridge had slowed down to a couple of times a week and Ma Annie couldn't stand not seeing Lawton and the kids every day. Then too, Ma Annie's health wasn't too good. She was having problems with high blood pressure. Anyway, Lorene didn't care that she lived much closer to them as long as she kept her nose out of their business. Virgil and little Doris were happy to have Ma Annie closer, and Lorene had to admit, she was very good to them.

That same fall, Lorene and Lawton took Virgil back to school at Danville. He was glad to be back in school, which made the trip and their farewells much easier. It still pained Lorene to leave him, but he no longer cried and clung to her as he had in his earlier years. He had made a lot of friends and was trying hard in his subjects. Virgil had learned several words such as thumb, nose, ear, face, eyes, hair and from pictures he was learning the different means of transportation and farm animals. He seemed to get along well with most of his instructors, however, he did complain somewhat about a Miss Lawson whom was the "House Parent" of the boys his age.

A new program was being incorporated into their schedule that year. The students at Danville were given the opportunity to learn the details of what was now being called, "World War II." They were informed that the United States was at a slight risk of an attack. Although, the fighting was taking place "overseas," the students had drills, instructing what to do and where to go in the event of an attack or a blackout. Virgil and the other students as well were frightened in the beginning, but the instructors kept assuring them an attack was not likely. However, they wanted them to know how to react just in case.

Back in Golden Pond little Doris had, once again, entered school. She made a friend that year that would be her friend all through her elementary years. Her friend's name was Edna Hooks. You see, Lawton screened Doris' friends very closely. He was careful that she didn't bring home children from whose families did not cater to the bootleggin' business. It could cause a peck of trouble for him, but, he did allow her to have a few friends. One of her favorite friends was Edna Hooks. She came from a large family who lived over on the ridge, and with so many youngens to feed and clothe, Edna didn't have as much, materially as did Doris. Edna was a quiet and well behaved little girl and thoroughly enjoyed visiting with Doris and playing with Doris' toys. Lorene knew the family, likely, did not have an abundance of food, so she always fixed something special when Edna came to visit. Edna was a year or so older than Doris, but because she was needed at home to help care for her younger siblings, she had missed a lot of school. Therefore, she was in Doris' class. Doris mentioned to Lorene that many times Edna came to school without any lunch, so Lorene began packing an extra sandwich in Doris' little red, tin lunch pail for Edna.

One Doris came home very upset. The County Health Nurse had made her annual visit to inoculate the students. Well, little Doris had been ill at the end of the summer and had been given a shot and also prescribed some other medication, and obviously she thought she did not have to take the typhoid shot. She flat out told the health nurse she was not going to have the shot because her parents did not want her to have it. Well, the health nurse flat out told her if she didn't take the typhoid shot that her daddy would go to jail. Needless to say, the distraught Doris let the nurse give her the inoculation, but cried the remainder of the afternoon and was still crying as she started walking the short

The Higgins Family, 1940.

distance home. To add to her dilemma, as she neared the curb just beyond the school, she encountered a group of dirty, odd-looking people on the side of the road unloading broken down chairs, blankets and pots and pans from a rickety wagon pulled by two of the grubbiest, skimpiest mules she had ever seen. Obviously, they were setting up camp for the night. Doris was frightened as she approached the strange bunch. There were three small children, two men and a young woman. All were ragged and skinny as the mules. They glared at her as she proceeded in their direction and she thought of turning around and running back to the school but she knew no one would be there so she quickened her pace and crossed to the other side of the road, ran past them and did not stop running until she had reached the kitchen door at home. By this time she was crying hysterically. Lorene came running from the bedroom where she had been at the sewing machine and it took her a full twenty minutes to calm Doris enough for her to explain why she was so distraught. Lorene walked a short distance down the road until she came in sight of the strange intruders, and neither could she figure out who they were. When Lawton came home that night she confronted him with the subject and he informed her they were Gypsies. He said he had seen them camped along the road in various communities under the shade of a large tree usually near a stream. They would stay around for a week or so, then they would move on.

No one had complained of any major harm being done by them. However, some folks had noticed some of their chickens had come up missing. One man near Turkey Creek had a side of middling missing from his smoke house and a woman on the other side of Golden Pond had several pieces of her washin' missing when she went to bring it in off the clothesline. But, there was no proof that the Gypsies did the taking and since they were camped on the side of the road which was state property, they couldn't be ordered off so the citizens just had to tolerate their presence until they decided to move on. Well, needless to say, Doris was escorted to and from school until the Gypsies moved on which was about a week later. Luckily, nothing was missing on the Higgins' property, but having two noisy bird dogs and a large yellow "mutt" of a variety of breeds, which would turn it's bristles wrongside-out at anybody strange, might have contributed to the Higgins' property being secured.

Autumn once again lost it's battle to "old' man winter", and the cold weather brought on the usual winter illnesses. Doris was sick almost all winter and missed quite a bit of school. Lorene worried she would have to take the fourth grade over the next year.

The war "overseas" was consistently heating up and as folks all over the country feared, the draft was initiated. Young, single men in good health were now being inducted into every facet of the military. Guy, Lorene's younger brother, received his notice to report to Louisville for his physical examination the first of December. The whole family was up in arms about it, but there would be nothing they could do except pray for his safety. The news commentators were saying able bodied married men with no children would be next for the draft, then if the war progressed, even able bodied men with children would be called. Farmers would be among the last to have to serve. This was the advantage Shaw had over Guy, who was now on the State Police Force; he was still farming with Ed and also doing some share cropping. Lawton, of course had his physical handicap and being a family man and a farmer of sorts, would decrease his chances of having to serve military time. As for his primary business, bootleggin', causing him to be exempt from serving in the war "overseas'. Well, if that issue was brought into light it likely would cause him to spend time somewhere else. Lawton had already declared was not going to go "overseas' and fight a bunch of "furiners" and if it came down to it he'd put on silk stockings leg and act like the craziest man on earth if he was called to Louisville for a physical examination. Lorene's answer to that remark was, "As for the crazy part, you won't have to do much acting."

Chapter Eleven:
Changing Times

World War II left it's mark on almost every facet of society in the United States, even though actual combat did not transpire on American soil. The attack on Pearl Harbor on December 7, 1941, when the Pacific Fleet lost eight battleships, three light cruisers, three destroyers and four other vessels along with one hundred and seventy U. S. planes, and killed or wounded 3,700 people, brought about the signing of the declaration of war by President Franklin D. Roosevelt. This gesture also brought about one of the largest draft laws ever known in U.S. history. Every state, county and community in the country gave up their young men to fight in the war "overseas," which has been considered the mightiest struggle that mankind has ever seen. Major changes and developments came about in every country as a result of World War II. Estimates of the cost of the war exceeded one billion, one hundred and fifty four million dollars and damage to property exceeded two hundred and thirty five billion dollars. The causalities in the U.S. alone reached 1,215,00 men and women.

People on the home front spent the war years building weapons, producing food and clothing, buying war bonds and paying taxes to help aid in winning the war. There were many shortages in consumer goods, therefore in the U.S. the rationing of butter, sugar, canned foods, gasoline, shoes fats, coffee and canned goods was enacted in 1942. Congress also gave the President power to freeze prices, salaries and wages. Opportunities for work in the building of aircraft and sea vessels caused many people to move about during the war. Several families had left the land between the rivers and moved to larger cities such as Detroit, Michigan and Evansville, Indiana to work in the ship-yards during the war years. May and her second husband, Stewart Cunningham, along with Maxine also moved to Detroit where Stewart went to work at the Ford Motor Company.

Guy was inducted into the Army in February of 1942 and was shipped to Europe after his six weeks of basic training states side. During his three years he spent most of the time in Europe where he incurred three major injuries. The Army awarded Guy several medals including the Purple Heart for bravery and unfaltering service to his country. Shaw was called into service during the latter part of the war. Shaw, whom had worked some in construction, was experienced in operating heavy equipment so he was sent to Okinawa to help restore the Island from the ravages of battle. During his hitch on Okinawa he contracted malaria and was hospitalized several months. Needless to

Lorene (top) with sisters Viona and Reba.

The Turner brothers: Shaw, Guy, and George.

say, it was a great day of rejoicing in Golden Pond as well as elsewhere throughout America on September 2, 1945, when General Douglas MacArthur and Yoshijio Umeza of Japan aboard the U.S.S. Missouri in Tokyo Bay, signed the peace treaty ending World War II.

During the War years, state funds had been cut back and the Kentucky School for the Deaf had only been in session for three months in 1943 and two months in 1944, but regular sessions resumed and continued through out the whole term in 1945. It was during the War years that Lawton and Lorene became acquainted with Willard and Margaret DePriest, who were from Benton, and had enrolled their son Jerry in the school at Danville the same year Virgil was enrolled. Jerry was a twin, born with some birth defects which caused him to be deaf. His twin sister, Ernestine, was born with perfect hearing. The DuPriests' were wonderful people who shared the same trauma as Lawton and Lorene. They began making the trip to Danville together, which was a great comfort, as well as a convenience for both families. Virgil and Jerry got along well and took comfort in each other, which eased Lorene's mind a great deal. It seemed that Virgil having a friend from close to home made him a little less lonely for home. Lawton and Willard drove Virgil and Jerry back to school in the fall of '45.

Virgil had a class in carpentry and woodwork that year. He also had a class in the tailor shop and learned to sew pants and shirts. Virgil enjoyed the shop classes. He did well also, in science and geography, but had trouble with math and English. He tried to play football when he was seventeen, but did not catch on to the game very well and after a season of sitting on the bench, he decided to give it up.

A tragic thing took place in the summer of '48 that left it's mark on the Higgins family for the rest of their lives. On July second Lorene, Virgil and Doris had paid Ed and Duck a visit to spend the day. Around four in the afternoon, Lorene purchased several items from the small grocery store and fish market her daddy owned and operated, then she and the children got in the '47 Olds and headed for Golden Pond.

The heat of the July day had not cooled much as they drove over the country roads toward their home. All of the windows in the car were open and Virgil and Doris had gotten into a push and shove "ruckus" as to whom was going to ride next to the open window in the front seat along side Lorene. Virgil won, leaving Doris to sit in the middle next to her mama. They were coming around the bend and starting up the straight stretch just out of sight of their place, some fifty yards from the house, when Lorene saw a '36 Ford coming toward them in the middle of the road. She began pulling the Olds to the side of the road as far as she could without dropping into a steep incline to get out of the way of the on coming vehicle, but the on coming car proceeded toward them at a high speed, swerving from the middle of the road to the side of the road on which Lorene was driving. Frantically, she tried to break enough to stop, but it was to no avail. The '36 Ford was zooming head on toward the Olds at "break-neck" speed as though there was no other car on the road.

Struggling desperately to swerve out of the path of the on coming car, Lorene said between clinched teeth, "That fool must be drunk," then, the sounds of Doris screaming was the last thing she remembered before she felt the terrible jolt against the Olds, pushing it out of control. The rear end was sliding downward into the deep gully she had tried frantically to miss only seconds ago. The sound of metal scraping against metal and a loud thud mingled with the sound of breaking glass and a sudden jerk of her head against something was the last thing she remembered.

The next thing Lorene knew she was looking through a blur into the faces of George and Mary Edna Blight, the neighbors. They were trying to get the car door open. "Hurry, we gotta get em out, it might blow up!" One of them was saying, "We've gotta get help! I'll get to a phone!"

Pain was racking the whole left side of her body and her face and eyes were burning as though someone had thrown hot grease in her face.

"Get...get...kids...," she mumbled, going in and out of consciousness. Someone was pulling on her and it hurt something fierce. Everything was blurry except for the terrible pain of her burning eyes and face.

"Th...th...kids." She then heard voices all around her as she was drifting in and out of consciousness. The kids was all she could think of, "Where were the kids?" Then all was darkness.

Lorene awoke hours later in the Murray Hospital with Lawton, Duck and Ed at her bedside.

"The kids! Where's the kids?" She asked, trying frantically to raise from the pillow.

"The kids are all right. They're here in the hospital too, but they're gonna be all right. Now you lay still," Lawton was saying as he gently pushed her back down in the hospital bed.

"Th..them sons—of————s dr..drivin' that Ford..was dr..drunk...Th..they was..in...in..the middle of th' road," Lorene mumbled as she tried to focus her eyes on the two other people standing behind Lawton.

"It's us, baby, me an your mama," Ed said coming closer and taking her hand.

"You're gonna be all right, Renie," Duck said, patting her arm. "You've just had a terrible wreck and you're stove up a right smart, but the doctor says you'll get over it in time. You need to get plenty of rest, though. Now you need to go back to sleep."

By this time Lorene was more alert and sleep would have to wait, for she had to know about Virgil and Doris. "I want to see the kids. What all is wrong with them?" She asked, once again trying to raise up in the bed.

"Now, Renie, you can't get up. Here, here, lay down and Lawton will tell you all about them," her daddy, who was standing closest to the bed said, pushing her gently back against the pillows. Lorene noticed tears in her daddy's eyes.

"Well," Lawton started. "Well, I don't remember a whole lot after I got down there, just that the back end of the car was in that deep gully and the front and left side was bashed completely in and there was all three of you in the front seat and there was a lot of blood. To tell the truth, all of you were knocked out an' I thought you all were dead. I just remember I was never as scared in my life as I was then. George and Emma was already there, I remember, an' I think they was tryin' to get the door open. The two in the Ford were scrambling out of the car, which was headed down in the gully, too. The back end still laid into the rear fender of the Olds. Glass and gasoline was everywhere."

"Tell me about the kids, Lawton. Then you can tell me more about the wreck," Lorene interrupted, now fully alert.

"Well, Virgil's head went through the windshield and he's got a bad cut under his chin. Lots of stitches and he's got other cuts and bruises, but they're not too bad. Doris got a bad cut on her knee. The doctor says her knee cap is cut in four pieces and it will be a good while before she can get around on that leg. She's got some pretty bad cuts on her face, in fact the Dr. said he took twenty four stitches."

"Which room are they in? I want to see them. Who's with them?" Lorene said, looking desperately from one to the other of the three at her side.

"Mammy and Clara's with them an they're just down the hall in the same room. Th' doctor says all three of you can be in the same room when you all gain some more strength; probably in another day or so," Lawton answered, trying to console her.

It was then Lorene noticed her voice sounded muffled and it was hurting her fiercely to move her mouth. She was also becoming aware of the burning of her face and severe pain through out her left side. When she took a deep breath, the pain in her back on the left side was excruciating.

"Then what all's wrong with me," She finally asked.

"Well," Lawton began once more, "they hit you on the driver's side, and it looked like the arm rest just bent into your hip. Your jaw bone is broke and the doctor said some ribs are pulled loose from your back muscles. You've got cuts and bruises on your face and arms and breast and the jolt knocked the battery loose. Acid flew through the broken windshield into your eyes and face and breast. Fact is, it plumb eat up the front of your dress."

Lorene began to cry. The salty tears burned her eyes so badly that she tried to stop. Instead, she only cried more until her painful body racked with sobs. Her mama and daddy and Lawton all tried to console her, but she kept thrashing about on the bed and sobbing, "I'm hurtin' all over. I'm hurtin' so bad an' I know the kids are too. I need to go to them."

"I'm gettin' a nurse. They need to give her another shot, ain't no need her sufferin' like this. I can't stand it," Lawton said, wheeling around from the bed and heading for the door.

Well, the days that followed were painful and nerve wracking for Lorene. She had nightmares about the wreck. The boy who was doing the driving had a broken leg. Lorene discovered later that he disappeared in the night, from the hospital, the day following the wreck and no one knew of his whereabouts. Lorene figured he thought if Lawton ran into him, he might kill him. The sheriff had told Lawton he had no license, no insurance and no money. The Sheriff thought his leaving the country was good riddance. That didn't console Lorene, though. She was very adamant toward both of them. She and her children were lying in the hospital and suffering with injuries, some from which they would never fully recover, while both the drunks had gotten away scott free. It made her feel very little better when Lawton and her mama and daddy kept telling her how she and the children were lucky to be alive from the looks of the Olds. It was totaled.

Virgil was released from the Murray Hospital in a week. Dora May came down from

Michigan to stay with Lawton and Virgil. Lorene's old boy friend, Sidney Rhode's sister, Suzie, was on the nursing staff at the hospital at Murray and she was a great help and comfort to Lorene and the children while they were hospitalized.

Two weeks after Virgil's dismissal, Lorene and Doris came home. Dora May stayed on another week until Lorene was strong enough to do light housework and help Doris get around. Lawton stayed close to home for the next several weeks. Ma Annie and Duck were in and out regularly to help out and the neighbors brought food and checked on them every day. It was a time, not only for physical recovery, but for emotional recovery also and Lorene knew in her heart the emotional scars would be there long after the physical ones had healed.

September rolled around and Virgil was well enough to return, once again, to the school at Danville. Doris' facial cuts had healed well, but her knee injury was healing slowly and putting even her scant poundage on it was a major chore.

Virgil's new school year brought about new challenges, among them were girls. The school had always been coed, but up until that particular year Virgil had just looked upon the girls as either friends or nuisances, depending on the nature of the girl. Well, he became interested in a girl from the Eastern part of the state named Coreen Brock. In fact, he was totally smitten by her dark hair and eyes, her pretty face and sweet smile. He would take her to the movie and on one occasion, while on campus, he got caught kissing her by one of the faculty, Mrs. Middleton, whom was pretty angry with Virgil. He found out that later he wasn't the only boy caught kissing a girl. Several others were caught, also and all of them, Virgil included, were given a stern lecture and a stout warning as to what the consequences of their behavior could entail if they continued. Lorene remembered how amused Lawton was when he found about Virgil's dilemma.

Meanwhile, back in Golden Pond, Little Doris, who was soon to turn sixteen, was seeing Kelsie Calhoun, a boy she had known for many years. Now, Doris had had several other beaus and Lorene and Lawton had even allowed them to visit the house on occasion, but that fall following the tragic accident, it seemed Kelsie kept showing up very often. He was the son of Roy and Mary Calhoun, who lived near the Cumberland River. Lawton had known Roy for many years. Lawton and Roy hunted together quite often. It was during those years that Lawton expanded his moonshinin' and bootleggin' business to include the installation of slot machines in some the small stores in the adjacent communities. Roy owned one of the stores that contained one of Lawton's slot machines. Roy and Lawton spent several afternoons in the bottom behind Roy's store shooting their rifles, shotguns and pistols. Lawton was a good marksman. He practiced religiously. He would purchase a box of shells for ten cents and shoot the whole box in one day.

Lawton always joked around with Kelsie, and Kelsie really thought a lot of Lawton. In fact, as time went on, Kelsie even idolized Lawton, even wanted to grow up to be just like Lawton. So, it wasn't hard to understand that as he and Doris grew older that the two of them could become more than just friends. Kelsie was a pretty nice looking boy, too, in his teenage years and the dark featured, petite Doris had turned out to be one of the prettiest girls in Golden Pond. They made a right fine looking couple. Kelsie had one thing going against him though. He was terribly shy. He had settled it in his mind by fall that Doris was the girl he was going to marry. He had hung around her house all summer during her time of convalescing from the terrible accident. In fact, he had come upon the wreck that tragic afternoon and when he saw the ambulance workers taking Doris from the car, Virgil thought she was dead. He recalled what a dreadful feeling he had. He told Doris sometime later, that he guessed that was when he first realized how much he really thought of her. Yes, Kelsie seemed to turn up at the Higgins' door step at any given time. In fact, he was coming across the yard so much of the time, Lorene declared she couldn't even throw out the "slop-jar" without hitting him.

Well, Doris slowly regained the use of her knee and Lorene still experienced stiffness in her left hip. She guessed, she was thankful the injuries were no worse than they were, however, she still harbored a lot of bitterness toward the careless boy who had caused her and her children such pain. She also harbored bitter feelings toward Lawton for selling the liquor that put people in the stupor that caused them to be unaware of their actions.

A sharp North wind rustled the leaves in the back yard as Lorene made her way to the chicken yard to feed the chickens that afternoon. The early November day had been bright and crisp with a few clouds floating across the sky and as the day drew to a close the hint of frost was in the air. Lorene paused to gaze at the hillside beyond the barn. A hawk flopped it's wings and flew from the large sycamore tree at the edge of the chicken yard, startled by Lorene's presence. "Hem," Lorene mused to herself, "that's likely what happened to my two best layin' hens. Lawton will have to get out here with his rifle."

A dense woods made up the hillside beyond the barn and a small creek ran beneath which emptied into the river a few miles away. Lorene pulled her sweater closer about her as she stood, drinking in the beauty of the world around her. Yes, this was her world, here in Golden Pond. They had lived here for more than ten years now, and she loved this, the first home she and Lawton had ever owned, even more now than the first day they moved in. Standing there in the lengthening shadows of the autumn afternoon, Lorene's thoughts, as many times before, drifted to bye gone days.

Some of the stress of Virgil's handicap had been lifted as she watched him progress from the clinging little boy of the first years at the school at Danville to his development, both in stature and ability to interact with others. He was now learning skills that would

Doris and best friend Wallene Chambers.

Renie and the kids with the '46 Olds.

enable him to be productive in society and in the job arena so he could provide for himself. He was even becoming interested in girls. Lorene smiled at that thought, yet had mixed emotions, for she knew the responsibilities that came with that area of the social pattern. Her mind then turned to Doris. Doris was no longer the little girl whose daddy had to flip the switch on the back of the slot machine in Ma Annie's store, so that the nickels come out so she could play. Doris was now keeping pretty steady company with Kelsie, and from the daze she was going around in these days, Lorene felt it wouldn't be long until Kelsie would pop the question. Ma Annie had seen the change too, in fact she had mentioned it a couple of times. Doris and Kelsie went to downtown Golden Pond and the old bank building, now owned by Ma Annie, quite often. Lorene giggled as she thought of a story Doris had told her only a week or so ago of how embarrassed she had been at Ma Annie's. It seems Doris and Kelsie had stopped in to see Ma Annie one afternoon and, being the character Ma Annie could be at times, she was joking with the youngsters and they all got tickled. Well, as mentioned "afore", Ma Annie was quiet a character and it seemed on this particular occasion, she laughed so hard she began expelling gas. True, she couldn't hear as well in her older days, but also true, just because the urge arose, she might have expelled the gas anyway. At any rate, it really embarrassed Doris. Lorene thought the story was pretty disgusting, while Lawton laughed and said, "that's Mammy for ya."

Lorene shook her head, letting her thoughts stray elsewhere…to Lawton. He was still in the bootleggin' business and she had resigned to the fact he would be as long as he was able. She never liked his liquor oriented profession, didn't like it now and knew she never would. It just seemed to Lorene anything illegal Lawton was bound to give a try. For example, hunting out of season. He and Shaw got all riled up talking about how a good mess of young squirrels would taste all fried up with gravy and biscuits. They couldn't wait for squirrel season to come in, "nosiree" they went over in the river bottoms the next day and killed a sack full of squirrels, only to get caught by the game warden. Well, that made Lawton good and mad, for sure, but what made him even madder was the fact the gamewarden gave the sack of squirrels to the Salvation Army. Lawton and several other of his regular buddies would kill deer out of season. Lawton would go on and on about how good that fresh deer meat was. Well, after a couple of years went by someone offered Lawton a deer he had killed during deer season and Lawton said, "Naw, he didn't care much for that dark wild tasting meat." Lorene remembered saying to him, "Well, it was the best tasting meat ever put in anybody's mouth, as long as it was killed illegally." Yep, that was Lawton, always living just beyond the boundaries of the law. But, Lorene had to admit, there was another side to Lawton. Now, he didn't have much of a religious side, but he was a caring and hospitable man. Lorene realized she only knew a fraction of the people he had be-friended down through the years. Word had gotten back to her at different times how he had given money to people who were down on their luck or how he had given some child a hand full of change. It had been said of Lawton to go out of his way to help a farmer broke down in the field during the busy season or stop to aid anyone with a car break down on the side of the road. He was always ready to help when there was a disaster in the community and quick to look in on the sick of the community. Yes, there was a lot more to Lawton than just a man who lived his life trying to beat the system.

Chapter Twelve:
Half a Century

The fifties! The era of electricity throughout most of the rural areas of the country; the making of faster and more luxurious automobiles; the birth of the fastest Jet planes in history; television; Elvis, bobby-soxers and rock and roll! What an era! It was a fact, all of these exciting new changes were taking place everywhere! World War II was history and America was recovering from its losses quite rapidly. There were more jobs available than ever before and the modes of transportation along with the new box now in the corner of almost everyone's living room...television, was bringing the world closer and closer together.

Well, Golden Pond was no exception when it came to experiencing some of the changes, but it was still a neighborly, little town in the heart of the region known as the "land between the rivers."

The beginning of this new and exciting era, the fifties, found Lawton and Lorene at the same place, doing basically, the same thing as before the calendar rolled over the half- century of the 1900s. Lorene was still taking in seamstress work for several regular customers and taking care of her family, garden and the house. Lawton was still in the bootleggin' business, shooting away a box of shells a day in order to keep his reputation of being a good marksman, and yes, engaging in a few hands of poker ever now and then.

Doris and Kelsie were a regular item now and Doris was about to complete her high schooling. Yes, Doris was now a grown up young lady. Her last year of school in Golden Pond, she was in a beauty contest, along with a fellow that lived up to the title he won, "The Ugliest Man Contest." Doris had gone from playing with dolls to, taking a vivid interest in clothes. She also spent a lot of time with friends, along with either refusing or accepting the company of the several boys in the community. It seemed, however, she spent most of her time with Kelsie Calhoun.

Yes, as that last year of Doris' high school education drew to a close, Lorene and Lawton came to accept the fact that Kelsie Calhoun would wind up being their future son-in-law and they felt it would not be long off.

In the meantime Virgil was nearing his time of completing his education at The Kentucky School for the Deaf in Danville. He was waiting to take his final examinations for graduation. He was worried he might not pass the exams because he had enrolled in the school two years later than most of his fellow students and he had missed a long period of time when he had German measles. Virgil had hinted on the subject a few times to Lorene that he was very serious about Coreen Brock. Lorene could not but have mixed emotions about Virgil getting married. He would have to find a job when he left school and even though a lot of marvelous changes were taking place in the country, it would still be hard for a deaf person to adapt and function in the working world.

The new half-century brought not only phone service, but electricity also, into Golden pond and Lawton and Lorene's household. The new and wonderful invention of electricity, also, added a whole new breed to Lawton's bootleggin' clientele. Since the end of the war, Fort Campbell, an army base less than twenty miles away, was housing and training several hundred young paratroopers. It did not take long for them to find Lawton's place of business on their weekend passes. True, the paratroopers brought in a lot of business which meant more money coming in, but Lawton and Lorene earned every nickel of it. The paratroopers were banging on their door at all hours of the day and night every weekend. Lawton hated to turn them away, but after a couple of months of interrupted sleep, sometimes even during the week, Lawton stopped going to the door after bedtime. Well, this did not set too well with the young paratroopers and one night they started rocking the house. It frightened Lorene and Doris out of their wits as the large rocks pounded the front and sides of the house. Lawton finally got them settled down by appearing on the front porch in his undershorts with his double barreled shotgun, where he gave them a good stern talking to as to the hours he was open for business. Soon after the rock incident, Gracey a town on the outskirts of Hopkinsville where they could purchase anything they were looking for, became their main place to purchase their beer. Lawton had become friends with several of the guys that respected his "business" hours and they continued patronizing him.

A few weeks after the rocking incident by the paratroopers, another nerve racking incident occurred. Lawton and Lorene experienced their second raid. Guy Crittenden, who was now a state trooper, called early that Tuesday morning and warned Lawton as to what was about to transpire. Lawton, who immediately went into a panic, barely had time to get the evidence secured in the attic space behind upstairs closets before two car loads of Feds pulled up in front of the house. Lorene, who was washing up the last of the breakfast dishes, was once again, scared out of her wits. Thankfully, Doris was at Ma Annie's.

Four men, three dressed in khakis and one in a dark suit paraded across the yard and upon the front porch. Lawton went to the door and greeted them in his best neighborly voice. The man in the dark suit introduced himself and the others, stated their business, produced the warrant and set to work searching the house. Lawton appeared cool as a cucumber, but Lorene could see the nervous twitch of his jaw as the men clamored through the house, especially when two started up the stairs. Lorene's eyes were scanning the kitchen to make sure no can of beer or half pint was visible anywhere. That was when it dawned on her that she had seen a pint in Lawton's old coat that was hanging on the back porch. She had to get to that old coat on the back porch some way and yet not arouse suspicion. One of the men in khakis was already going through the china cabinet on the other side of the room. If she made her move, she must do it before he got to the built in cabinets where she was standing in front of the sink, for he would be able to look directly out the back door and see the old coat hanging on a nail beside the door. Lorene glanced around quickly, looking for some excuse to go to the back porch and there on the counter set the pan of scraps left over from breakfast she had filled to throw out to the dogs. She glanced around at the Fed who was closing the bottom door on the china cabinet, then picked up the pan and started for the back door. He glanced up, but said nothing and paid no attention as she went out the door. As she closed the screen door behind her she glanced back in the kitchen and the Fed was beginning to open the built in cabinet doors, with his back to the back door. Quickly, Lorene snatched the pint of whiskey from the pocket of the old coat and without turning around, stuffed it in the bosom of her dress. She then walked to the edge of the porch and threw the scraps to the three waiting dogs in the back yard. She walked back into the kitchen with the empty pan in her hand and placed it in the sink. The Fed finished his search of the kitchen, then said to Lawton who was standing just in side the kitchen after coming from the living room, "Mr. Higgins, I'll have to search the out buildings." Lawton nodded, then crossed the kitchen and followed him out of the house. Soon the other three men completed their search of the rest of the house and went out to help continue the search outside. Lorene breathed a sigh of relief when they were all gone from the kitchen. She turned to the sink to wash the pan which had held the breakfast scraps moments earlier. The revenuers had finished their search and was getting back in their cars within twenty minutes of their arrival. Lawton came back into the kitchen and Lawton was all smiles and strutting like a peacock when he said, "We fooled them suckers again, didn't we Renie?" Lorene threw him a glare cold enough to freeze a lit firecracker on the Fourth of July as she reached in the bosom of her dress, pulled out the pint of whiskey and thrust it out to him.

"Well, I'll be a son of a gun! Look here, I knew there was a pint around here somewhere and I was a might worried it'd be found. Where was it Renie?"

"You wasn't very worried about it being found or you'd a known where it was before the Feds came snoopin' around. You beat all I've ever seen Lawton. That pint of whiskey could have cooked our goose had it been found," Lorene stormed as she stood at the kitchen table, hands on hips and fire flashing in her eyes.

"Well, I think it's time I get outta' your way, woman, till you simmer down some. Them Feds sure make you awful nervous, don't they?" Lawton asked, laughing as he made a quick exit from the kitchen. Lorene was so furious she threw the dish towel she was holding and hit the screen door.

The following Friday, Lawton came in early in the day with a pickup truck following him in the driveway. Lorene watched as Lawton and a man carrying a tool box and a roll of wire went toward the back of the house. "What's he up to now?" Lorene mumbled as she went into the kitchen to see where Lawton was taking the stranger. Lawton was taking him to the back of the house to show him where the electric wires ran into the house from the pole. He was pointing to the smoke house. Well, Lorene was to learn within the next few minutes what Lawton had up his sleeve. The electrician had no more than finished putting electricity in the smoke house and left till another pickup came pulling in the drive way carrying a cold drink box. The boy driving the pickup helped Lawton carry it to the smokehouse. Later that afternoon, after Lawton returned from Gracey and he and filled the drink box with beer. The next week Lawton had two refrigerators delivered and placed on the back porch. Those he filled with beer, also. Lawton allowed now that they had electricity he could accommodate his customers with chilled beer. Lorene just threw her hands up in despair. "Lawton Higgins, a body would think that after being raided not a week ago you'd be considerin' how to be gettin' out of this business, not how you are goin' to better accommodate your customers!"

"Aw, now, Renie. You just fret too much," he answered, trying to put his arm around her.

Well, less than a week later she found out the reason he was so cocky and confident. She over heard him telling her daddy that he had struck up a deal with a state policeman and a revenue man who he was paying fifty dollars a month, each, and he was also paying the local sheriff one hundred dollars a month to keep a search warrant off his property. Lorene's heart sank when she turned from the door of Ed's store that led to the living quarters where Ed and Duck now lived. Ed and Lawton had been in the store at the time Lawton told him about his pay-offs and Lorene had been in the back visiting with her mother. Lorene had been on her way to the front for it was time for she and Lawton to be heading back to Golden Pond. Needless to say, the trip home held some stout friction along with some strong language which, as usual and to Lorene's dismay, accomplished nothing.

Later that same afternoon, for the sake of getting her head cleared and her thoughts collected, Lorene walked down to the small creek that ran beneath the hillside behind the barn. The sun was warm on her back as she sat on a stump on the bank of the shallow creek. Spring rains from a few days before left the creek running and the gentle trickle of the clear water slipping over the rocks that lined the bottom began to calm the storm Lorene was experiencing inside. As many times before her thoughts began to wander back to by-gone days.

When Lorene and Lawton first married, Lawton was getting one dollar a gallon for his fine "brew" or if the customer chose to buy it in the bulk, he could get four gallons for three dollars. Times had changed from those days in many ways, but it seemed the exasperated feelings she had experienced the past week were feelings she'd had for such a long time and she was about to concede in her heart that they would never go away. Lawton got such pleasure in telling younger men and boys like Kelsie who were interested in how real good moonshine should taste and just how he made his or how some "old timer" he'd run into somewhere concocted his fine "brew." Several men and boys would congregate on the front porch in the summertime now and then and their conversation would always wind it's way around to moonshinin'. Lawton would have his audience totally captivated, so much so, you could hear a pin drop. He would rare back in his chair, rearrange his hat and begin, "Well, I run into this old feller from the Eastern part of the state about eight or ten years ago and he made his moonshine a little different than I do. He say's, I always make mine the old fashioned way, none of that "pison" tastin' Whiskey. Nawsiree, a liked to use good, fresh white corn, yep, corn made the best mash. Best way's t' put th' grains in a grass sack an' soak em' in water till they swell up twice th' size. After that, ye need t' put em' in a good spot where th' sun's on em' fer a spell. When er' good n' dry, ye wanna grind em' up real good, fore ye' put em' in th' mash barrel. Sprang water s' th' best. I'd fetch fresh water from the sprang an' put in a littl' rye malt, nuf' water to cover the top an' then I'd cover it up, to keep it all clean an' all. When it'd "worked," I stiri an' thin it out with th' sprang water. Now, you gotta be shore th' mash is a'cookin' right, can tell by lookin' at th' steam comin' from the worm. Ya'see, iffin' ye heat the still too fast, it can blow up, blow plum apart! Knowed a greenhorn over

Renie and the '34 Chevy in front of Ma Annie's house.

'36 Olds with Lawton's sister Dora Mae behind the wheel.

on th' Ridge, one time, built th' fire too hot and th' thang 'sploded and blowed his hat clean offen' his haid! Burnt his face sum, too. Yep, shore gotta watch how hot you get th' cooker. That's a 'portant part uf' it all. Now boys, I'm a'gonna tell ye somethin' bout makin' corn whiskey. It's all bout bein' serious bout' what yer a'doin'. If'n ye ain't, ye might's well not start, fer bad corn whiskey is th' worse thang, ever. If'n ye sell a body bad stuff, ye can git yerself killed. Nawsiree, people don't want no bad whiskey. I'll tell ye one other thang, too. Moonshinin' ain't against the Bible, it's just against the law." That's when the laughter would cut loose.

Young and old alike enjoyed being around Lawton. Lawton attracted people. That's just the way he was. Lorene often wondered how much influence he would have had if he had gone into the ministry. Yep, Lawton was one of a kind. Lorene guessed it was all of those reckless, daredevil ways of his and his winning personality that attracted her to him in the first place, but it seemed the older she got the more she wished he could just settle for normal work like other men and be satisfied with a normal day to day life and not always out on the edge like he was just daring trouble to knock him off.

Sitting there beside the creek in the sunshine of the spring day Lorene began thinking of all the cars Lawton had owned since they had been married. The first, of course, was the '27 Chevy Coupe, then it was a Ford, which Lawton didn't like and traded off for a Chevy four door. In one year he had put so many miles on it, he replaced it with a tan Studebaker, which he didn't care for, so in less than a year he got another Chevy four door. Almost a year to the date he traded the Chevy for a '38 Olds, four door sedan because the Chevy needed new tires. He had told Lorene he was taking the Chevy to Hopkinsville to get new tires and when he returned with the Olds he said, "Well, since the Chevy needed new tires, I figured if I'd run her enough to wear out the tires, no tellin' what all else was fixing to go, so, I just traded er' off for a new one."

"But, Lawton, you haven't had that car a year. No wonder we can't have nothing. You're all time buyin' a car!" Lorene remembered storming at him. And, of course, a heated argument began and Lawton stormed out of the house like a puffin' bull, only to

Lawton and Lorene with the '46 Olds.

come back around midnight two-thirds drunk, which prompted the heated argument all over again. Now, Lawton didn't drink much. It took very little alcohol to make Lawton "knee-walkin" drunk. Lorene could remember only a few times in their younger days that Lawton had thrown a "bender", and it was usually after he and Lorene had had a fight. Lawton just couldn't hold his liquor. On one of the few occasions when Lawton came in tipsy Lorene watched him get out of the car and come staggering across the yard, so when he reached the back door she was ready for him. She slammed into him feet first when he came through the door. He put up a defense, trying to justify the state of his inebriation as he staggered into the kitchen, Lorene remembered he said, "Now Lorene, I am NOT drunk." Then he leaned against the door facing to steady himself and pulled a half-pint whiskey bottle two thirds full from his pocket and waved it in her face, saying, "See, this is all the whiskey I've had all night."

"Well, I can believe that!" was her reply. "All a body has to do to get you drunk is hit you in the a— with a rotten apple."

"Yes, those younger years were "doozies'," Lorene recalled as she sat there on the creek bank. Paying off the law and cars was where most of their money had gone. In less than two years he had traded the '38 Olds for a 1940 Olds, then the next year he got another Olds, a '41 model, claimed he just had to have it for it would do one hundred and ten miles an hour. In addition to the '41 Olds he bought a three quarter ton pick-up and on down the line every single year a new car or truck or both. "Well," Lorene thought to herself, "he's had the '48 Chevy he bought to replace the '47 Olds I wrecked for nearly two years now. Guess he'll be comin' in with another one any day now." She sighed, pulled her feet up higher on the creek bank, put her arms around her legs and rested her chin on her knees, gazing at the lazy stream.

Lawton was crazy. He could do the most outlandish things and Lorene had to admit, most of the time they would turn out down right hilarious. Maybe not at the time, especially to her, but after a time, someone would again mention something crazy he had done or been involved in and she would be bound to laugh. At the end of the story

Lawton would usually say when he saw her laughing, "See Renie, there's one thing, at least I ain't dull!"

One particular story came to mind as Lorene continued to reminisce. It was springtime and of course, the rainy season. During the depression days many necessary things were hard to come by. Since it took a lot of sugar and barrels to make moonshine, when a person got the opportunity to load up on a supply he took advantage of it. Lorene and Lawton were living at Ma Annie's and Virgil was just a few months old. Well, Lawton had stewed and stewed because he didn't have sugar to start the mash that spring. He finally got word of a man who was coming through Golden Pond with a truck load of sugar, but the man could not be seen unloading the sugar. Therefore, Lawton and the other moonshiners would have to meet him in some obscure place to purchase the sugar. Well, a time and place was set that was both convenient and obscure for Lawton. The time was early one morning and the place was on the back side of one of the moonshiner's farms about seven miles east of Oak Ridge. Well, Lawton had to take the wagon, for the back roads that led to the designated spot were not graveled and would be too muddy to go in the Chevy Coupe. Anyway, they couldn't have carried many bags of sugar in the coupe, so he and Jake hitched up the two old mules, and they were stubborn old mules to start with. Well, of course they took the most remote route, which took them hours to get there and back. It was early afternoon when they returned with a wagon load of sugar, covered with a tarpaulin. The wagon wheels were caked with mud and so were the mules, as well as two men. The mules were lathered up and looked as if they were so tired they would drop any minute. Now, instead of Lawton unhitching the mules and letting them rest, he decided he and Jake would make this the day they would move the still from it's present place on the wooded hillside by the spring beyond Ma Annie's barn, to a more secluded place down in the holler where the spring branch emptied into the creek, which was about the distance of a quarter of a mile. They unloaded some of the bags of sugar at the house but left on the wagon enough to make up two barrels of mash. Then they took the wagon and the two tired mules and went up the hill to load up the barrels and other still "paraphernalia", after which, they started down the holler. Well, things went well for a good piece and Lawton and Jake thought they had accomplished quite a lot in one day, but no good luck streak never lasts forever. When the mules, wagon and it's cargo got to the foot of the hill there was a small creek they had to cross to enter the bottom land, beyond which was the wooded area and the spring branch. Now, the old mules, being tired from their long journey before noon and the trip up the hill and down, were simply not in the frame of mind to exert the necessary energy it was going to take to pull a wagon loaded with one hundred pound bags of sugar, barrels and other still "paraphernalia", along with two grown men and two wet coon hounds. Lawton directed the mules into the crossing which was nothing but a shallow, muddy "loblolly" and no sooner had the back wheels of the wagon rolled into the creek, they mired to the hubs......And that was it for the mules. It was as if they had it planned. They were in perfect timing, when one balked, they both balked. All of the raving, cussing, driving, pulling or stomping Lawton and Jake could muster would not prompt either mule to budge! The coon hounds even took their turn making a racket, but they soon gave up. Likely, they were a bit sympathetic with the mules. Well, after about a half hour Lawton and Jake decided they had only two alternatives: number one, they could unhitch the mules and get them on out of the muddy creek. This would leave the wagon setting in the middle of the creek till it dried up some. While on the other hand, it being spring of the year, it was more likely to rain more than dry up some. Alternative number two: they could "hoof it back to the house and try to round up some trusting soul with another team of mules they could hitch up to the ones already hitched and hope the two teams could pull the wagon out to solid ground. The latter alternative was the one chosen. Needless to say, it was well into the night when the "frazzled" men, mules and dogs finally got to their sleeping quarters.

A chill was beginning to set in when Lorene rose from the creek bank and started back to the house. Coming up the path beside the garden, she noticed the maple trees around the house were beginning to show tiny leaves, while patches of green grass was clumped here and there over the back yard. A robin strutted proudly across Lorene's path; her approach deemed it to flutter it's wings and fly to the limb of a nearby tree. The old jersey cow bawled from the barnyard, waiting to be milked and the chickens flocked to the fence, awaiting their supper as Lorene walked past the chicken yard. Two of their three dogs met her, wagging their tails as she rounded the corner of the house and their gray tom cat jumped from a chair on the back porch to rub against her legs as she climbed the steps. Lorene sighed as she walked across the porch and paused a moment to glance back toward the serenity of where she had been. She then took a deep breath, opened the back door and went into the kitchen to start supper.

Chapter Thirteen:
Kelsie Pops the Question

❝Red in the mornin,' sailors take warnin.' Red at night, sailors take delight." Well, that Saturday morning in late June dawned red over the hills that banked the Cumberland River. Kelsie Brown Calhoun pushed his chair back from the kitchen table, walked toward the back door and paused only long enough to grab his cap from the nail beside the door. He stepped off the back porch onto the dusty path that led to the shed where he parked his truck the night before. He secured his cap, flipped up the bill as he walked and gazed at the Eastern horizon. The air was heavy and the slight breeze stirring was already hot, even though the sun had not yet made it's appearance over the tree tops on the ridge. The young man, clad only in khaki pants, his old white cap and work shoes was already brown from hours spent in the spring and early summer sun. His thin torso exposed wiry muscles in his back, shoulders and arms, a result of the hard, physical labor required to help his mama and step-daddy farm the three hundred and fifteen acres which lay a few miles away near the river.

Kelsie was born in a log cabin nestled near a small cedar thicket, only a short distance from the Cumberland River, on August thirty first in Nineteen and twenty nine; the first child of Roy and Mary Calhoun. Eighteen months later Edna, Kelsie's only sibling came along.

One of Kelsie's earliest memories was his mother telling the story of the last thing she remembered when she was giving birth to Kelsie was looking out the tiny window of the cabin as she lay in labor while the hired help was building the bonnet of the new stock barn. The bonnet was the wide overhang which contained a pulley where ropes could be attached to sharp pronged hooks that lifted the bales of hay from the wagons through double doors and into the loft to store for winter feeding of the stock. With ropes or cables stretching the length of the loft the bales could be stacked from back to front as the wagons brought it from the field. The other end of the rope was attached to one or more mules on the ground which provided the power to lift, and guide the bales to the desired place in the barn. Loose hay could also be forked from wagons through the double doors beneath the bonnet.

Kelsie began tagging along after his dad when he did the evening chores, while his daddy patiently instructed him how to do them correctly. Kelsie learned to drive a tractor as soon as he was big enough to maneuver the pedals. He was as much at home on the seat of the tractor by the time he was ten years old as he was on his old bicycle. He caught on fast to the procedures of farming and loved the work. His dad taught him the value of the dollar and that the material things he expected to have had to be earned. So, Kelsie was taking his place as a full-fledged farm hand at a very early age.

While Kelsie scanned the red horizon that unseasonable hot June morning he made the short trip from Golden Pond to the farm. He drove down the dusty lane to the shed where the hay baler was already hooked to the Farmall tractor, ready to bail the fescue in the bottom which had been cut the day before. He knew from the looks of the sky that rain was on it's way and he must make haste to get the hay bailed. Kelsie didn't see Zeek and Clyde, the hired hands, around anywhere, so he figured they were gone to the barn over on the ridge to bring the John Deer tractor and wagon to haul in the hay as he bailed. Kelsie's mind, however, was not totally centered on the chore before him. Kelsie had another matter pressing his thoughts. The matter taking precedence over the hay bailing just happened to be how he was going to get up the courage to ask the parents of his long time sweetheart, Doris Higgins, to allow her to marry him. He had been pondering the matter now for several months. He and Doris had known for the past year they were going to be married soon after Doris completed her last year of high school, however, they had not mentioned it to her parents, at least, not the two of them together. Well, school was now out and Doris was graduated. Kelsie had mentioned their plans to his mama and Seldon Ahart, his stepdaddy, whom readily agreed Doris would make Kelsie a fine wife. So, now there was only thing standing in their way of getting married, asking Lawton and Lorene's permission. To Kelsie, that was the hardest part. It wasn't that he didn't know Lawton and Lorene. Why, he had spent about as many of his waking hours at their house down the road in Golden Pond as he had here at home. Lawton had played a big part in helping Kelsie's daddy get elected magistrate of Trigg County back in '41. Yes, Kelsie had "plugged" around with Lawton and his daddy, up until the fatal car accident that took Roy Calhoun's life when Kelsie was only fourteen. It seemed after the accident Kelsie grew even closer to the Higgins family than ever, for he was already sparkin' Doris. Lawton sorta became a father figure to Kelsie. Yes, he knew Lawton and Lorene very well and liked them, like family, but it was the hardest thing he had ever tried to do, trying to muster up the courage to ask for their daughters hand in marriage.

"I've got to do it, "he mumbled to himself as he climbed on the Farmall, "an', I promised Doris I'd ask tonight. I've been puttin' it of for near a month now and she's 'bout to lose patience with me; thinks I don't care about her. I've just got to ask em' tonight."'

The sun was trying to peek through a haze of puffy clouds as Kelsie bounced along the rutted lane that led to the small bottom. He could see the mist rising from the river and spreading through the trees that lined the ridge. Darker clouds were forming to the southwest and the tall weeds along the lane were beginning to sway as the breeze began to pick up strength. He geared the tractor down as he entered the field and lowered the baler as he proceeded down the long rows of wilted fescue, then he let his mind wander to the happenings of the past.

Roy Calhoun had bought this hundred odd acre farm from Kelsie's granddaddy soon after he and Mary married. Within a couple of years, one which was a bad crop year, he and Mary left the farm to go to Michigan where Roy worked at public work in order to accumulate enough money to payoff the mortgage on the farm. When they returned they moved into the cabin and they not only acquired Kelsie and Edna, but also some cattle and hogs and managed to keep two or three hired hands to help tend the farm. Roy built what he called the "bungalow" house in the early thirties which was just across the field from the log cabin, but once again hard times hit so he and Mary and Kelsie, whom was less than a year old moved into Cadiz and rented on the shares the farm to a fellow who made a little moonshine on the side. That year was a good crop year and a good year for moonshine and within eight months they moved back into the "bungalow" house there on the farm. Large oak trees grew in the front and back yard while an apple orchard flanked the lane beyond the garden. Kelsie's mama had worked along side his daddy on the farm, making as good a hand as the men they hired. She also cooked for her family and the hired help along with caring for Kelsie and Edna, not to mention raising a large garden which she harvested by herself.

It wasn't long until Roy was buying up farmland in three directions adjacent to the original hundred-odd acres. At one time Roy owned six farms totaling over six hundred acres, all in the heart of the land between the rivers laying next to the Cumberland River.

One of these farms he bought was from a Wallace family and there was a two story house which Roy and his family occupied for about a year. In 1940, Roy decided he wanted to go into the general merchandise business since his farming operation had grown and supplies and tools were constantly needed. So Roy built a store building with living quarters up stairs. Roy moved his family from the "bungalow" house into the store building and Mary ran the store while Roy continued farming. This was where they were living when the fatal accident in the early fall of '44 claimed the life of Roy. There were large debts remaining after his death on the farms, equipment, cattle and buildings Roy had acquired over the years. Mary, in order for she and Kelsie to manage, sold all of the farm land except for the three hundred acres they now farmed, along with the excess machinery and most of the beef cattle to get them free of their creditors. Mary continued running the store until she married Seldon Ahart, also from Trigg County and who had a house and two hundred acres of land in Golden Pond. She then closed the store and she along with the children moved into Seldon's house.

This three hundred and fifteen acres of farmland near the Cumberland River was a productive piece of land for the most part, however there were times the backwater caused problems. Almost every year, this one being the exception, backwater had covered the small bottom that grew the fescue, as well as the larger bottoms where they planted corn. Kelsie and Doris had already made plans to renovate the now abandoned store building and use it for their home when they got married. Kelsie could hardly wait until he was living back out here on the farm.

The hum of the tractor as it chugged along before the hay baler and the simultaneous thud as a neatly shaped bail of hay hit the ground was the only sound penetrating Kelsie's ears as he moved back and forth across the small bottom. His thoughts kept slipping from the chore at hand to the even harder chore he was going to have to perform tonight. The thought had even crossed his mind a time or two these past few months, if getting married and being with Doris a lifetime was worth all of the agony he was going through trying to muster up the courage to ask her parents for her hand? And the answer was always "yes". All he had to do was envision the brown-eyed, petite girl whom had been his sweetheart since childhood, and he knew in his heart he could let no other man beat his time with Doris. Yes, Kelsie and Doris had spent many a happy hour together driving around the countryside and in Golden Pond in his old '41 Chevy pickup. The old truck was a TVA surplus vehicle he had purchased and "fixed up" himself. She had a V-eight engine with "grandma gears" and over sized tires. He had painted her black, highlighted with silver. He had even repaired the radio and installed a spot light. The younger guys in the community admired the vehicle and Kelsie would beam with pride as they would gather around when he had it parked in down town Golden Pond or at the local store or church. Yep, she was a sharp old truck and even Doris rode in it with pride. It didn't seem to matter to Doris if he hadn't had time to clean her out for their Saturday night date. Sometimes there was dust on the seat and mud or manure in the floor board, but Doris would just climb aboard all decked out in her starched blouse, can-can skirt and white bobby socks, snuggle up close to Kelsie and they would head out for the general store across the lake where the young people of the various communities hung out and they would share a Dr. Pepper and maybe later take in a movie, that depended on how Kelsie's funds had run that particular week. Sometimes they would attend a special country music festival put on at Golden Pond. There would be special performers which included, Goober Peanut, Lillie Belle and Cotton, Chubby Dink and Sister Lily. Occasionally, the Bisbies Comedians would perform. Sometimes, on a Saturday there would be a School

Fare and if the farm work was caught up Kelsie and Doris would attend the all day event. There would be activities of competition in which they would participate such as the high jumps, broad jumps, sack races and three legged races. A bar-b-que was held late in the afternoon, after which "The ol' fiddlers" contest would be the "grand finale" of the all day event. Then, there were times when they would just cruise Trigg County's back roads and listen to the Wayco Texas radio station or WSM in Nashville as the "Grand Ole Opry" came across the air waves.

Yep, Kelsie had to admit he lived for those times with the little gal with brown eyes and curly brown hair that wore only a slight trace of lipstick for was pretty enough without layers of make-up and he knew she could not belong to anyone else besides him. So, he simply had to swallow his pride, put his shyness aside and ask Lawton and Lorene for Doris' hand in marriage, and he had to do it tonight!

Kelsie glanced toward the thickening clouds to the west then he saw Zeek and Clyde coming around the bend on the John Deer. The "bungalow" house was in the distance behind them and catching sight of the house reminded Kelsie of a story his daddy had told when he was a small boy. He grinned to himself as he remembered when the Bennett family lived there a when he was a young boy. Old man Bennett helped with the farm work to pay for the lodging of his family and he had the use of a garden spot, an old stable for his cow and a small hog pen behind the stable for his sow and the four pigs he would fatten to kill for their year's meat supply. The Bennett's had a whole gaggle of youngens. When company would drive up, those youngens would pour out of the house and spread all over the yard like warmed molasses on hot butter. There was a bunch of em.' Ol' man Bennett was known to dabble in a little moonshinin' on the side, for he had a small still in the cellar under the house. Now, Kelsie was too small to remember the time the actual incident took place, but he had heard his daddy tell it so often he could picture it plainly in his mind. The incident transpired late one afternoon on a hot day in July. It seems a terrible thunderstorm came up that ran all of the Bennett youngens inside, for several of them were upstairs at the time. Now, old lady Bennett was in the kitchen preparing supper, while old man Bennett was in the cellar at the still. Well, it had been a long, hot dry spell and when a storm blows up during those conditions, fierce lightening is just to be expected. The youngens were "tearing up Jake," playing, hollering and fighting as a bunch of youngens put together will, when all of a sudden a terrible bolt of lightening struck the chimney of the house! It scared the youngens so bad it created complete still and silence among them. Rumor was it even addled some of them, anyway, the lightening charge shot straight down the chimney which was the vent for a fireplace in the stayin' room along with the vent to the wood burning cook stove in the kitchen. Well, old lady Bennett had just put her hand on the handle of a big pot of beans to take from the stove when the lightening bolted down to the main floor and when it hit it scared her so badly she threw the pot of beans into the air and went screaming out of the kitchen! Instantaneously, the lightening bolt streaked on down the chimney, through the floor and into the cellar where the ball of fire landed in the dirt floor only a few feet from the still where old man Bennett was standing! Needless to say, the old man moved faster than he had in years to exit that cellar! All of the youngens made an even faster exit, scrambling from doors and windows all over the house. Since the streak of lightening had traveled mainly down the chimney, no measurable amount of damage was done to the rest of the house. When Kelsie's daddy and a couple of hired hands went across the field to examine the damage after old man Bennett had relayed his story shortly after the storm, the one thing they took notice of more than anything else as a result of the lightening occurrence was the pinto beans they saw scattered in every corner of the kitchen!

Thunder began to rumble, loud enough to be heard above the hum of the tractors as Kelsie and the hired hands finished loading the bales of hay. A strong wind was now blowing and lightening played in jagged streaks across the dark clouds. Large drops of rain were beginning to splatter here and there on the dusty lane as they headed for the barn. Well, that's how it was with the life of a farmer, always at the mercy of the weather.

Kelsie got out of his truck at Doris' house shortly after sun down that evening. She was standing on the porch all dolled out in a pink dress with a matching bow in her hair. Kelsie felt his heart skip a beat as he started slowly across the yard. He didn't know if it was because Doris looked so pretty there on the porch or if it was the ordeal on which he was about to embark. His palms were sweaty and he could feel the hairs on the back of his neck rising under his shirt collar. He knew his face was beet red. His knees began to feel weak as he started up the steps to the porch. He gulped as he tried to swallow and finally managed a deep breath as he walked through the front door with Doris and into the living room where Lawton and Lorene were sitting. He managed to get through the usual, run of the mill conversation as to the weather, crops and so forth, then there was silence, dreadful silence, and silence among a room full of people had always made Kelsie nervous. He felt like if one was in the company of others they should be carrying on a conversation. Well, he squirmed around on the couch where he was sitting next to Doris, looking first at the floor, then at the ceiling, trying desperately to find the right words. Now, Doris had already told him some time back it likely would be easier for him if he directed the question at her mama. So, he took another deep breath which came out in rasping jerks. Then he rocked back and forth in his seat, all the while Doris was staring at him with that "well go on, do it" look and Lawton and Lorene whom were sitting across the room in rocking chairs, were also staring quizzically at him; Lawton with a sly grin on his face. So Kelsie thought to himself, "I've got to get this over with before I blow up!" So, he looked straight across the room into Lorene's face and blurted out in one breath, "Lorene, I've come here tonight to ask you if I can have Lawton to be my wife!"

Well, needless to say, Lawton all but hit the floor rolling with laughter, and it wasn't until Lorene and Doris broke loose that poor, frazzled Kelsie realized just what he had actually said.

While Kelsie was living down his "goof-up" the night he "popped the question," for Lawton just had to tell it to the first person he saw and of course it spread through out the community like wildfire, Doris was busy making plans for the wedding. They had made plans to be married in mid July, but Ma Annie, whom had been having health problems for the past several years, became very ill. This postponed the initial date set for their wedding. Lawton, Lorene, all of Lawton's sisters and Doris took care of her day and night as her physical condition steadily declined. Then one night in mid August, Ma Annie was called to her eternal resting place. Lawton mourned the death of his mother immensely, for he had always been very close to Ma Annie.

Well, on September 7, 1951, Kelsie and Doris had a quiet, private ceremony in Julian, Kentucky, by a preacher who had been the a friend of the family for years. Those attending were Lawton, Lorene, and Mary and Seldon Ahart. Mary and Lawton "stood up" with the happy couple. The bride wore a two piece, teal suit with a navy velvet hat and navy accessories. The groom wore a dark serge suit with tie and a spit shine on his brown Sunday shoes. The newly weds spent their honeymoon in Michigan, visiting with family and from there to Niagara Falls.

When Kelsie and Doris returned from their honeymoon, they lived with Mary and Seldon for two months. During those two months they were renovating the old store building on the farm, as planned.

Doris was excited and pleased with their first home. She fell right into cooking for farm hands, planting and harvesting a large garden and doing other chores common to most other farm wives in the land between the rivers. She, also joined Kelsie in going to the Cumberland River Baptist Church where he and his family had belonged all of Kelsie's life. Doris was afraid her mama and daddy, being of the Mormon faith, might have reservations about her going to Kelsie's church on a regular basis, but nothing was said to the contrary and Doris continued attending.

Those first two years of married life were a time of adjustment for Kelsie and Doris, as the case is with all young married couples. They worked very hard there on the farm on the Cumberland. The little store house was getting more comfortable with more modern conveniences added from time to time. Red brick siding covered the outside walls of the structure, while a tin room covered the roof. A porch extended almost the length across the front of the building, with the same in the back. The upstairs portion of the little store building consisted of one room, extending the length of the house. Kelsie and Doris converted the grown floor into a living room, dining room, bedroom and a small kitchen with a back room which they used for storage. Kelsie bought Doris a deep freezer to put in the back room. This they filled with meat from butchered hogs and calves they grew there on the farm, along with many of the vegetables from the garden. A large basement which had two large doors leading into the back yard, was beneath the house and Doris filled pint, quart and half gallon jars with vegetables and fruit and filled the shelves that lined the basement walls. There was a cistern on the hill, beside the garage and a hand pump in the kitchen brought water into the house. When the weather favored rain Kelsie or Doris would go up to the cistern and put the gutter that extended from the over hang on the garage into the small opening on the top of the cistern to allow the fresh rain water to be caught.

A small chicken house was beyond the backyard, and Doris had acquired a dozen or so hens and a red rooster by the end of their second year of marriage. Now, Doris had been around chickens all of her life and she had no "hang-ups" about fearing them. But, it was evident from the time she brought the red rooster from her mothers, that he had a strong dislike for Doris. When she went to gather the eggs in the late afternoon that rooster would chase her from the edge of the yard into the house. There were times when she forgot to pick up a stick that she would have to throw some of the eggs she gathered from the nests at the rooster to "shoo" him away so she could get back to the house. One morning when Kelsie had no eggs to go with his toast and bacon he inquired as to what was happening to all of the eggs? Well, Doris confessed about the problem she was having with the red rooster. Well, Kelsie thought that was one hilariously funny and ridiculous story! He even got members of the family teasing her about the red rooster. Well, Doris didn't care how much they laughed at her, she couldn't help but be scared for the rooster had spurs as long as her finger and he did sincerely enjoy making her daily trip to feed the chickens and gather the eggs totally miserable. There were times she had knocked him "winding" with a tobacco stick, in all honesty, hoping she had killed him. Well, the old saying "what goes around comes around," came to pass over the red rooster early one morning the following fall. Kelsie and Doris were awakened by a loud clap of thunder at daylight. They both realized at the same time that the gutter needed to be put up at the cistern and Kelsie climbed out of bed, threw on his shirt, pants and shoes and rushed toward the garage, for the storm cloud was right up on them and it was likely to start raining any minute. Doris also climbed out of bed, slipped her robe on and made her way to the kitchen, where she was in the process of starting breakfast, when Kelsie came through the kitchen door holding the lifeless form of the notorious red rooster by the feet. Doris' mouth fell open but Kelsie spoke first, "This infernal rooster fought at me all the way to the garage an' when I turned my back to put the gutter in place, he jumped on me for the last time. I reached down and grabbed the first thing I could get my hands on, which was a pitman rod, and put that sucker out of commission. Here, guess we'll have chicken and dumplings for dinner, huh?" he concluded, holding the dead foul out to Doris.

"Oh, I thought you thought I was just being silly cause I threw eggs to get him off me when I was tryin' to get back to the house? Now, you're the one ready to eat em'?" Doris answered smugly, enjoying every moment of the present scene.

Well, in 1954 Tracy Brown was born into the Calhoun household. Doris had a very difficult time with birthing Tracy. She was in labor two days before the seven pound, twelve ounce boy came into the world. Kelsie was overjoyed to have a son, and the son had a lot of Kelsie's physical similarities in looks. At birth, as with most babies, Tracy had blue eyes, which later changed to brown like Doris', but he had a head full of dark hair like his daddy's.

Kelsie was so proud of "my boy", as he called him, that he could hardly wait to take him out in public to show off. One of the first places Tracy was taken by his parents was to the Cumberland River Baptist Church. Doris had made a profession of faith during her pregnancy and made her request to their young pastor, Rev. Ervin Darnell, to be baptized. When she was fully recovered from giving birth to Tracy, she, along with an elderly man of the community, were the candidates to be baptized in a small lake near the church. The lake was muddy from previous rains, but Doris did not mind. She was their young pastor's very first candidate to baptized.

Meanwhile, Virgil was had finished his schooling at the Kentucky School for the Deaf in Danville, and was living in Detroit. Virgil and Coreen had gotten a divorce within the first year of their marriage, and Virgil went through a traumatic time. It appeared to him, as well as Lawton and Lorene and the rest of the family, that Coreen had used Virgil and the kindness of his family, somewhat, as a way to get away from her home in Eastern Kentucky. Virgil had since been transferred to the Dearborn Stamping Plant, where he used two press operating machines. It was hard work and a dangerous work for workers who could hear. Virgil had to be very careful and during his first months of adjustment at the plant there were times he wanted to quit the job. Dora May and her second husband, Red Cunningham, kept encouraging him to hang on to the job, that in time it would become easier. Virgil had bought a new '53 Pontiac, his first car, and he was very excited with his new purchase! Dora May worried about him driving in the heavy traffic, but Virgil was determined to become as self sufficient as he possibly could, so he joined the Motor Club for the deaf and made a lot of new friends along with adjusting to driving in the city.

Back in Golden Pond, Lawton and Lorene were alone now. It saddened Lorene when Doris moved the last of her things into the storehouse they had renovated down on the farm. Lorene kept busy with the routine chores and her sewing and of course, assisting Lawton, yet there were times when the house was quiet and only the ticking of the clock on the mantel was the only sound that Lorene heard as she gazed out the window and wondered where all of the years had gone. They truly had sped by.

Chapter Fourteen:

TVA

The special session of Congress called by President Franklin D. Roosevelt in Nineteen thirty three that lasted Ninety nine days and the important laws passed during that special session, which included the Tennessee Valley Authority or (TVA) Act, did not, at the time, cause much concern for the inhabitants of "The land between the rivers." Fact was, many living there twenty years later in fifties were now enjoying the electricity generated by the Kentucky dam, built by TVA on the Tennessee River, which was completed in 1944. Other than that, little thought, or conversation was given, if any at all. Now, Kentucky Dam extends one and a half miles long and is some two hundred and six feet high, creating a massive lake approximately one hundred and eighty five miles long. TVA's Kentucky Dam project required the purchase of many land owners bottom land, which was of little use because of the constant flooding. Those residing beyond the immediate area were not directly effected. Their only connection with TVA and the building of Kentucky Dam was the electric power it provided for the citizens. When the phrase TVA began making the headlines of the news papers and the air waves again, it wasn't long, however, until it became the main topic of conversation among the residents between the rivers. It was talked on the street, at home, in the field, at social and church gatherings and on the phone lines. TVA was, aging, making plans to build another lake on the Cumberland River and this idea, alone was not what was disturbing the people living between the rivers... It was the "talk" that TVA was planning to take the rest of the land between the rivers and develop into a wild life reserve...If this rumor proved true, it would take, not only people's flooded bottom land, but every home, business and farm that made up the various communities in the area. Yes, by the late fifties the phrase TVA had passed through the lips of almost every adult and many youngsters among the people making up the population of the land between the rivers.

TVA was created in Congress during that special session in 1933 as a Federal Corporation. It's main purpose was to conserve, develop and utilize the natural resources of the near forty one thousand miles that made up the Tennessee Valley. Dams were to be built to control floods and to deepen the Tennessee and Cumberland rivers for commercial shipping, along with creating electric power. The power and mineral resources to be developed by TVA were to be an important part of the country's defenses in the event of war. New forests were to be added and those still standing preserved. Farmers and manufacturers were to be encouraged to take advantage of the many natural riches of the Tennessee Valley.

The original plans TVA had for building dams on the Tennessee River were to make possible a continuous chain of lakes from Paducah to Knoxville, Tennessee. These dams would be equipped with locks that would allow towboats and barges to raise or lower from one lake level to another. This procedure would allow for faster water transporting of various manufactured goods, along with iron ore, lumber and coal.

TVA was to build large steam-electric generating plants to aid the hydroelectric plants at the dams to meet the ever increasing demand for electric power.

Millions of seedlings to re-forest the thousands of acres of woodlands in the area would be supplied through TVA, while the lakes would attract tourists, thus enhancing business and trade throughout the Tennessee Valley. TVA even had a program of water level control that would stamp out the malaria carrying mosquitoes. Well, all of these marvelous developments sounded wonderful when heard over the airwaves or read in the newspaper, and for the most part they were. However, there was only one catch for those living between the Cumberland and Tennessee rivers; these new and wonderful developments which were, obviously, going to come about in the near future would destroy many homes, farms, businesses and even some of the towns, forcing the inhabitants of this unique and self-sufficient part of the country to uproot, totally change their life style and find other means of survival where ever they could.

"Now Lorene, there's no need gettin' all tore up before anything happens," Lawton said as he pushed back from the supper table. "It's like your daddy said, them TVA people say they'll pay the fair market value for any piece of property they buy."

"Oh, Lawton Higgins, you don't understand one thing!" Lorene stormed out in reply, tears streaming down her cheeks as she stood before the sink. "There's not a fair market value to this place as far as I'm concerned! It is not for sale!! Not at any price! No amount of money the TVA or anybody else on God's green earth could pay what this place is worth to me! This is our first home and our only home and we ought to have the right to decide whether we want to get rid of it or not. It's not right for a bunch of outsiders to come in and tell people what they can and can't do with a place they've worked hard to get. Nothin' right about it! And if enough people set their foot down to these dadblasted government people and flat out say their not sellin' out and not leavin,' I think the TVA would go elsewhere and run somebody else out of their homes. I don't want to get rid of this place and furthermore, I'm not leaving here! They can just drown me when they flood the place with their dad-blasted dams and lakes. I am NOT leavin' an' they can't make me!!!" By this time Lorene was boo-hooing.

"Now, Renie, it's a law; passed by Congress durin' Roosevelt's time back in the thirties, and there's not much any of us can do about it if they want our places," Lawton started, but he began to change his approach when he saw the look on Lorene's face, for she looked mad enough to start throwing the stack of dishes she was holding.

"Since when have you got so all-fired concerned about what's the law?" she stormed out at him.

"Now, Renie. It's not like they're comin' in here to start all this stuff tomorrow or the next day," Lawton began again, trying to think of something comforting to do or say. Lorene turned to the sink and began shaking her head. Then he continued, "It'll be a long way down the road. Why, you might even be ready to move by the time it comes about." He went on, but Lorene just cried louder, for it seemed everything he did or said only made matters worse, which got him flustered, also. So, finally, out of desperation, he shook his head, threw up his hands and stalked out of the kitchen, leaving her standing at the sink crying in the dishwater.

Meanwhile, over on the Cumberland, Doris stood in the door way and watched Kelsie as he headed across the back yard toward the barn with three year old Tracy at his heels. Doris folded her arms across her swollen mid-drift and smiled. She had not mentioned it to Kelsie, but she had been having sharp twinges in her back all day and now they were beginning to move around to the lower part of her stomach. Doris was determined not to go to the hospital as soon as she did with her first baby, so she would just not tell anybody and tough it out until she was sure the pains were coming good and hard and five minutes apart.

She turned back into the kitchen and began straightening the kitchen chairs left askew by Kelsie and Tracy then she began to clear the table.

Doris mulled several things over in her mind as she went about the chore. She too, had heard the talk about TVA and had a lot of thoughts of her own about giving up this, their first and only home to own since she and Kelsie had married. Life was good here in the little store building on the farm Kelsie loved, even though the work was hard and tiring sometimes. She knew it would be very hard for Kelsie to leave this place on the Cumberland River, for it had been his home place for his entire life. She too, had grown to love this place. Late on summer afternoons she, Tracy and Kelsie would pile in the pickup, or if the weather was warm, on one of the tractors, and drive over the fields and hills and hollers and Kelsie would tell them what he was planning to do with this field or that bottom, much as they had done when they were going together. Again, she smiled as her thoughts reflected on a few years prior.

Back in their sparkin' days, she and Kelsie used to write letters to each other when Kelsie was so busy at the farm he couldn't get over to visit Doris for several days. Doris would send her letter by her daddy to the post office so he could put a stamp on it and mail it for her. She had since that time learned that several times her letters did not require a stamp for they never got mailed. Lawton had run into Mary Ahart more times than one at the post office and much of the time she would be bringing a letter from Kelsie to be stamped and mailed to Doris, so Mary and Lawton would just exchange the letters and save the three cents for the stamp. The letters also got to their destination a day early.

Doris remembered how she hated to see Kelsie enroll in College at Murray after he graduated high school while she was just a sophomore. His daddy had always said he wanted Kelsie to have a good education and even if Kelsie wanted only to farm, he still needed schooling. Kelsie had commented on his daddy's wishes several times to Doris after the tragic accident that took Roy's life. So, the next fall after high school graduation he enrolled at Murray State University to get the college education his daddy had desired for him to have. Well, two weeks to the day of his enrollment at Murray, Kelsie was back at the farm on the Farmall tractor, once more cutting hay. He laughed and told Doris when he went to pick her up for a date that first night back home, "most people take four years or more to get all of the college they need. I got all of the college I needed in two weeks." Doris "kinda" liked to think the farm wasn't all that caused him to drop out of college in two weeks.

A horrifying incident she knew she would never forget came to Doris' mind as she finished cleaning the tiny kitchen. The incident transpired the first spring they were married and the first spring they were living here in the old storehouse. Now, back water had always been some what of a problem on the farm and that particular spring there had been more rain than usual. In fact, it began raining in mid April and rained every day until the last week in May. Water was everywhere! The first week of May the storehouse, yard and garden spot were almost totally surrounded by muddy water. Kelsie was still able to drive the big Farmall tractor down the lane and over the rise to get out to the main road. Doris' mama was worried sick about she and Kelsie, and begged them to stay at their house until the rains let up and some of the water ran off, but they did not want to abandon their home. Kelsie needed to be near the stock and they felt as long as they could get in and out to the main road they needed to be at home. Well, one Saturday morning, to their dismay, when they got up and looked out the window only a small portion of the front yard was above water and there was water at least a foot and a half deep in the basement with more running in by the minute. There was no way to get into the basement except through the two large doors that opened into the back yard, and since the back yard sloped down the water there was even deeper.

Evidently, it had rained all night, although at that present moment it wasn't, but dark clouds were blocking the suns rays and it looked like it could start again anytime. Doris began to worry about the cans of fruit and vegetables on the lower shelves that lined the basement walls. If they set in the water long they would come unsealed and Doris would lose all of the fruit and vegetables she had worked so hard to preserve. What were they to do? They mulled over the situation while Doris fixed breakfast. Kelsie was worried about the stock, which he could see huddled together in the stable lot which set on a rise. The stable was still above the water and although Kelsie couldn't see the hog pen which sloped down from behind the stable, he knew that most of it was likely under water, but there was a small door leading from the pen into the large stall inside the barn, so he felt sure the sow had taken her five pigs inside out of the flooded hog pen. There was no way Kelsie could even drive the tractor out that morning, for the lane, by which he had come home the night before, was now covered by at least three feet of muddy, swirling water. Well, there was still one mode of communication still accessible, the telephone.

Doris had already talked to Lorene, who was still worried sick over them and was quick to tell them they should have come over to Golden Pond with them two days ago instead of waiting around until they got hemmed in by the flood. Doris told her Kelsie was trying to come up with something and that she would call her back as soon as they had figured something out. Well, Kelsie decided to go up Hwy. 91, to Mam Sherberts who lived in the two story house that set around the bend on a hill there on the place. Kelsie knew one of her boys had a boat for he did a lot of fishing on the river and he figured he might have come over to check on Mam Sherbert. Luckily, her son, Charlie, was there at the time. He had rowed over in his old aluminum fishing boat from his place a quarter of a mile up the river to bring her some groceries. She said he would be right over to get Doris and Kelsie. She also said for them to come prepared to stay for a few days, for the weather was calling for more heavy rain and flooding for the next three days. Well, this time, Kelsie didn't argue the issue, for he had lived next to and gone to battle with the Cumberland River enough times to know when the river had him licked. In less than a half hour Charlie was rowing across what used to be the corn field, in Doris and Kelsie's direction. Doris, who was still worried about her canned goods in the flooded basement asked Kelsie, as Charlie approached them where they stood on the back porch, if he thought they could get the boat through the double doors of the basement and move the canned goods from the lower shelves to the higher ones. Well, Kelsie wasn't too thrilled with the idea, but he did ask Charlie, who was more than willing to try. Well, after much maneuvering and splashing they managed to get the boat through the doors and transfer the jars of fruits and vegetables to a dryer location.

When the ordeal in the basement was completed, Kelsie and Charlie maneuvered the boat as close to the back porch as they could get and loaded Doris, who was carrying a sack of the necessary clothing they would need to stay a couple of nights, into the boat and began the trip to Mam Sherberts, delaying only long enough for Kelsie to throw some hay and corn out on to the stable lot to the mules and cows and go inside the stable to check on and feed the sow and pigs. They were in the stall as he had anticipated, and after throwing several ears of corn into the stall he headed back to the boat, leaving the stable doors open for the mules and cows.

It was only a few minutes later that they were scrambling out of the boat and making the climb up the muddy hill to Mam Sherberts. Her plump form filled the front door way as she welcomed them into the house. Now Mam Sherbert was one of those rare individuals that once you saw and met you'd not likely forget. She always wore a shirt waist, printed dress, over which was a freshly starched apron. Mam Sherbert had helped to birth many babies into the world in the various communities in which she had lived there in the land between the rivers. One characteristic she had that always fascinated both Doris and Kelsie, was the smoking of a stone pipe. Not that smoking a pipe was an out of the ordinary thing among elderly women of the area, but it was how she lit it that was fascinating and amusing. She would take the pipe along with a pouch of tobacco from her apron, fill the pipe, then reach into her pocket once again, bring out a match and strike it on the seat of her dress, hold it to the top of the pipe and puff until the tobacco inside had ignited, then she'd lean back in her rocking chair, cross her legs, smooth her apron and blow the smoke into the air. Now ready for a leisurely conversation. Sometimes she would dip coals up from the fireplace with her pipe to light it, but most of the time she struck the match on the seat of her dress.

Well, the next afternoon Doris and Kelsie were able to return home. The heavy rains and flooding forecast by the weather man the day before had gone to the North of the Cumberland River valley. With the exception of a few sprinkles that afternoon while Doris and Kelsie were at Mam Sherbert's, no more rain came. The next day dawned clear and before noon the sun was out and the air fresh and crisp. The water began abating about as fast as it rose, so Charlie was only able to row them only about half way to their house. The rest of the way they waded through mud and debris. The stock would have to remain in the barn and stable lot for another day or so and it would be some time before the basement would be drained enough to enter. The back water had drained from the front yard and Kelsie thought he could get the Farmall out of the shed by the next morning, for it looked as though the lane out to the main road would be passable by then, also.

The sound of a Kelsie's pickup coming up the lane from the barn brought Doris back to her senses. She went to the back door as Kelsie, with Tracy standing beside him on the seat, stopped the truck at the edge of the back yard. "We're going to Golden Pond for a few minutes, want to come along?" Kelsie yelled from the truck window.

"Sure," Doris answered, tossing the drying towel she was holding on to the back of one of the kitchen chairs.

"Goin' to see Nanny, mama!" Tracy yelled excitedly as Doris climbed into the truck.

They visited for a couple of hours with Lawton and Lorene that evening in early June and during the visit Doris told Lorene she wasn't feeling too well. The pains in her back and stomach were increasing in intensity as the night wore on and Doris just couldn't get comfortable enough to go to sleep. She was in such discomfort by ten o'clock Kelsie wanted to take her on to the hospital, but Doris was determined to hold out as long as she could before going, however, within the next hour or so the pains were coming so hard and fast, she consented to get her bag and the bag she had prepared for Tracy's stay with Lawton and Lorene and they headed for the hospital. Well, Doris had a somewhat easier time birthing her second child than with her first for by three a.m. on that Ninth day of June, little Michael Wayne Calhoun came into the world weighing seven pounds and six ounces. It was a toss up as to which baby was the prettier, Tracy or Michael. It was evident from the start that Michael would likely have lighter hair than Tracy, and his eyes were now blue, but Tracy's had changed from blue to brown and Doris wondered if Michael's would also.

Well, it seems that many times as the cycle of life revolves, sadness follows joy and "vice-virsa," in sequence and old timers used to say dramatic events seem to come in "threes," This old adage proved true for Lorene. Lorene was still basking in the joy of having a second grandchild that third week after Michael was born when Duck called to tell her Ed was very ill. Duck went on to explain that he had barely been able to be up and around for the last few days, but she had hesitated to call anyone until he had just gotten to the place where he could not keep food on his stomach. Lorene usually visited her parents who still lived over at Edgars Ferry Bridge where Ed still ran the small store and fish market every couple of days, but she had been so busy with harvesting her garden stuff and the seamstress work that it had been over a week since she had seen them. She knew her daddy was in ill health, although no one in the family, not even she, herself, could persuade him to go to the doctor. He had lost the twinkle in his eyes and it seemed everything he did tired him out. She had watched the color go out of his face and although, Ed was always wiry thin, he had, in the last several months lost even more weight. Lorene had almost come to tears the afternoon they took little Michael by on their way taking the new baby and Doris home from the hospital. Ed was sitting in the shade of one of the oak trees that grew in the yard there at the store and as Lorene laid Michael on his lap she saw tears in her daddy's eyes as he gazed at the tiny bundle, his second great grand child. Lorene and her mama had discussed briefly in the past, the way Ed's health was declining, however, he kept on running the store and fishing. So, Lorene was not surprised when she received the call that early summer day.

When she finished washing the dinner dishes Lorene went over to spend the afternoon with her daddy and mama. Ed was in bed and her mother was very worried. She called Lorene aside out of earshot of Ed and told her that he had not kept a bite of food on his stomach for almost two days. She also told Lorene he was having trouble getting his kidneys to act and that he had had that problem, off and on, for some time now.

"Well, Mama," Lorene said when her mother finished, "we are taking him to the doctor in the morning." Duck just nodded her head in agreement. Then Lorene turned and went into the bedroom where her daddy lay on the bed and was opening her mouth to tell him of the decision she and her mother had made but he spoke first. "Renie, I believe I'm gonna have to break down and go to the doctor. I'm just feelin' awful poorly."

"Well, daddy, that's what me and mama were just talking about; we think you need to go," Lorene said gently sitting down on the edge of the bed.

The next day Ed went to the local doctor in Cadiz who informed him he needed to go to Vanderbilt Hospital in Nashville for a series of tests. Ed was, at first, reluctant to go, but he knew he had no choice, so a week later he was admitted into Vanderbilt and two days later he was diagnosed with cancer of the stomach and prostate. The doctors there did not give he or the family much faith in Ed being cured. He began a series of treatments and stayed in Vanderbilt for ten days. Duck then called Lorene and told her he wanted to be transferred to the hospital in Cadiz where he would be close to home. The doctor's consented to his transferal. Ed was never able to return home. His condition steadily declined. It was evident that the cancer had reached an advanced stage before Ed ever gave in to go to the doctor, for on July twelfth, in that year of Nineteen and fifty seven Lorene lost, not only her daddy, but the dearest friend she had ever had in her life. She knew as she watched the caretakers lower the casket into the ground there in the little cemetery at Turkey Creek that she had lost a great portion of herself and her grief for her daddy would end only when she joined him some day.

The late 1950s not only brought about the promise of change for the land between the rivers, it also brought new happenings into Virgil's life. It had taken Virgil a long time to recover from the divorce of his first marriage which only lasted eleven months, in fact, he was so devastated in the beginning and missed Coreen so much for several years afterward, he felt his heart simply could not love again. But, to his surprise, one sunny afternoon when he was visiting in the home of some friends, the Mullins, he met Shirley Cox, whom was also visiting with them. Virgil remembered Shirley from years past, for she too was deaf and had attended the school at Danville, however, Virgil had not met or gotten to know her personally. They visited with the Mullins for the afternoon and got acquainted. Virgil and Shirley had a lot in common and it seemed they hit it off from the start. Virgil learned that Shirley baby-sat with her brother Chuck and sister in law Alice's two children while the couple both worked. Chuck and Alice lived in Roosevelt Michigan only a few miles from the Mullins home. Shirley asked Virgil if he would mind taking her to her brothers house later that afternoon. Virgil assured her the pleasure would be all his. So that was the beginning of a beautiful relationship. Virgil and Shirley began dating on a regular basis. Shirley was a sweet and warm person and very easy to know and be around. Virgil had not been so happy since he and Coreen had met and it took only a few months into he and Shirley's relationship until he was over Coreen. Virgil brought Shirley home to meet his family and they were well pleased with the choice he had made in his second wife. Later, in their relationship, Lawton and Lorene met Shirley's parents. They were from Louisville and very nice and warm people. Her father Ed was pastor of the Church of Christ in Louisville, and her mother Delta was a homemaker.

Well, much as Lorene and the rest of the family had suspected, on September the fourteenth of that same year, Virgil and Shirley were married in a small, church in Detroit. The family was thrilled for Virgil and Shirley. They were so happy and Virgil had spent such a long time anguishing over the disappointment of his first marriage that Lorene felt a burden had defiantly been lifted.

When the ceremony was over and everyone was leaving the church, Lorene had walked a short distance from the others of the wedding party to spend a few moments alone with Virgil. He gave her a hug and assured her this was the happiest day of his life. Lorene patted him fondly on the jaw, then smiled as he ran to the edge of the church yard where Shirley awaited him. They would soon be on their way to Niagara Falls for their honeymoon.

How long she stood there under the golden leaves of one of the several maple trees that grew in the church yard, staring down the road from which Virgil's 1956 Olds had vanished from sight, she didn't know. Her thoughts had drifted to years ago when Virgil was first born and to the look on her daddy's face as he held Virgil, his first grandchild in his arms, much the same as when she lay Michael in his arms only a few months ago. Hot tears burned her eyes as a faint breeze rustled the crisp leaves above her. She heard the sound of Lawton's voice coming from the church parking lot and when she turned she saw him patiently waiting for her to join him for the short journey home. She and Lawton talked of the ceremony, of Michael's birth, then the death of her daddy; three dramatic events, all in a row, in the same year, confirming the truthfulness of the earlier spoken "adage."

Chapter Fifteen:

Life on the Farm

The perfect circle of a harvest moon had barely lifted above the thicket that lined the ridge overlooking Kentucky Lake. It was a pretty sight to see. The moon's reflection on the slightly moving water was shimmering like a long, white, silk skirt flowing against the thigh's of a slender young maiden swaying to and fro on a dance floor. The hoot of an owl and songs of the katydids mingled with an occasional splash as a wave, stirred by the subtle breeze, lapped against the rocks on the lake's edge, created the only sounds that penetrated the early evening air.

Meanwhile, a few miles away, in the Cumberland River Valley, Doris tucked four year old Tracy into bed, then went into the living room and took one year old Mike, whom was ready for bed also, from his playpen. Doris had warmed and placed a full bottle of formula on the small table beside the rocking chair that faced the television in the corner of the room. Mike was beginning to get fussy, but when Doris snuggled him on her lap and gave him the bottle of formula, he immediately became quiet and began to relax.

Kelsie had not returned from the far bottoms where he and two hired hands had been picking corn since sun up. Harvest time on a farm was a busy time and not a moment could be wasted. The crops had to be harvested before the fall rains set in or the bottoms would flood with back water and the corn, beans and grain would be lost.

Doris sat rocking baby Mike and watching "The Lucy Show" on the television, every now and then, letting her thoughts slip back over the past six years. She and Kelsie

Shirley, Tim, Virgil, and Matthew Higgins, early 1960s.

123

Doris, Tracy, Mike, and Kelsie Calhoun, early 1960s.

had a good life here on the farm in the Cumberland River Valley, for the most part. The back water did propose a problem from time to time, creating a shortage of income on which to live. Doris and Kelsie were hearing talk, much as her parents in Golden Pond, that The Tennessee Valley Authority, along with the Corp of Engineer's were going to take over the whole area of land between the rivers. The news saddened Doris and she was concerned to some extent as to where they would go and what kind of work Kelsie would find, for after all, he had farmed all of his life. But, the news did not propose as much of an upsetting threat to her as they did her mama. Yes, it would mean she and Kelsie and the boys would have to leave the valley and relocate somewhere else, but she didn't know if it was because she was so busy with the children she didn't have time to dwell on the matter, or because she was younger and had not developed the strong attachment for her home as that of her mama. The house in Golden Pond where Doris grew up was the only home she had known since she was five years old, at which time her mama and daddy purchased it and moved from Ma Annie's house. It was her mama and daddy's first and only home to own after living with Ma Annie for the first eight years of their married life. It was her mama, Lorene's dream house and it was killing her to think of having to give it up. Every time Doris had been in the presence of Lorene since the news began to spread about TVA buying up the land for another lake, in addition to the Kentucky Lake which was completed in 1944, and utilizing the remainder of the land that would not be flooded between the rivers as a wildlife and game reserve, her mama had come to tears. It disturbed Doris to see her mama so distraught at the thought of loosing her home in Golden Pond. But, every other resident of the area was experiencing a degree of frustration and insecurity, also. They too, did not think it was fair for rank strangers to come into the various communities and give those whom had cleared and farmed the land, built homes, along with towns and various businesses no choice, not even a vote, in making the decision as to the drastic changes that were obviously coming about. Neither would the inhabitants who occupied the land between the rivers have the option to negotiate a price for their property. They would be forced to take what the government conceded was "the fair market value."

"Yes, it does seem unfair in all respects," Doris thought to herself as she sat rocking her now sleeping baby in her arms. She sighed, slowly arose from the chair and made her way to the bedroom where Tracy peacefully slept in the half bed across the room from the baby bed. She lay her lips against the silky, soft flesh of the baby's cheek as she gently laid him in the crib. She, then turned to the half bed, tucked the covers around Tracy, who had already kicked them off, and kissed his forehead. She straightened to leave the room, pausing long enough to gaze, fondly in the dimly lit room, at her two sleeping boys, then with a sigh, she shook her head and whispered, "if you two little angels would just sleep the entire night, just one night, in your own beds so your daddy and me could get one good night's sleep, how wonderful that would be."

Well, it didn't happen that night, nor for many nights to come. Yes, it seemed every morning around two o'clock, when Mike's feeding time came, a crying session began that ended only when both boys were in the double bed, snuggled between Doris and Kelsie.

Meanwhile back in Golden Pond, life continued much the same for Lawton and Lorene. The house was now empty of the children, but Doris, Kelsie and the boys visited frequently, and Virgil and Shirley made their way to Golden Pond as often as time away from their jobs would permit. Lorene was still busying herself with the house, sewing, garden and yard work. Lawton was still in the same "business," conducting most of his "business" among the regulars that had patronized him down through the years, but he had slowed down considerably in the number of out of town trips he made. He stayed pretty close to home with the exception of a poker game now and then in the creek bed and a trip or two a day to the business section of Golden Pond where he caught up on the neighborhood news, world news and politics. Lorene began to notice toward the end of summer in 1957 that Lawton just didn't seem to be his same active self. He went to bed earlier and got up later. He was turning down the opportunity to be out and about with the old "cronies" he had always run around with. Most of the time they would just sit in the shade of the trees in the front yard or on the porch and talk. Lawton wasn't laughing and joking a lot as he was previously accustomed to doing. He even took up whittling as he sat in the shade during the Indian summer days. Lorene noticed also, his crippled leg was bothering him more and it was a major effort for him to get up from a chair or out of bed. He complained a lot of not feeling good and he had lost much of his appetite. She had insisted he go to the doctor, but he would just shake his head and make the comment, "If you've got one thing wrong with you when you go, when they get through with you, there'll be two or three. It's just the heat, I'll get to feelin' better when fall gets here and it cools up."

Well, fall came and then winter but Lawton wasn't feeling any better. He finally, on his own, decided to visit the doctor, only to discover his blood pressure was very high and severe arthritis had set up in the left side of his back and crippled leg. The doctor prescribed medication for the high blood pressure and put him on a diet. The doctor explained there wasn't much he could do for the arthritis, except for Lawton to take aspirin on a regular basis and he also told him the arthritis would progressively get worse. He suggested that Lawton stay as active as he possibly could. Well, it was hard for Lawton to be up and about any more than he was accustomed to, but he began walking the short distance to the downtown section of Golden Pond instead of driving the car. It was very difficult for Lawton to adjust his eating habits. He had always loved to eat and Lorene, being a good old fashioned country cook had always seasoned their food highly and fried much of the meat they ate. Lawton complained that the broiled and baked meat tasted like shoe leather and the bland vegetables needed to go into the slop bucket for the hogs. Yes, it was quiet an adjustment for the two of them.

Back on the farm on the Cumberland Doris was busy taking care of the boys, along with cooking for hired hands, helping Kelsie with feeding the stock and milking their old cow "Bessie." Bessie was the only diary cow they owned, but they had several head of beef cattle. Doris got broken into the perils involved in the beef cattle business the first year she and Kelsie were married. It seemed to Doris the cows picked the worse time of the year to calve. It was nothing for Kelsie to come in from the stable on a cold snowy night, fill a pail with lard, grab the lantern from the back porch and yell to Doris, "Come on' we've got to head back to the stable and pull a calf! That heifer can't make it by her self." Well, Doris never got used to helping "pull a calf", but she was always amazed at the miracle of birth, and the way the new mother, instinctively cared for her young. Then too, Doris accepted her part of the chore as being a part of her duties in contributing to their livelihood.

Yes, Doris considered herself to be a fairly resourceful and reliable farm wife. She didn't mind helping with the feeding, not even when the snow was a foot deep or the rain pelting down, but she did hate milking that old jersey cow. It never failed, regular as clock work, once a week, Bessie would set her foot in the milk bucket. Sometimes there would be only an inch or two of the warm milk in the bucket, yet sometimes the bucket would be almost full. It was also, a constant chore as Doris squatted under the cow to dodge mud or manure soaked tail as she swished it from side to side. Then, there was the ever present complaint by Kelsie that she wasn't stripping all of the milk from Bessie and she was going to "dry up."

Much of the time while Doris was squatted there in the process of completing the most despised of all of her farm chores, she would let her mind trail off onto more pleasant matters.

One such incident that always lifted Doris' spirits occurred back in the spring. Now, Tracy was definitely an animal lover. Anything that had four legs and fur that he could catch and pet, he was after, however, at four years old, about the only critters he could manage to catch was Lassie, their two thirds coon hound and one third bird dog, and the old mammy cat. Now, upon one of Tracy's visits to Nannie's house in Golden Pond, she had drug out some of Doris' old toys for him to play with; one of which was a doll buggy. Well, Tracy had had such great fun with the doll buggy while he was at Nannie's that he insisted on bringing it home with him.

Now, Lassie, took every step Tracy took and it was apparent that the dog admired and totally obeyed his young master. But, when Tracy insisted she get in the doll buggy, that was stretching it a bit too far, for after several minutes of Tracy grunting, straining and pushing against Lassie's gentle restraints, the little boy finally gave up on getting the big dog into the doll buggy. Lassie retreated to a shady spot under the lilac bush and watched as Tracy began looking around for a more suitable sized passenger. Well, Tracy had only one other visible option, and she lay napping on the back porch. Yes, that's where their very much pregnant old mammy cat spent most of the day, and she was a perfect fit for the doll buggy. So, Tracy began pushing her around the yard and back and forth down the path to the garden. This was an every day ritual. The mammy cat didn't seem to mind, for she'd just lay right there in the buggy, bouncing along and sleeping away as Tracy entertained himself.

"I guess the mammy cat is just too tired being as pregnant as she is to put up a fight. I know just how she feels." Doris had commented late one afternoon in May as she and Kelsie sat on the steps of the back porch watching Tracy at his great new game."

"Yep, you and the ol' mammy cat have somethin' in common don't you, hon? Both ready to deliver anytime." Kelsie replied, laughing.

"I'm apt to have this baby squattin' under old Bessie and the mammy cat's apt to have her kittens in that doll buggy." Doris said, shaking her head and laughing. Kelsie laughed with her. Little did Doris know true her statement concerning the mammy cat might be.

Well, a few days later, Doris was clearing the table of the breakfast dishes when the piercing sounds of Tracy yelling "Mama!" penetrated her ears. He had gone outside as soon as he had finished his breakfast and the last time Doris had looked out the kitchen to check on him, he was once again pushing the mammy cat down the garden path.

"Mama!" he called again.

Doris went running to the back door, where Tracy met her yelling and pointing to the doll buggy at the foot of the steps. "Mama, th' mammy cat's got a baby! She's got a baby!"

"Oh, my Lord!" Doris gasped as she dashed across the porch to peer into the buggy. Sure enough, the old mammy cat was busy cleaning up a tiny, wet, yellow kitten.

Well, Doris didn't quite know what to do, or more like it, didn't think it a very good idea to allow Tracy to witness any more of the birthing process, so she began to look around for a solution.

"Well, I'll say! She does have a baby, don't she? I'll tell you what we'll have to do. We'll have to fix her and her baby a good bed in the smoke house." Doris explained, looking around on the porch for something in which to put the mammy cat and her baby.

"Oh, no Mama!" Tracy protested, beginning to cry. "I have to push her, she'll be afraid in the smokehouse."

"Now, Tracy we have to put her in a safe place, she will likely have more than one baby," Doris said, picking up a box from under a shelf at the edge of the porch.

Tracy showed signs of more tears, but when Doris told him he could help her put mammy cat and her baby in the smoke house and that they would check on her every little bit, it seemed to console him. So, Doris, along with Tracy's help took the box, lined the bottom with some rags they found in the smoke house and transferred the mammy cat and her new baby from the doll buggy to the safety of the smoke house.

"Mama," Tracy asked as they closed the smoke house door, "how many babies will she have?"

"Oh, she may have as many as five," Doris said, holding up one hand, "or she may have three. How many is three?"

Tracy held up three little fingers and Doris tousled his hair and they started toward the house.

"Mama?" Tracy asked as they reached the back porch, "how many babies are you gonna' have?"

"Only one, I hope," Doris answered laughing and holding up one finger.

The seasons came and went leaving behind them the planting, the growing, the harvesting and the harshness of winter's fury. TVA, along with The Corps of Engineers was still the main topic of conversation among the residents between the rivers. It was a settled fact there were drastic changes coming about, but no one knew just when. Funds for various projects had already been approved by Congress and plans were being laid. All of this talk was a definite "thorn in the flesh" to Lorene. Just when times were getting easier with all of the modern conveniences, it seemed everything was about to change.

The people between the rivers had adapted well to the changes brought about by the booming fifties. Although many areas of their lives had been made easier, it seemed all of the modern conveniences had also brought about a distance among neighbors. The time saving devices that had come into existence in the communities, seemed to leave less time for one another. Practically every family now owned a vehicle which eliminated the dependency of travel on one another. Farmers had numerous pieces of machinery with which to farm their land and since money was more plentiful they hired needed help rather than use the barter system that had bound neighboring farmers for many years. Neighbors did not visit to pass the time as they had in the past. The amazing gadget known as the television which almost every family now had in their living room had brought about an in house entertainment that took the place of the gathering of friends and neighbors. It was taking the most of every man's daylight hours to work to pay for all of the new conveniences they were now enjoying.

Now, Lawton and Lorene still had quite an influx of people frequenting their home, but the majority were customers and they definitely had a lot more in common with Lawton than with Lorene. Sometimes she would become very adamant about them congregating to "shoot the bull" with Lawton, especially when Tracy and Mike were there. Lawton did not condone drinking the fruits of his labor around the house as they loitered, but he would do a lot of entertaining with the tales and escapades of his younger years. Lorene had voiced her opinion to him several times about talking that "stuff" in front of the boys, but Lawton would laugh it off and say, "Oh, Renie, quit your frettin,' them boys won't ever do any moonshinin' or bootleggin' there's too many other easy money making jobs out there, it's not like in mine and your day."

Well, Lorene still didn't like it, even if "conjoling" with his old "cronies" did seem to be one of the few things Lawton enjoyed doing these days.

Virgil and Shirley were now living in Taylor, Michigan where they had bought a nice house and they were expecting their first child. Of course, Lorene was excited because she was, once again, going to become a grandmother, however, she had the same old reservations she had concerning all of the other responsibilities Virgil had incurred. She consoled herself that he had gotten his schooling, found his place in the job market, endured a devastating divorce, managed to have a productive relationship and marriage and she guess Virgil would succeed in filling the role as a good father. But, how in the world would he and Shirley, both being deaf, ever be able to communicate with a child? This was a question that entered Lorene's mind frequently. Then too, there was the ever present question in the back of her mind, "would the baby be deaf also?"

Kelsie pulled his old blue pickup into the driveway at Lorene and Lawton's one Sunday afternoon in the spring of 1959. Doris and Kelsie made their way toward the house while the boys went running toward the back of the house where Lawton was coming from the barn.

The visit was not an unusual occurrence and the line of conversation began much in the norm. It was when Doris and Kelsie had been there for about an hour and they were all around the kitchen table, having a piece of Lorene's apple pie and playing with the boys that Kelsie broke the news of he and Doris' startling decision.

"We talked to a man from the Corps of Engineers, fact is, we've talked to him three times," Kelsie began, "and me an' Doris and mama and Edna have decided to sell most of the farm to the government. They plan to do some land movin' to try and control the floodin'."

"You all have made up your minds to sell out to the government, to TVA?" Lorene asked, astonished by Kelsie's statement.

"Well, Mama you know what a time we've had just about every year with the back water. We lost three bottom fields of corn last year and we know it's not going to get any better," Doris added.

"But, you all know people sellin' out to them here and there only encourages them to take all our places. There's more and more talk of it ever' day," Lorene said earnestly.

"Well, now Lorene they're gonna' take everybody's land that they want anyway," Lawton began, obviously entertaining a more sympathetic view toward Kelsie and Doris.

"Well, I just reckon they will for sure if people start givin' in to them!" Lorene answered sternly.

"Well Mama, we've been havin' a hard time on the farm and it seems the last three years have been the worst," Doris began again, seemingly trying to convince Lorene that their choice was inevitable.

"Lorene," Kelsie began, "it's been about all we could to keep our heads above the water in more ways than one. When them bottoms flood and wipe out our corn and bean crop that leaves us with nothin' to feed the stock in winter, not to mention, nothin' to sell. Maybe if we sell off our bottoms and they do something to stop part of the floodin' it will help some of the other farmers."

"Aw, I know you all have been havin' it rough these last few years, and I don't reckon we'd do any different if we were in your shoes, but it just seems the Government has already took land and built the Kentucky Dam and now they are takin' your land, then God knows who else they'll be wantin' next," Lorene said in a calmer voice. "I just get the feelin' it won't be long till we'll all be run out of our homes and this part of the country has survived many a' year before these blasted Government projects come around."

"That may very well be Lorene, but it cost's more to live now than it used to," Kelsie said. "Seems like the more we've got of modern conveniences, the more money it takes comin' in to pay for them. Up until the last few years people could make out on a few tillable acres, a couple of mules, a cow, a few hogs and a garden. It's not that way any more."

"No, I know it's not and I don't know as all these new-fangled modern conveniences are all they're cooked up to be," Lorene flat out declared.

"Well, I don't reckon you'd be any to thrilled at goin' back to carrying water and cookin' on a wood stove," Lawton said, putting his two cents in.

"Well, I can tell you one thing. Life was a lot more simple back then. At least people took the time to stop and talk to a body," Lorene answered. "Now days people are in too big of a rush to much more than speak."

"That's a fact, Lorene," Kelsie agreed. "Bad thing about it is, I have a feelin' it's going to get even worse."

"What do you plan to do, Kelsie, when you sell your land?" Lawton asked.

"Well, since I'll still have the hills and some timber still left, guess I'll keep some cattle and still put out enough corn and hay in the fields on the ridge to feed them in winter," Kelsie answered. "Then too, I'm goin' to try to find a public job somewhere."

Doris and the boys left about middle of the afternoon and Lorene thrashed their decision around in her head for the next several days. She could see the predicament they were in. She knew it took more money coming in to meet expenses. She knew also that educating two children would be triple to what it cost she and Lawton when Virgil and Doris were growing up, but she also knew that if families gave in to the Government and let their land go, there would soon be no more "land between the rivers."

Chapter Sixteen:

The Family Continues to Grow

The North wind's fierceness forced Lorene to pull her old gray sweater tighter about her as she stepped off the back porch and headed for the smoke house. Glancing to the sky she noticed dark clouds low on the horizon and she thought she felt a drop of sleet or snow hit her face. She quickened her steps and as she reached quickly for the smoke house door, at which time she definitely did see tiny snow flakes floating, light as the down of a thistle, in the blustery air.

"Oh, my goodness!" She whispered, "I hope Virgil and Shirley and that baby don't get stranded between here and Michigan."

Lorene grabbed the cured ham, her reason for making the short trip to the smoke house, from the hook that hang from one of the rafters, turned quickly and rushed out the door. She secured the wooden latch, ran back across the yard, then dashed across the back porch and into the house. The warmth of the kitchen was a welcome recluse from the December chill.

Cold weather had set in early that year and Kelsie and Doris had had a hog killing shortly after Thanksgiving. Lawton had quit raising hogs several years past, for he had gotten to the place where he was not physically able to take care of them. Then too, pork was not on the diet the Dr. had put Lawton on for his high blood pressure and the two strokes he had incurred. But, considering Lawton's "always living on the edge nature", he had purchased the biggest ham in Kelsie and Doris' smoke house, once they had finished smoking the middlins, shoulders and hams. He brought it home and hung it in their smoke house to save for the Christmas Holidays.

Lawton was coming into the kitchen from the living room as Lorene placed the ham on the counter.

"Looks like Kelsie did a pretty fair job of smokin' the ham," he commented as moved up to the counter where the pungent aroma of the hickory smoke that had saturated the browned ham was beginning to fill the warm kitchen air.

"Law, my daddy would sure enjoy a slice of this country ham if he was here," Lorene said mostly to herself, with an expression on her face mixed with both softness and sadness.

Lawton mumbled a reply as he moved on to look out the window above the sink, but Lorene wasn't listening. Her thoughts were turned to years ago and miles away in the Fenton Community when she was a little girl. Many had been the time this same aroma had teased her senses when Ed had brought a ham from the smoke house and began slicing it on the old wooden cook table that set beside the wood cook stove. Duck would have two iron skillets on the stove, ready to lay the perfectly carved slices into the hot circles where the meat would immediately start to sizzle. Ed would always leave enough fat around the edges when he carved out the hams on hog killing day to create enough grease for the ham to cook tender. Once the slices were browned on each side, Duck would scoot the skillets to the cooler burners to let the meat simmer until done. Meanwhile, she would go to the cabinet and sift a sizable amount of flour in to the wooden biscuit bowl that set beneath the sifter which was at the bottom of the large bin that was contained in one side of the white, wooden, kitchen cabinet. She would then remove the bowl from under the bin, round out a hole in the middle of the heap of flour, fill the hole with fresh buttermilk, add a sizable scoop of lard, a pinch of baking soda along with a pinch of salt and begin mixing the ingredients by hand, slowly working in the flour, until she had a large round dough ball. She would sprinkle a heavy amount of flour on the wooden dough board she had placed on the metal counter top of the cabinet, lift the dough ball from the bowl and begin completing the kneading process. Then she would take the rolling pin, spread the dough over the circle of flour until it was approximately a half inch thick and with a tin biscuit cutter she cut the dough into two dozen or so perfectly shaped biscuits. Next, she would place the un-baked biscuits, one at a time, in the large, greased baking pan and take them to the stove to put on the "finishing touch," as she called it. The "finishing touch," was brushing the top of each biscuit with some of the fat dipped from the skillets of still cooking country ham. The biscuits were then placed in the hot oven, where Lorene could remember so clearly, it seemed to take forever to bake.

Duck would take the ham slices from the skillets and place them on the large, iron stone platter when the biscuits were about half done, then pour the bigger part of the grease from the skillets into a bowl she had placed on one of the cooler burners. She would then scoot the skillets back on the hotter burners, let them heat until they were sizzling well, then pour an approximate half cup of water into the remaining grease and ham "drippings", then stir. When the mixture came to a boil it was ready to be poured into the bowl of grease on the cooler burner, thus creating the succulent "red gravy" that was almost as good spread over an egg or hot biscuits as the perfectly browned ham slices awaiting consumption on the platter beside it. Now, it was time to fry the eggs, for the biscuits were beginning to brown. You see, perfect timing was imperative to produce a good, between the rivers, country breakfast. If the entire 'entree wasn't served hot all at once, it took away from the pleasure of the much anticipated first "mess" of country ham. Duck even had the plates stacked on the warming closet shelf so the grease from each fried egg didn't chill the minute it touched the plate, as it would if they were setting on the table. Sorghum molasses and fresh churned butter, along with the silverware were waiting on the table. These were the only other ingredients needed to complete a thoroughly satisfying and minutes later, completely consumed breakfast.

Lorene smiled as she remembered how she and her younger siblings enjoyed those breakfast's on a cold winter morning! Sometimes the North wind would be howling around the corner of the house and sometimes there would be snow flakes swirling in it's havoc, but no chill was felt in the warmth of mama's kitchen. She could see, in her mind, the expression of love on her daddy's face as he, at the head of the table, and she next to him to his right, watched his little brood lick the last drop of sorghum molasses mingled with country ham fat, from their fingers.

"Yes, Daddy always loved to see us well fed and happy." She mumbled as she busied herself about the kitchen. Then, she began to chuckle to herself as she recollected a time when she was very small and went to the barn with Ed to do up the night work. It was one of those many times she followed her daddy around, just enjoying being outside and in his company. She had helped her daddy feed the mules, fed corn to the hogs while he milked their two cows and Ed had gone to the loft to fork down some hay to the mules and cows. Lorene had wandered into the tack room beyond the stalls where they kept the mules at night. Soon after entering the tack room, she spied a birds nest in the corner of the rafters above the pegs on which the mules harness hang. She quickly assembled a make shift ladder so she could closer investigate the contents of the nest by stacking a crate, then an old tin bucket on the top of a large wooden box where Ed kept numerous, miscellaneous tools. Then she scrambled, ever so cautiously to the top of the bucket, only to realize she still had several inches to go before she was at eye level with the bird nest. She glanced around trying to find another foot hold and discovered a wide crack between the boards that braced the partition between the tack room and the mule stalls. Holding onto the pegs that held the harness, she hoisted herself the few inches she needed to see into the nest. There was movement in the nest which she did not instantly identify, but as she peered closer and her eyes adjusted to the dimly lighted corner, she found herself staring into the eyes of, not the downy softness of a baby bird as she had hoped and expected, but the beady eyes of a snake! Well, how Lorene made it back down the make-shift ladder and to the floor without falling and becoming mortally wounded, she could not, to this day tell, but she did, screaming all the way! Ed, alarmed by the piercing howls, met her by the time she had rounded the corner of the mules' stalls.

"What on earth is the matter, Renie?" He called, reaching his arms out to her.

"Oh Daddy! I...I saw the awfullest snake! It's in...in a b..bird nest in there!" She gasped all in one breath, falling against him and pointing toward the tack room.

"Aw, it's likely an ol' chicken snake. Probably the rascal that's been suckin' all the eggs in the hen's nest up in the loft," Ed said holding her little trembling body against him and patting her head. "I'd go see what kind it is, but I know with all that screamin,' that snake took off in the opposite direction 'bout as fast as you did." He went on as he chuckled at his wide eyed little girl. He then took her hand and said, "common' mama'll be waitin' supper on us." Lorene remembered telling Ed the whole story as they walked up the dusty path to the house, then she told it again to Duck and the youngens when they sat down to supper. How brave and important she felt at having endured such a danger-ous incident unharmed! She could, still to the day, see the grin on her daddy's face and the amusing winks he gave her mama as Lorene, who was sitting across the table, re-layed every detail of her ordeal. That was her daddy, always good "natured", always taking the time to attend to even the small mishaps. Lorene could remember only a few times Ed showed annoyance.

One of those few times was when they lived on the ridge in a little frame house not far from Uncle Joe and Aunt Rhodie. The Tennessee River lay some hundred yards to the front of the little house and a corn field was to the back with a slew between, just a few yards from the back yard. Well, it was well on into the summer, with the weather fairly dry, but the slew had about a foot of murky water standing in the deepest places. It was the perfect place for the breeding and thriving of misquotes. And, that they did, in fact, they were so dense, it was virtually impossible to open the windows and doors or be outside without constant swatting. Lorene, vividly remembered the terrible whelps on she and her siblings legs, faces and arms. That was the same summer she contracted Typhoid fever and the doctor confirmed it was the mosquito bites that had infected her. One of the first things she remembered when her fever finally broke after days of being so sick she was hardly aware of what was going on around her, was seeing her daddy waving burning rags in the air as he ran around the house in an effort to run the mis-quotes. He was in a rage, yelling and swearing as he went! That was one of the few times she saw her daddy show any display of anger. It was after a couple of days of the waving of burning rags that he came stomping into the house panting and sweating, stamped his foot and declared he was looking for another place to live. Well, later that same year, a drought hit, causing the river to go dry and Ed had to give up his muscle fishing, which took away from, their already hard pressed, income. Yes, those were hard times, yet it seemed during those times there were less hurried days. People worked hard at their livelihood whether it was fishing, moonshinin' or their crops and gardens during the spring, summer and fall, but they always managed to find time for a neighborly chat. When the bad weather set in and the crops no longer demanded their attention, friends and relatives from other communities would pile in the buckboard, wrap the small kids in blankets and brave the elements to pay a visit for two or three days at a time. The men would usually hunt, the children would play and the women would unroll the long quilting frames from ceiling of the stayin' room, pull up chairs and spend their spare time chatting as they would "turn out a quilt."

Lorene missed those times. There were other occupants now, at the home place and there had been for sometime before Ed died. TVA had bought the three hundred acres Uncle Joe and Aunt Rhodie had left to Ed and Duck when they passed on. The three hundred acres now lay under the lake created when the Kentucky Dam was built. Ed and Duck had bought the store building near Edgar's Ferry Bridge where he operated both the store and fish market, along with working running the ferry in Calloway county. Shortly after Ed's death, Duck rented the store out and moved into a small house she purchased in Cadiz.

"Where have the years gone?" Lorene thought. In some ways those times seemed like only yesterday, yet in other ways it seemed like such a long time ago. The old song came to Lorene's mind as she pondered the past, "Tell me the tales that to me are so dear. Long, long ago. Long, long ago…"

Virgil and Shirley had been living in the house in Taylor, Michigan for almost two years when Shirley gave birth to their first son on May first of Nineteen and fifty nine. Timothy Bruce weighed eight pounds and eleven ounces. Virgil being deaf could not talk on the telephone, of course, and he had Dora May call Lorene as soon as the great event transpired. When Lorene received the news she could hardly wait to catch a plane out of Paducah to see her new grandson! The garden she and Lawton had planned to get planted that next week would just have to wait or Lawton would just have to plant it by himself. Well, Lorene made the trip fine and Timothy Bruce was everything and more than she expected. She stayed several days with Virgil and Shirley to help with the housework and the baby Timothy until Shirley was able to be on her feet once again. It was a delightful stay for Lorene, however, she was exhausted when she returned to Golden Pond. Lawton had, flat out, refused to go to Doris' house or to let her come and stay with him while Lorene was in Michigan. During Lorene's entire stay with Virgil, Shirley and baby Timothy she was under constant stress worrying about Lawton. She knew he was, definitely, not able to be alone, but she felt such a strong need to be with Virgil and Shirley during their time of need that she went, but she was relieved when she was home once again.

Early in following fall, Virgil had vacation time coming, so he and Shirley brought baby Timothy down his first visit to Golden Pond. How he had grown and changed since the last time Lorene had seen him, which was his first week in the real world. All of the relatives, both Lorene and Lawton's, that lived close enough to visit, including Doris, Kelsie and the boys, of course, kept a constant stream of traffic coming to Lawton and Lorene's to see Timothy Bruce. Well, that was had three months ago and now, they were coming for Christmas! Their spending the Christmas Holidays in Golden Pond would be one of the best Christmas presents Lorene could ever have. She could hardly wait to get her hands on the baby again even though she was concerned about them traveling in the bad weather.

The new year of 1960 rolled in and the state of Kentucky was still basking in the industrial revolution that had come about since the end of World War Two. Many farms, especially in central and western Kentucky were prospering. Tourism was fast becoming very popular and the good roads the state was constructing was affording easy access to the various lakes and recreation areas that were being built throughout the state. Kentucky Lake, on the Tennessee River which was completed in 1944, had already reached fame as being the largest man-made lake in the United States. It was now an established fact that the government was in the final stages of completing the plans for the lake they planned to build on the Cumberland River.

Meanwhile, in Golden Pond, things had returned to an even keel, after the holidays; as even a keel as they usually got, for Golden Pond, that is. Lawton was still in the liquor "business," although, he was barely able to get around. The two strokes, especially the last one, had taken their toll on Lawton's legs and back. Naturally, this only aggravated the already existing, arthritis. Lorene, as well as Doris, Kelsie and even their two little boys, Tracy and Mike, could tell a big difference in Lawton. He was depressed much of the time and no longer felt up to teasing and playing with the boys when they came for a visit. His patience was short because of the pain in his back and legs and it frustrated him that he could no longer get around as he could before the strokes. He had become forgetful and would get very irritated if Lorene contradicted him in a discussion, even if he knew she was in the right.

Talk of the TVA project was still rampant, in fact, it was rumored in Golden Pond that several other families farther West in the Tennessee River Valley had recently been bought out by the TVA. This disturbed Lorene to no end, for she still felt, very strongly, if all of the residents whose properties were beyond the boundaries of the lakes, held together, they could discourage the government from taking their land.

Winter gave way to spring and Lorene began planning for their yearly garden. She knew, without discussing the matter, that Lawton's input into the project would be minimal that spring since he could not be on his feet for a long period of time. Kelsie and Doris had tried to discourage Lorene from even trying to plant a garden, volunteering to plant enough to share with she and Lawton, but Lorene could not stand the thought of not having fresh vegetables growing in her own garden. Why, she never remembered a time in her whole life when there was not a garden growing in the back yard. So, Kelsie got the ground ready and Doris and the boys helped Lorene get the garden seeds in the ground. Lawton was able to help plant some of the seeds, but his legs just would not hold up for him to be on his feet for any measurable length of time.

The warm spring days with their sudden showers and balmy breezes soon turned into long, hot days of summer. Rain grew scarce toward the middle of July, causing crops and gardens to suffer. Lorene was now having several vegetables from her garden which supplied the table, but without a refreshing rain soon there would be little to preserve for winter. Lorene had gotten word from Virgil that he and Shirley and Timothy would be coming for a visit soon. Virgil always enjoyed coming to Golden Pond in the summer when the fresh vegetables were in. Lorene, of course, enjoyed cooking the fresh green beans, yellow squash, sweet corn and new potatoes, all seasoned with hog jowl and accompanied with a large "pone" of perfectly browned corn bread and fried chicken. Although Shirley was a good cook and fresh vegetable were accessible in Michigan, it just seemed the vegetables grown in the Kentucky soil there in Golden Pond and cooked by his mama were always a much anticipated treat for Virgil. So, the third Monday in July brought Virgil, Shirley and baby Timothy rolling in the driveway around four in the afternoon. Timothy Bruce was now walking, jabbering and into everything. Everyone's concern and fear that Timothy might also be deaf had been evident throughout his first year, for the doctor had told them, although everything looked normal and he definitely was not totally deaf, after his first year they would know for sure if his hearing and speech were impaired. At the end of his first year's check up, Virgil and Shirley were assured their little son had perfect hearing. This was a great relief to Lorene, also.

Virgil expressed his deep concern to Lorene about Lawton's condition several times during their stay and as they were leaving the following Saturday. Lorene noticed tears in his eyes when he turned from his daddy to get into the car.

The last week of July brought several good rains in succession that extended into the second week in August and Lorene found herself up to her elbows in trying to keep the weeds out of her garden, along with caning and freezing the vegetables which were fast coming in. By the first of September, she was totally exhausted. Lawton had helped as much as he could and likely more than he should, while Doris had been able to contribute a little time toward helping Lorene fill her jars and freezer bags, but the brunt end of the work fell on Lorene's shoulders to complete. When the three rows of the peas, along with the late corn was put up and the last of the apples dried and stored in white feed sacks in the basement, then, and only then could Lorene breath a sigh of relief. By this time she was so far behind on her seamstress work, she didn't know when she would ever get caught up. It was a relief when the fall rains set in, bringing with it cooler weather and the promise that frost would soon nip the grass to put to an end the chore of mowing the lawn.

Kelsie and Doris were now looking for a house, for they had signed the deed turning their three hundred acres of low land on the Cumberland over to the government. They only had approximately ten acres of hills and ridges left and Kelsie had already accepted a part-time job at the Goodwin Funeral Home in Cadiz. This transition saddened Lorene, however, she was well aware of the money they had lost the many years that the back water destroyed their crops.

It seemed to Lorene that things were changing so fast that she felt as though she was in a whirlwind most of the time. How good it would be if time could stand still when all was well and one was experiencing peace of mind. Those time were few and far between for Lorene, though. Lawton was steadily becoming more incapacitated. Most of the time she had to help him from his chair. He growled and complained about everything. The weather, the food on his diet, too many commercials on the television; just name it, Lawton complained about it. Lorene knew he was suffering, both physically and mentally over his physical condition, but so was she! It seemed he didn't see her suffering, though. There was only one time when Lawton would be his old self and that was when some of his old "cronies" and customers would stop by to make a purchase and stay awhile. Lawton's eyes would light up as he began to entertain his audience with tale after tale, how many and the length of each, depending on how long his audience would tarry. Lorene would mull over in her mind as she went about her sewing or housework, "I don't know which is worse, his complaining or his story telling."

Well, once again, pleasant weather lost it's battle to colder temperatures. The yard was filled with multi-colored leaves from it's dozen or so oak, elm and maple trees. Lorene had spent most of that early November morning trying to rake the leaves down to the shallow ditch at the edge of the yard where, later they would be burned. While she was raking, the mail carrier slowed down as he approached their mailbox. Lorene leaned the rake against a tree and started across the yard. The mail carrier stopped at the box and waited for Lorene to accept the letter he was holding out the window of his car, rather than put it in the mailbox. She glanced at the return address as she accepted the piece of mail and saw it was from Virgil. She exchanged greetings with the mail carrier and chatted briefly with him, then thanked him and went to the edge of the porch to read what Virgil had to say. Most of the contents of the letter were as usual, but there was one bit of news that was a total surprise to Lorene. Shirley was expecting again! The doctor thought it would come toward the last of June. Of course Lorene was happy to know she was going to be a grandmother again, but again, she had that feeling of uneasiness as to the huge responsibility that another child would bring to Virgil and Shirley.

Lorene finished reading Virgil's letter then rose from the porch and took it inside for Lawton to read. When he finished he looked at Lorene who had sat on the edge of the couch and said with a grin, "Well, Renie, looks like our family just keeps growing and growing, huh? I think it's about time one of these youngens was named after me, course', unless this one's a girl, then maybe they'll name her after you."

Chapter Seventeen:
Predicted Fears Come to Pass

D awn broke with a fair sky. The red ball of sun that illuminated from a rosy red glow on the eastern horizon now cast it's red and golden rays through the mist that was, slowly, rising from the Tennessee River; marking it's path on the lazy current as it rolled on it's never ending journey to the sea. Birds, in the thickets, began their morning calls, while furry critters scampered to their lores to escape daylight and predators while they rested from a long night's hunt. The reeds among the rocks along the river's edge began to sway as a gentle, southern breeze blew across the bottoms, lifting the rising mist higher and higher until it spread and mingled, soon, to be undetected in the vastness of the atmosphere.

Meanwhile, in Golden Pond, Lorene and Lawton finished their breakfast and left the house together to climax the planting of their garden. They had put slips and seeds, for early production, in the ground some two weeks prior, and now they were planting some late corn, peas and tomatoes. They had learned from many years of experience, some of their own, some from earlier generations, that staggering the planting, provided fresh vegetables until frost.

Lawton's condition had stabilized, somewhat, but being on his feet for long periods of time was a thing of the past. Lorene's health, except for the hip she had injured in the terrible car accident in 1947 was good, as far as she knew. Lawton had had to make so many trips to doctors and have so much medication, along with her attention, that she had not had the time to bother with concentrating much on her own health.

They were bent over their planting, there in the garden just beyond the back yard, when they heard the sound of a vehicle stopping in front of the house. Lorene, being faster on her feet, headed toward the house. Lawton followed. As Lorene rounded the front corner of the house, three men were stepping upon the front porch. They saw Lorene and the older of the group spoke, "Mrs. Higgings?"

"Yes, I am," Lorene answered, as she walked around the porch to the steps. Lorene's eyes narrowed into tiny slits and she felt a flush coming to her face, for she knew exactly who these three strangers were and what they represented.

"Mr. Higgins?" The same man who spoke to Lorene, asked, looking beyond Lorene to Lawton who was now, coming around the corner of the house.

Lawton nodded and continued making his way to the steps, all the while, trying to "size up" the three, early morning, visitors.

"Mr. and Mrs. Higgins, I am Bob Hunter. This is Vernon Hardin and Charlie Wagner. We're appraisers representing the Tennessee Valley Authority. We're here to appraise your property," the older, and evidently the spokesman for the group, began.

"We don't need our property appraised. We don't intend to be sellin' it any way soon," Lorene answered, her tone as cold as a well digger in Utah.

"Well, Mrs. Higgins, I'm afraid you nor us, either one, have a choice in the matter. I'm sure you've heard from the news media that Congress has passed the bill that entitles TVA to buy all of the land between the Tennessee and Cumberland Rivers?" He continued.

"Yesser, we've heard it, but, it don't mean we have to like it!" Lorene answered, her voice rising and fire blazing from her eyes. "We bought this place almost thirty years ago with hard earned money and we've fixed it up and put a whole lot more money into it, and it's our home and we don't plan to leave it or sell it no matter how many bills Congress or the government or anybody else has passed! Now, you two can take yourselves back to where you came from and quit wastin' our time. We've got a garden to finish plantin'!"

The older man, again, opened his mouth to speak, while the two younger stood with their eyes wide and mouth's slightly ajar, but Lawton then spoke from where he stood at the foot of the steps. "Hush up, a minute, Lorene. Let's hear just what these "fellers" have to say as to what the place is worth, not that we have the idea of sellin'."

"Thank you, Mr. Higgins," the older man said, nodding at Lawton.

Lorene opened her mouth to speak, but Lawton threw her a glance, shook his head then nodded to the appraiser.

"Now, we're just doing our job, here", the older appraiser continued, in what Lorene thought was the most fake display of a sympathetic voice she'd ever heard. "We're not the ones to make the final decision on anything, and we can sympathize whole hardily with you people for not wantin' to give up your home and move, but like I said, we're just doing our job."

"Of course you are! You're just getting paid by the Government to do their dirty work!" Lorene wanted to say as she stood rigid, her teeth and fist's clinched as Lawton motioned for the three men to have a seat on the porch. Lawton stepped past Lorene, climbed up the two steps onto the porch and sat in one of the two rocking chairs near the middle of the long front porch, while the man doing the talking, followed suit and took a seat in the other chair beside him. The two younger of their unexpected visitors, moved toward the swing at the end of the porch. Lorene, reluctantly, climbed the steps and sat stiffly on the edge of the glider which set on the opposite end of the porch from where the two men sat on the swing.

Well, in Lorene's estimation, the older man doing the talking had missed his calling. She thought he should have been a car salesman. He came across with all this "mumbo-jumbo" as to how wonderful the project was going to be, what with protecting the environment, along with all of the flood control, and on and on he went, each moment and each word making Lorene more and more sick to her stomach. "And to think Lawton had the "gall" to tell me to shut up, then invite these three men, who are settin' a price on our place, forcing us to let the Government take what we've worked nearly thirty years to have, to have a seat on our front porch and engage in this b—s—t conversation." Well, Lorene, at this point, had had all of the situation she could take! She jumped from the glider, darted in the front door and slammed it behind her! Hot tears burned her eyes as she stomped through the living room and into the kitchen. As she stood at the back door, fighting back the urge to either sob or get the shotgun, she could hear the monotones of the TVA men mixed with Lawton's voice, but she couldn't distinguish what any of them were saying, and furthermore, she didn't want to. That was her reason for making her exit from the front porch in the first place.

She was still standing motionless, her arms folded across her breast, at the back door staring, with unseeing eyes, through the screen, when she heard Lawton coming into the living room. She then, heard the slamming of car doors and the roar of the motor as the men made their departure

"I don't want you to open your mouth to me Lawton Higgins!" She began as Lawton came into the kitchen. "I don't want to hear you try to tell me one thing about them three men and their business!" She continued as she wheeled to face him, her voice low, through clenched teeth. "You're just as low as they are, telling me to hush up! Maybe you don't care to give up our home and maybe you don't care if every home and community between the rivers is done away with, but I do! And I'll tell you another thing or two, I am not a coward! I can't believe you'd sit there and give them two s—of b——s the time of day! They're just stealing our home! That is exactly what it boils down to, and I'll tell you somethin' else, I'll fight it to the finish to stay right here where I belong, come hell or high water, whether you are in it with me or not!"

With that she turned on her heel, stormed out the back door, slammed it behind her while tears streamed down her cheeks. Lawton, feeling tired and helpless, just sighed, shook his head and followed her. He knew, at this point, there was no way trying to comfort her. Her hurt was too deep, at this particular moment, for anyone to give her comfort. He simply and quietly picked up the small sack of seed corn and bucket of fertilizer that he had placed, earlier, at the garden's edge and moved the short distance from where she bent over the tomato plants, to start planting the five rows of late corn.

Well, the days that followed that spring of 1965 were stressful, not only for Lorene and Lawton, but for the residents of the Golden Pond community as a whole. There was an array of mixed emotions among all of the people of the community. The appraisers from TVA had pretty much canvassed the whole community the same week they paid their visit to Lorene and Lawton. The appraisers were not allowed to inform the residents as to what their property was valued. That was the job of the "adjusters," whom would make their rounds as soon as the appraisers had finished their job and turned in their report. Very few home and business owners felt the "fair market value" would be what they deserved for their property, for most of them felt as strongly as Lorene about having to give up the homes and businesses they had worked a life time to acquire. The issue at hand was not about money; it was the principal of the matter. The total overthrowing of the basis on which America was founded as stated in the Constitution. All men created equal, with the freedom to pursue his dreams; the "free enterprise system," as it was later translated. "What's happened to a person's rights and freedom? Shouldn't a body have the right to a say in whether he wanted to sell or keep his home?" Those were the questions that haunted Lorene's mind throughout the days that followed

The residents of Golden Pond, as well as others of the various communities between the rivers, strongly voiced their feelings at organized meetings. Many conferred with lawyers who could offer little encouragement in their favor. They even circulated partitions which resulted in acquiring dozens of signatures opposing the issue, proving the number of those opposing the TVA project greatly out numbered those who had consented to sell. Many letters of protest were written and mailed to their Congressman, State Representative and State Senator, but to no avail. By early June, that same spring, each property owner was paid a visit by inspectors, whose job was to validate the reports turned in by the appraisers. A short time later, they were visited by, what Lorene called "enforcers," for the latter group quoted them the price they would be paid for their properties. There was no discussion, no recourse. They were told flat out, they were expected to be moved out by the following fall. Lorene's sanctuary, her dream home of nearly thirty years, was appraised at the "fair market value" of $18,500.00.

The days and weeks that followed were some of the most trying times of Lorene's life. She had, not only cried a river, but she had totally lost her appetite. Lawton and Doris were, actually, becoming very concerned about her. They had tried to reason with her as to how little power the people between the rivers had against the Government's Tennessee Valley Authority project. This had only made Lorene's attitude more hostile.

She could reason the fact that this house she loved so much, in essence, was a wooden structure. She could reason the fact that another one somewhere else would give her a roof over her head with similar comforts and conveniences, but another house, somewhere else, would never be the same as this house they purchased in 1937 here in Golden Pond. This was her first and only home. This, her home, had been her shelter from the storms of life, her recluse. It just simply, was not fair for the Government or anyone else to force her out of this home of her dreams. Where would they go? She had been so distraught for the last couple of weeks, she hadn't even thought about where they would go, or what kind of a place they would need to look for, or anything about moving somewhere else. She just could not imagine living anywhere other than here, in Golden Pond.

Lorene went about the chores in the house, yard and garden as though she were in a daze, much of the time, during those next few weeks. Her seamstress work was piling up because she just could not seem to concentrate on anything she simply didn't have to. Lawton, whom, for the most part had just tried to stay out of her way, however, as time went on he rationalized the fact, they must start deciding what they were going to do. So, he made an attempt to get her to sit down and have a conversation about finding a place to move, but she refused to talk about it....She stormed out at him for admitting defeat. So, he retreated, once more and began discussing the situation with Doris and Kelsie whom, were now living in Cadiz. Their suggestions to Lawton seemed to make sense. They thought Lorene would, likely, be more satisfied with another house if it was one she and Lawton had someone to build, rather than trying to buy one. They also suggested, they might consider having one built in Cadiz. Lawton, however, knew he would have to wait until Lorene was in the right frame of mind before he could approach her with Kelsie and Doris' suggestions.

Well, defeat finally began winnin' it's battle with Lorene's strong will. She was, slowly, entering the grieving process as the spring days wore on into summer. Her emotions, were on a roller coaster. She was experiencing times of anger, then sadness, then denial and from there to despondency. She was on this emotional roller coaster some three weeks before she came to the place where she could have a civil conversation with Lawton. The conversation came about one Saturday morning at the breakfast table.

"Lawton, what are we goin' to do?" Lorene finally asked as she sighed and pushed away from the table.

"Well, I've been tryin' to get you to talk about it for nearly three weeks now," he answered, laying his fork on his plate." Now, here's what we're up against. We've got about three months to find somewhere to live. Now, there's some right nice-sized lots on Main street in Cadiz, with several new houses already goin' up and I've inquired into the price of the lots and their fairly reasonable. I've even got the name of the fellow who owns them. Kelsie knows a contractor that does a good job building a house, so…"

Lorene turned her head, looked out the back door, then sighed and said without lookin' at Lawton, "Just go ahead and do whatever has to be done. It don't matter to me."

"Now, Lorene," Lawton began with urgency in his voice, "Look at it this way, you can have a house built like you want it. Why, you've complained about the stairs ever since we've been here, an' the leaves, you know how you hate to fight that leaf raking every fall and spring. We'll get a lot without trees and big enough for a garden. Why, we'll just make a whole new life. We'll be just be startin' all over, ever' thing brand new. A whole new lifestyle." He then noticed tears in Lorene's eyes, "Lorene, it ain't like somebody's died."

"Lawton, just hush up!" she interrupted, in a somber yet matter of fact tone of voice, blinking back the tears, "I've told you to do what you have to. You don't have to try and sell me on another place. There will never be another place like this one, but I know when I'm defeated. And, I know too, that nobody has died. Now, what else I do know is this, I know we have to do somethin', so, I'm just tellin' you, go on an' do what has to be done. Ain't that enough said?"

Lawton took a deep breath and opened his mouth as though he was going to pursue the conversation, but he didn't, for Lorene, who had rose from the table, was making her way toward the back door. Besides, he guessed she had said enough.

Two days later Lorene gave in to go with Lawton to look at the lots. Well, after about an hour of looking at the track of land that had been divided into nice sized lots, varying some in size, they decided on one of the larger lots still available. They, also, agreed to meet Mr. Moore, the owner of the property, at his lawyer's office there in Cadiz the following Monday to draw up the papers. When Monday rolled around and Lorene and Lawton found themselves going over the details of the contract there in the lawyers office, Lawton was in for the shock of his life when the lawyer read the next to the last paragraph of the contract. It read, "In agreement, upon the request of said property owner to the containing parties here to fore mentioned, this contract is valid only if purchasing parties adhere to the stipulation that no forms of the making or dispensing of illicit or legal alcoholic beverages be practiced on the properties this day transferred."

Lorene saw Lawton's eyes widen and his mouth open to speak when the lawyer finished reading the contract. She held her breath, not knowing what Lawton was going to say. Finally, when the lawyer looked around those seated in his office, Lawton meekly asked, "Will you read that part again about the alcoholic beverages?" The lawyer did as he was asked. Lawton made no comment, but Lorene saw the muscle in his jaw tighten and she knew it was time for them to get the papers signed and for her to get him out of there, fast.

Well, needless to say, the signing of the deed for the property was a turning point in Lawton's personality and attitude. He, simply, could not handle giving up his liquor business. All of the way back to Golden Pond that afternoon after signing the deed, he raved. He cursed the Government. He cursed TVA. And last but not least, he cursed and accused Lorene of telling Mr. Moore to have the clause put into the deed. Well, Lorene did not have a thing to do with the clause getting put in the deed, however, she was glad it was done. Lawton had said they would make a new start. Have a whole new lifestyle and she guessed it was meant for him as well as her. Now, it was his turn now to be adamant about leaving Golden Pond, but for a different reason and, a trifle too late.

Lorene was still going about her chores methodically as July rolled in. There were so many things churning in her head and so many different feelings in her heart that she didn't know, much of the time, what she was feeling or thinking. Lawton had simply pulled himself into his own cocoon, moping and grumbling about his liquor business fate, which left Lorene totally, in charge of completing the chore of getting a house built. Coping with buying another piece of property, hiring a contractor and figuring out a set of blue prints, had only added to Lorene's already, sleepless nights. Sometimes she would get out of bed, leaving Lawton snoring away and go quietly, from the bedroom, through the kitchen and out onto the back steps in hopes of the night air clearing her head.

The many times her thoughts would drift to by-gone days as she sat there under a full moon in the sultry, summer nights. She thought of her daddy a lot. She even envisioned the different expressions on his face and the gentleness of his hand as he would pat her on the head or give her a hug when she was obedient to him. She could, some-times, hear his laughter and the sound of his voice when he would be distraught over something she or one of the other youngens did of which he did not approve. "If Daddy were only alive now…" He'd know how to comfort her. He'd know what to say to make some of the hurt go away. Then her thoughts the losses she had experienced down through the years. She thought of Jewell. Jewell, being the next of her siblings, was her first playmate whom she lost to influenza when she was only five. Lorene could see her running through the tall grass in the meadow, her long, light, brown hair blowing in the wind as she was laughed and called back to Lorene, "Run, Renie! Come, catch me!" Then, she'd think of baby Clyde, whom they lost to meningitis when he was only a year old, and she'd relive the terrible guilt she carried for many months after he died, thinking because she dropped him, it had been the cause of his death It was during those very young years of Lorene's life that Aunt Rhodie fell sick with cancer. Dr. Rollins paid many visits to the house. He gave Aunt Rhodie many different kinds of medicine and on one occasion he prepared a poultice of several different kinds of herbs and placed it on her breast in order to deteriorate her breast, hoping to destroy the deadly tumor. Months of Dr. Rollins visits of administering medication and applying the poultices did little good, for the tumor kept raging, uncontrolled, until her whole body racked with pain which even the heavy doses of morphine could not ease. At dusk, one spring evening, Aunt Rhodie slipped into eternity, leaving behind a life that had been a blessing to many people, especially Ed, Duck and the youngens. She had also received, from life, many blessings with the exception of the last two years, at which time the dreaded disease, cancer had imposed upon her such agony, she was eagerly anticipating the time when her call to leave this world would come. Lorene remembered, very vividly, how much she missed Aunt Rhodie after they laid her to rest in the little cemetery in the Fenton Com-munity.

Yes, it seemed this was a time when Lorene was so sad she could only count the many losses that had been hers down through the years. At the present time there was no light at the end of the tunnel, no portion of a silver lining shining behind the many clouds that hung above her. Defeat was a bitter pill to swallow, especially for someone with the strong will of Lorene Higgins, the will that had always kept her going.

By the end of July, the framework was beginning to go up on, what would be Lorene's new home, on the outskirts of Cadiz. It was a time when most women would have been totally elated, but, not Lorene. She and the contractor had several fiery words the first week they were putting up the frame work, for he wasn't going by the changes in the floorplan they had agreed on in the beginning. When his workers began putting up the two by fours for the walls, they were not leaving the hall and door ways wide enough. The doctor had told Lawton and Lorene that Lawton would likely be confined to a wheel-chair in the near future and she had discussed the matter with the contractor on the on set of his hiring, but he obviously hadn't discussed it with his workers. Well, of course, it was costing him time and money to tear down and reinstall the two by fours, but Lorene couldn't have cared less. This project was not of her doing to start with. Her nerves were on edge. Her temperament in the pits because Lawton had buried his head in the sand, leaving everything up to her to get done, and furthermore, her heart was far from being in the whole situation.

She was having to make the trip to Cadiz every day for one reason or the other. Most of those trips were by ferry, for the Corps of Engineers and TVA were building the new dam on the Tennessee River and the old bridge had been destroyed. There were shingles for the roof to decide on, along with whether to choose rock, brick or siding for the house, neither of which she knew anything about and none of these decisions would Lawton even discuss with her. The tables had totally turned. He was, now, the one grieving and despondent. She even threw the remark up to him he had previously made to her, that nobody had died. His response was only a grumble or a slur about the clause in the deed.

Well, during the days that followed, between trips to and from Cadiz, she managed to find a little time to began packing some of the smaller items. She packed several tears in the boxes along with them. Everyone in the family tried to get her excited over the new house. Doris, Kelsie and even Tracy and Mike, all went about in an "up-beat" mood when they were around her, hoping she would come out of the terrible depression she was in. She knew she was a burden to them, the way she moped around, but, to save her life, she couldn't help it. "Maybe, in time I'll come to like the new place, but I know I'll never love it. The only place I'll ever love and call my real home is right here in Golden Pond."

Meanwhile, Lawton began to get out of the house some and to Lorene's surprise, he pulled in the driveway late one hot afternoon with a pickup following behind. He and a younger man from an adjoining community, who Lorene had seen do business with Lawton in the past, came across the yard. Lorene thought nothing of the man's visit, at first. She figured he was there to make a purchase, however, when Lawton began showing him around the grounds, she became curious and walked out on the back porch to watch as they went toward the barn. Well, after several minutes, when they did not return to the kitchen, Lorene went inside to finish warming supper. It was near dark when the man left and Lawton came into the house. Lorene, then, questioned Lawton as to what the tour of the place was all about. He simply told her he was planning to rent the place to the young man, if his wife liked the house. After all, the TVA people had told them the house would not be destroyed immediately. The young man was to bring his wife back to look the house over the following Saturday. Well, Lorene thought it was a pretty good idea, renting the place. It would bring in some extra money, but it would also be one the hardest things ever, to see someone else living here in her house.

Now, Lorene should have noticed Lawton was in unusually high spirits after the young couple confirmed they wanted to rent the place, but, evidently, she was so busy she hadn't had the time, until one Saturday afternoon a couple of weeks later. Lorene inadvertently caught wind of what Lawton was up to. The situation occurred when two of his regular customers had stopped by and tarried awhile on the front porch. Lorene was in the front bedroom, cleaning the closet and packing some items, when through the open window, she could hear the men's conversation. Lawton, as usual, had his audience captivated, with past moonshinin' tales. Lorene, being busy about her chore, wasn't paying much attention to the men's conversation, other than hearing Lawton as he began "speeling" off the history of cars he had owned down through the years, "Now, I had this '51 Chevy coupe I traded off in 1953 for another brand new Chevy. It was another coupe, good car, one of the best I guess I ever had, an' I kept er' till 1956. Guess that coupe was among the longest I ever kept any car I've ever had. Well, I traded er' off in 1958 for another one, only this one had air suspension. That car rode like a dream, 'specially when I had er' loaded up. She was a runner, too! She'd hold to the road, man; smooth ridin' automobile. Now I kept that one till '60. I'd put well over a hundred and thirty miles on that ol' gal and I'd wore out four sets of tires, but she still run good when I traded er' off. That's when I got the '60, and I remember, me an Kelsie came out of Gracy with that Chevy coupe loaded as full as she'd hold, with cases of beer. Boys, we had er' level! Man, when I patted that accelerator, she rolled on out just like she's empty an didn't miss a lick with us doin' eighty n' eighty five all the way back here. She's a good runnin' car, till I tore the transmission out of er' one night when I backed off in a ditch between here and Cadiz, an' she never did run the same, so, I got rid of er' and got a '61. That's the one I had before this '64 I've got now. I dunno' bout these newer cars; seem's they don't make em' like the older ones. You don't have em' no time till their rattlin' and clangin' and usin' oil."

One of the two men laughed and remarked, "Well Lawton, You drove em' all to death. How fast would you say you averaged driving one of em' cars going from here and back to Gracy or Hopkinsville?"

Lorene heard Lawton chuckle and reply, "Hell, Clyde, you don't want to know, just be glad you wasn't in there with me. Reckon I've seen that speedometer needle go out of sight a time or two."

"I'll bet it's been more than a time or two, don't you Al?" Clyde said laughing as he nodded his head at the third man sitting on the porch.

"Yep, I've heard you could, flat out, burn them roads up between here an' Hopkinsville and Gracy," Al said, laughing along with Clyde. Lawton laughed with them, then his tone grew rather somber. "Yeah, boys, them was the good ol' days. Can't keep up that pace no more, tho. Times have changed a whole lot. My health's give out on me. The law's got harder to outsmart. Lotta changes have come about in the last several years. Lot different now from them days."

"Just how much longer do you plan to stay in the "business?" Lorene heard Clyde ask.

"Aw, I donno. Probably do a little, long as I have people wantin' to do business with me," Lawton answered. "I won't be able t' do any myself when we get in Cadiz. Seems them high faloutin' city people there on Main street don't cater t' havin' a bootlegger in their neighborhood an' Lorene, well, she's bout got a lot of high faloutin' ideas about it too, so guess you boys will just have to patronize th' boy that'll be rentin' here when we move. He's gonna carry on for me. Everybody knows where th' place is an he's a likable feller. He'll do right by you."

Well, Lorene didn't hear the rest of Lawton and his old "cronies" conversation for that's when Lorene could feel the flush began to come to her face and that fire began to spark in her eyes! She started stomping across the bedroom and was almost half way through the living room on her way to the front porch to give Lawton a piece of her mind, but she stopped, short. If this was what it would take to wean Lawton away from the illegal livelihood he had practiced all of his life; if letting someone else bootleg for him for the remainder of time the house stood kept Lawton's disposition bearable for her to be around, then, so be it. Lorene couldn't say she liked it, but, had Lawton's mental state, since the signing of the papers for the lot in Cadiz, had continued much longer, she knew he would become completely bedfast within the near future. Lorene then, turned, went back into the bedroom to finish her chore.

Chapter Eighteen:

Lorene's Greatest Loss

S hades of night were falling fast as Lorene sped along Highway 68 in route to Golden Pond. She had spent the entire afternoon at the house they were having built in Cadiz, trying to decide on floor covering and kitchen cabinets. She had incurred her third "run-in" with the contractor that afternoon, because, again, he had not told his workers of some of the changes he and Lorene had discussed when the plans were gone over in the beginning. Needless to say, by the time she started home, she was running on her last nerve. "He's the "hard-headest" man, next to Lawton Higgins, I've ever tried to talk to in my entire life. It's his own doin's that's costing him time and money, not mine," Lorene mumbled to herself as she proceeded home.

"Where in the "Sam-hill" have you been?" was the first question Lawton popped to her when she walked in the front door. He was sitting before the television in his old easy chair with his feet propped on the ottoman.

"Well, now just where in the "Sam-hill" do you think I've been?" she answered, with icicles hanging on each word. Then, before he could speak again, she added, "I've been doing what you should be doing instead of sitting down in that creek bed playing poker!"

"I've not been playin' poker today, I'll have you know, I've been drummin' up some new business for when our renters move in," he answered, defensively.

"Well whooped-de-do, what else is new?" Lorene threw back at him as she stomped through the living room toward the kitchen. "I've had about as much of this house building and that contrary, smart-elic contractor as I can stand. Every piece of floor covering I picked out he didn't know if he could get that particular kind or not. Well, why in the devil did he have me look at five hundred different kinds, anyway. Why didn't he just say, here's what you have to choose from and let that be it? I'm sick to death with building this house that I don't even want to start with!"

"Now, Lorene, you know I'd be no help in picking out what's to go on the floor or what color of paint to go on the walls or what kind of cabinets you want," Lawton started.

"Oh, just hush up, Lawton. Just hush up. I don't want to hear it. I've had, practically all of it to see to, up to now, and you know the rest will be up to me, too. I just don't want to hear any more of your excuses," Lorene said wearily, as she walked on to the kitchen to start supper.

The days of summer flew by. Mid September's warm days and cool nights were splashing blotches of red and gold here and there among the green leaves on the elms and maples scattered along the countryside; some, of which, were already falling to the parched vegetation beneath. Farmers were, once again, beginning the harvest, but the lack of enthusiasm was evident. This would be the last harvest for many of the farmers between the rivers. Neighbors, who had depended upon one another during harvest time for many years, either by swapping labor or the lending of equipment, or both, would be scattered following this harvest. The leisure conversation which often came about at the end of an autumn day, before neighboring farmers parted to do up the night work, sometimes, at the edge of a freshly harvested corn field or beneath a loft of sweet smelling hay, would be missing after this harvest. Many veteran moonshiners, along with beginners, had made their last batch this year. Those, whom the revenures had not put out of business, were now being put out of business by another branch of the government. No longer would favorite recipes, flower slips and seeds, or dress patterns, be exchanged among the women folk. The distance, brought about by TVA was, quickly bringing an end to all of these cherished, old traditions that had been practiced and assured the survival, for generations of this, now scattering, self sufficient breed of people "between the rivers."

Lorene rose early that Monday morning two weeks later and went to the garden to gather the last of the black-eyed peas, as soon as breakfast was over. Lawton left for Hopkinsville, "on business," he said.

Dew clung to the pea vines as Lorene, quickly, proceeded down the rows. The air was crisp and hinted of frost. Lorene rose from her bent position when she reached the end of the third row, stretched her aching back and rubbed her wet hands against the skirt of her dress. She paused, still longer, to let her gaze drink in the beauty of the familiar surroundings that had brought her comfort for so many years. A portion James W. Riley's poem, which she learned during her school years, came to her mind, "There's something kind o' harty-like about the atmosphere when the heat of summer's over an' the cooling fall is here. Oh yes, we'll miss the flowers an' the blossoms on the trees an' the mumble of the humming birds an' buzzing of the bees, but the air's so appetizing in the landscape thro' the haze on the crisp and sunny mornings of the airy, autumn days. Tis a picture that no painter has the colorin' to mock. When the frost is on the punkin' an the fodder's in th' shock." A dark mask of sadness was plainly visible on Lorene's face as she, once again, bent over the dew covered pea vines to finish her chore.

The last week in October brought about the completion of Lorene and Lawton's house in Cadiz. The packing was finished, with boxes varying in size, stacked throughout the house, some of which she had already taken to the new house in Cadiz. Lorene was totally exhausted and Lawton claimed the same, however, she doubted that, for he had done nothing any different than his usual routine, except, make trips to Hopkinsville and Gracy with their future renter, who was planning to move into the house, immediately upon it's vacancy. The two of them were refurbishing the cold drink box in the smoke house, along with the two refrigerators on the back porch, which would be the extent of the items Lorene and Lawton planned to leave behind.

That cloudy, Halloween morning in 1965 was a blur for Lorene. The neighbors with their pickup trucks along with Kelsie arrived around eight o'clock to transport Lorene and Lawton's plunder to their new home. She was in a daze as she watched the men carry piece by piece, of their plunder from the house she loved so dearly. She was still in a daze as she tried to inform the Kelsie and the others where to place the furniture and remaining boxes which they brought into the new house. She was too sad and drained to give much thought as to where they put it. She just wanted them to get the ordeal over with. Her heart was simply not in it.

Lorene stood in the sparkling new kitchen amid the boxes of dishes and cookware, but there was no sparkle about Lorene. She sighed as she stared out the small windows over the sink. A drizzling rain had set in and night was falling. How strange the sounds and smell of the new place. So different. There were no stately oaks, nor golden maples in the yard. No grass, just the brown ground, slightly, sloping the short distance from the front entrance to Main street, which and been leveled, tilled and sewn, hopefully producing life come spring.

The weeks that followed brought more exhausting days for Lorene. Although, Doris helped with the unpacking and arranging of the furniture, Lorene was worn to a "frazzle" every night. Lawton had not missed a day returning to Golden Pond. She knew the weaning away from Golden Pond and his bootlegging business would be as much of a transformation for him as when they moved from Ma Annie's house in the Oak Ridge community almost thirty years ago. He had left behind his still, which was worked by others on the shares, in Ma Annie's woods. And now, the legal liquor that Lawton had sold, illegally, as their livelihood for nearly thirty years, was left behind in the smoke house and on the back porch at, what had been, Lorene's dream home in Golden Pond.

Time, as it always does, went on, waiting for no one, and every new day, for Lorene, began with the pain of home- sickness and the anger toward the government of her country. True to fact, she had a lovely new home. Large, spacious and airy rooms. The neighbors and the town of Cadiz, as a whole, were friendly and charitable. And, true to fact, her hurt had dulled,

Those were the days ... Lawton and Lorene in Golden Pond.

somewhat. The first spring they lived in their new home, Lawton and Lorene put out a small garden. The soil in their garden spot, however, was poor from the lack of previous years of fertilization, and did not produce, that first year, nothing to compare to the quantity or quality of vegetables as did the garden at Golden Pond. The garden, did however, add to making the new place a little more homey, along with giving Lorene something to occupy her mind. Doris, Kelsie and the boys were in and out, almost daily, which helped the place seem more like home, also. Occasionally, old friends, some of whom had also, moved from between the rivers, along with some who were awaiting their orders to move, came by for a visit. Those visits, however, were sometimes painful for it seemed the line of conversation would always get around to the mutual hurt each one was presently experiencing. Virgil, Shirley, the two boys, along with baby Lori, whom had been born the previous spring on Lorene's birthday, all visited during the Christmas holidays that first year Lawton and Lorene were in Cadiz. Lawton, whose health was steadily declining as time went by, was still making his daily trips back to Golden Pond. Word was, that the house in Golden Pond would likely, be torn down within that next year or so. It pained Lorene so much to pay a visit to the old house that her visits were few. She threw herself into her seamstress work, taking on more and more new customers from the town of Cadiz. She had also, taken up crocheting and knitting. It seemed, anything she could do to keep her hands busy helped to ease the pain in her heart and mind.

Lorene and Lawton had been living in Cadiz for nearly two years when they decided to buy a small business that went on the market in the fall. It was, The Handy Andy Laundry. Lawton had been at a loss as to knowing what to do with his time and was driving Lorene nuts, so she was hopeful the Handy Andy Laundry would occupy Lawton's, otherwise, useless days. Well, this new business venture soon proved to be more than a mere outlet for Lawton. Within a short time, the Handy Andy Laundry had evolved into a full time job for both of them.

One Saturday morning, a few month's after she and Lawton, on their way to Paducah one Saturday, drove through, what was left of Golden Pond and witnessed yet, another devastating occurrence in Lorene's lifetime. Their timing could not have been more perfectly, or maybe better described as imperfectly arranged, for just as they were driving down Highway 68 and approaching the old home place, they witnessed TVA's bulldozers pushing Lorene's beloved house to the ground. Their renters had been ordered to move a few months prior and Lawton had been told by TVA's construction crew foreman that they would soon be demolishing the house and outbuildings, however, the foreman had not given a specified date. How ironic that the day and time Lawton and Lorene had chosen to make the trip to Paducah would be the day and time TVA would turn the house they had lived in and loved for nearly thirty years, into rubble. Needless to say, a renewed gloom hovered over Lorene for a time to come.

The years of the Sixties rolled into the Seventies and Lawton progressively grew more feeble. He had, by this time, gotten out of the "bootleggin'" business. He was, once again, having much difficulty getting around. He was now using a cane most of the time. His doctor had told him, when he went for his last visit, he would likely be dependent upon a walker within the near future.

Well, same as any other legal venture that had occurred during their married life, Lorene had, on her shoulders, most of the responsibility of operating the Laundry. She was having a lot of trouble with her hip injury and five years of working on the concrete floor only complicated matters, so by the mid Seventies they gave up the Laundry.

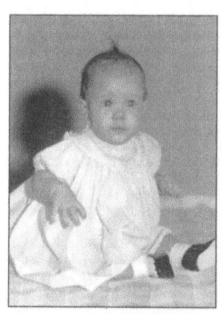

Virgil and Shirley's daughter Lori, 1965.

Everything was changing with time. Lorene and Lawton's grandchildren were fast growing up by the mid Seventies. Tracy was interested in his school work, while Mike was already getting the girls on his mind. Timothy, Matthew and Lori were busy getting their schooling in Michigan, while Virgil kept putting his work days in at the Ford Motor Co. factory. Shirley had worked at various jobs for short periods of time, but, having her hands full with the children, she devoted most of her time to being a housewife and mother. Kelsie was still working, part time at the Goodwin Funeral home in Cadiz, but he and Doris were considering taking on the job of running the new IGA Foodliner and an ice business adjacent to the IGA building that was owned by the Sanders family, also in Cadiz. Lorene,

50th Anniversary photo taken in Cadiz, Kentucky, 1978.

once again, had returned to her seamstress work since she and Lawton had gotten out of the laundry business.

Lorene and Lawton began having a lot of trouble keeping up the grounds and house on Main Street. The lawn mowing chore had fallen to Lorene some three years prior and with the on going problem with her hip, by the late Seventies, she had to discontinue mowing the large lawn. When the spring of 1978 rolled around and Lorene saw the many other things that needed to be done in addition to the lawn that would soon require starting up the mower again, she expressed her frustration to Doris and Kelsie, concerning she and Lawton's inability to maintain the place. She had also mentioned how she would like to have a smaller, new house, with a smaller lawn, built in a near by sub-division. Doris and Kelsie, whom had always loved the big roomy house Lawton and Lorene had built on Main Street, made them an offer to purchase the big house if they could sell theirs. Well, in less than two month's Doris and Kelsie had a buyer. Lawton and Lorene, along with Doris and Kelsie went the following week to look at a small brick house that had just been completed on Warton Road. in the new sub-division. Lorene liked the house with it's small yard, immediately, so the four of them went to the lawyer's office and transferred the deed to the big house on Main Street to Doris and Kelsie, then, a few days later Lawton and Lorene purchased the house on Warton Road and set the last of October as the time they would move in.

A tragedy occurred the day before Lawton and Lorene were to celebrate their Fiftieth wedding anniversary in '78, which marked the turning point for the remainder of their lives. Lawton, whom had been having trouble urinating from time to time for several months previously, awoke that morning in such intense pain that Lorene, immediately called Doris. When Doris arrived, only moments later, and saw the condition Lawton was in, she told them she thought he had no alternative but to go to the emergency room at the local hospital. He stayed in the local hospital and received treatment to ease the pain, then he was transferred to Ginnie Stewart Hospital in Hopkinsville.

Shortly after their arrival at the hospital in Hopkinsville, Lawton was taken in the operating room for surgery. When the surgeon had finished the surgery, he came to the waiting room and explained the extent of Lawton's condition to Lorene and Doris. He told them the muscles in Lawton's body were in a progressive state of deterioration due to a muscle disease similar to muscular dystrophy. Not only were the visible muscles in his body deteriorated, but those inside his body were equally as weak. The doctor farther explained, even though he had performed the surgery that removed a huge tumor from his prostate, which would relieve his condition to some degree, he would continue having trouble with his kidney's acting, and if the condition continued progressing at the rate it now was, he would also have trouble with getting his bowels to move. And, of course, the muscles in his arms, back and legs were deteriorating equally as fast.

Well, Lorene brought Lawton home from the hospital a week later. He was very weak from the surgery and his week-long stay in bed. As the weeks went on, it seemed Lawton just could not manage to gain back the strength he had before the surgery. Kelsie brought him a walker which seemed to help some, however, Lorene still had to help him walk from the bed to the bathroom, the table for meals and to his chair in the living room. She was hardly out of his sight the remainder of the summer, at which time she was, once again, trying to do some packing, all the while, wondering if Lawton would be recovered enough for them to move into their new house. Finally, when the weather began to cool down he seemed to show some signs of improvement.

Well, once again, on Halloween day they moved. Lorene left behind some pieces of furniture for Doris that she did not have room for in the smaller house. Although, Lorene was several years older and the packing as well as the unpacking was all on her to do, with the exception of the short periods of time when Doris could help, the move to Warton Rd. was much easier on Lorene than the move to Main Street. Yes, physically, she was exhausted, but mentally, she was in much better condition than she had been on Halloween day fourteen years before.

Lorene liked their new house fine. It was much easier to keep, as was the lawn. Their house, with the exception of the people owning the property in the sub- division, was the only one there. Word was, that the lots were selling fast and more new homes were expected to start springing up in the near future.

Lawton's condition was slowly getting worse. Within three years after they had moved to Warton Road, Lawton did not have the strength in his arms and legs to lift himself, with his walker, from his chair, nor hold himself up enough to walk without help. One morning, in the early spring of 1982 Lorene had gotten Lawton settled in his chair before the television and gave him specific instructions to stay put until she returned from her beauty shop appointment and the weekly trip to the grocery store. She, went the short distance to the beauty shop, which was operated by her sister-in-law Dot and before she left for the grocery, Lorene phoned home to check on Lawton. He was fine, so she left the beauty shop and stepped next door to an outlet store, intending to go to the grocery shortly. When she entered the outlet store, the lady in charge was on the phone. Lorene was soon to learn she was talking to Doris. She was also soon to learn that one of Lorene's customers, whom she sewed for had brought a dress for Lorene to alter and found Lawton on the floor and immediately called Doris. Doris rushed the short distance from her house to the outlet store and she and Lorene rushed home. Lorene knew immediately when she saw Lawton whom, was in extreme pain, either his leg or ankle was broken. Doris, quickly called the ambulance and he was taken to the Trigg County hospital, where he was examined and it was confirmed his right ankle was broken. He was, then, transferred to Ginny Stewart Hospital in Hopkinsville. Several times, previous to Lawton's fall, Lorene had caught him trying to get out of his chair by himself, at which times, he had almost fallen. It seemed he just couldn't accept the fact that he could not get out of his chair and on his feet with the help of his walker only. Lorene had explained, sternly to him, his muscles just were not strong enough to support his weight to rise from the chair. So, that particular morning she, once again, reminded him, sternly, to stay in his chair until she returned. But, he hadn't listened, nor obeyed. She could not help but feel, somewhat, responsible for his fall, especially, during his stay in the hospital as she watched, helplessly, while he agonized with the pain and dealing with the fact, he might never be able to walk, even with the help of his walker again.

The healing process was very slow for Lawton. Needless to say, neither was he a very good patient. He began wanting to go home as soon as some of the initial pain went away, and demanded Lorene talk to the doctor about his release. That was when she was to learn, Lawton's injury would never heal properly because of his muscle disorder, along with the condition of poor circulation in his lower extremities. The doctor, upon acknowledging Lorene's hip injury, explained to her that Lawton would be bedfast and suggested entering him in a nursing home. Lorene knew she could not put up an argument, for there was no way she was strong enough to lift and attend to him in the manner his condition required. When she related to Lawton what the doctor had told her, he was devastated at the thought of going into a nursing home. He became so up set that he blamed Lorene. He said he knew it was her doings, that she was now going to put him where she had wanted him to be for the last five years. On and on he raved and carried on, until he finally became resigned to the inevitable and he was transferred by ambulance from the Ginnie Stewart Hospital in Hopkinsville to the Shady Lawn Nursing home in Cadiz.

Lawton hated the nursing home, in general, but he complained most about the food, so Lorene started cooking his food and taking it to him every day. It seemed, Lawton began to adjust, somewhat, to his surroundings after some three months, however, Lorene began noticing some strangeness about his conversation, from time to time. She mentioned it to Doris and Kelsie, who also visited him often and they admitted they had noticed it too, but had hesitated to mention it, for fear of upsetting Lorene. By the end of the first year of his stay in the nursing home, Lawton had almost completely lost touch with reality. The muscle condition, inside and outside of his body, was gradually taking it's toll. It was an effort for him to even, raise his hand. It seemed, every medical effort administered bore no results of stabilizing his fast deteriorating muscles.

The seasons came and went for two years, all the while, Lawton hanging on with the same old will that had sustained him as he fought the battle with polio in his young years. Lorene went for her usual visit to the nursing home around mid morning on July fourth of '85, only to find Lawton in terrible pain and much weaker than her last visit only two days before. The head nurse entered Lawton's room soon after Lorene arrived and informed her that Lawton's bowels had been unable to move for several days. The nurse suggested he be admitted into the hospital, for without immediate treatment, the results would be devastating. Lorene called Doris, then asked the nurse to get in touch with their doctor. Lawton was admitted into hospital by early afternoon. An hour or so later, the doctor came to the waiting room and relayed to Lorene and Doris, the inevitable. It would be just a matter of time. He farther explained, there was nothing medically to be done, except keep him as comfortable as possible. Doris called Dora May in Michigan and asked her to get in touch with Virgil as soon as possible. The next day Lawton Higgins slipped from this life into eternity, leaving behind a legacy which displayed strength and personal courage, along with, the wit and will to grasp life and live it "his way".

During the days that followed, both before, during and after the funeral, Lorene could not grieve over loosing Lawton to death, for she had been loosing him gradually for the past several years. When Lawton got to the place where he could not walk,....could not be about his "business," as usual, that was the time she started loosing him. Then, almost three years prior when she had to place him in the nursing home, which was the time that was the hardest time of all, she watched Lawton Higgins, the crippled boy she came to know and love. The Lawton Higgins, to whom she gave her hand in marriage, whose children she bore and to whom she stood beside through out the good times and the bad, she watched him, because of his inability to be in control of his life any longer, slowly sink into such deep despair, both in body and mind, that his spirit had already left this earthly plain to take up residency, somewhere in that unknown realm. Lorene's tears were now just a continuation of those she had shed for months. They were not tears of grieving for Lawton drawing his last breath. No, she had prayed for God to take him, to end his suffering. Yes, Lorene's tears were just a continuation of those already shed for a time. Tears of loneliness.

Chapter Nineteen:

A Time of Adjustment

A cloud of gloom hovered about Lorene as she began her regular routine following Lawton's funeral. Virgil, Shirley and the children, who had arrived late in the afternoon the day of Lawton's death, stayed for a week. He and Doris, along with Lorene had gone through some of Lawton's personal things and divided the things each wanted. Virgil was unable to take many of the things home with him, since he and his family had flown. They were planning to drive down in the fall when Virgil got his two week vacation, so Lorene stored the remainder of the things Virgil wanted.

Once the house was empty, the gloom seem to hover even heavier. Lorene had been accustomed to making the trip to the nursing home almost every day to take Lawton food. She would now, have to find something else to fill her days. There was one advantage to Lawton having been in the nursing home for the past three years, it had made his death a little easier to bear, for she had gotten used to being alone in the house. Some few month's after Lawton went to the nursing home, Lorene knew he would never be home again. His being confined to the bed after having broken his ankle, had taken it's toll on him mentally, as well as physically. So, at the present time Lorene's major adjustment would be, trying to find something that would fill the time she had used preparing and delivering his food to the nursing home.

Well, Lorene did as she had done in the past, only for a different reason, she threw herself into her seamstress work. She took on more new customers every week, not only for an escape from her loneliness, but she needed the extra money. Many nights she would fall asleep from exhaustion after a long day at her sewing machine. Then, there were nights when she would lie in bed and gaze through the semi-sheer curtains at her window into the night and reflect on things of the past.

Life had been hard for Lorene in many ways since she married Lawton. He was used to having his way with Ma Annie and his sisters and without the example and strong hand of a father, Lawton had taught himself most of the things he knew and practiced concerning life and survival. Nothing ever stood in the way of Lawton doing what he wanted to. Not Lorene, nor his family, nor even the law, at least not for long. The one time he did ninety days in the Paducah jail taught him a lesson about getting caught at his moonshining trade. He paid his cousin Jake and Shaw, along with other younger men to work at the still. Since a person couldn't be arrested unless he was caught at the still site, working, several of the younger men, including Jake and Shaw, had taken the rap for him. Numerous times, Lawton had even spent money needed for the family to pay the law to stay out of his woods. Each year a new car, some times two and one year even three, were bought with money needed for the family. Lorene, for years at Golden Pond, had taken care of customers after Lawton began bootlegging legal alcohol, a job she detested. But, Lorene had to admit, she nor the children had ever gone hungry or been without a roof over their heads, nor gone without decent clothes. Lawton, despite his quick temper and his many days and nights away from home tending to his illegal means of livelihood, had always thought his kids "hung the moon." He always wanted them to have equal to other children, and his concern for Virgil's deafness was as deep as Lorene's. Sometimes it was difficult for Doris to accept the fact that her daddy had to screen her friends, closely, however, she was never without close friends, who were always from families with similar backgrounds as Doris,' and they were always welcome at the Higgins' home.

Lawton always wanted Lorene home when night came whether he was there or not. Her mind went back to the time Dora May called her from Michigan late one afternoon to tell her Virgil and Shirley were having a terrible time with Timothy, who, at that time, was three. Matthew was just a small baby and whether it was because of jealousy or because of the fact Timothy was trying to talk and since both his parents were deaf he was frustrated, wasn't determined, however, he had become so unruly he had kicked out the picture window and knocked a large hole in the wall plaster in the hall. Well, needless to say, Lorene knew she had to go to Michigan to see if she couldn't be of help in the matter. The next day she bought a plane ticket and had Lawton take her to Paducah to catch the two o'clock flight out to Michigan. Lawton thought it was a waste of time and declared he didn't know how he'd manage with her away a week. Lorene stood her ground, tho and went to help Virgil and Shirley with Timothy and baby Matthew. Her effort did prove productive, for she was able to give Timothy the extra attention he needed, giving Shirley more time to devote to caring for the new baby, Matthew. A short while after Lorene's return home, Virgil and Shirley were able to enroll Timothy in a nursery school, which became a marvelous help to the frustrated little boy. He soon learned to talk, which made a tremendous difference in his understanding and interacting with both, his parents and school mates. And, Lawton managed to live through the ordeal of Lorene being gone for a week.

Another instance, concerning how much Lawton depended on Lorene, came to mind as she continued reflecting on the past. Lawton loved to hunt, especially out of season. One year before squirrel season came in Lawton decided he and one of his regular customers would go down in the river bottoms and kill some squirrels before other hunters came in when season opened and killed most of them. Well, they did not want to take a vehicle to have to park somewhere for fear the game warden would get suspicious or have someone else drive them who might just might turn them in, So, Lorene was appointed to be their designated driver. Her instructions from Lawton were, to drive them near the vicinity in the woods where they were to hunt, she was to return home, having been given a specific time to return, but not by the same way as they came and drive throughout the river bottoms until she saw a limb lying across the road, which would be her signal as to where to wait for them to emerge from the woods. Needless to say, Lorene hated having to do these daredevil stunts for Lawton, but, he just had to do what he set his mind to do and his will, at times was stronger than hers.

Yes, true to fact, Lawton Higgins had his faults, along with his good traits, same as any other man. Lawton and Lorene had shared life for nearly fifty seven years and a great part of her was now gone, but she must continue as best as she could, till her maker called her to join Lawton in that vast expanse, known as eternity.

The old saying, "Time heals all wounds," proved to be, somewhat, true in Lorene's case of grief. Lorene, now, had more time to spend with her mother, Duck, who was now living in Cadiz. Duck had been having a lot of trouble with her eyes and the eye doctor had informed her, she might have to under go surgery for cataracts in the near future. Lorene knew she, living the closest to her mama, would be the one to do most of the taking care of her when that time came. Lorene also, turned her thoughts and attention to Tracy and Mike, to whom she had been close since they were born, because they had lived close by, unlike Virgil's children in Michigan. Tracy was now thirty one and Mike twenty seven, but they still seemed like little boys to her. They visited her often which always gave her a lift. Often times, after one of their visits, her thought would return to days of their childhood. Particular instances came to mind, such as the time Tracy's faithful old dog Lassie got killed. Tracy was in the first grade in the Elementary School at Golden Pond and rode the bus the few miles from where he, Kelsie, Doris and little brother Mike lived on the Cumberland River. One afternoon, early in the school year, while it was yet warm weather, Tracy got off the bus to find his faithful old dog Lassie, waiting at the designated spot where she always waited for him to emerge from the bus. He patted her head and scratched her ears and went bouncing down the hill, the short distance to the house. A short while later he came back outside to play with Lassie, but she was nowhere around the house. Then, he caught a glimpse of her up near the road. He called for her, but she did not come, obviously because she was chasing a rabbit or some other small creature through the weeds along the side of the road. Tracy took off up the hill just in time to witness a very devastating sight for a small boy. One of the many big trucks, loaded with logs that traveled the road in front of Tracy's house had hit Lassie. When Tracy made it to the top of the hill, there lay Lassie in a motionless heap on the road. Doris, who had started across the front yard, heard Tracy's anguished cries. She ran as fast as she could up the hill and what she saw through the tall grass was little Tracy sobbing as he tried to lift Lassie, who was as big as he, into his arms. Needless to say, Doris shared the same anguish as Tracy. She could tell at a glance that Lassie was dead. There was not a spot on the animal's body; obviously, the lick had been to the head. Doris helped Tracy drag the dead animal from the road and was frantically trying to get Tracy away from Lassie when Kelsie came up the hill. He looked Lassie over and confirmed the fact that Lassie was dead. Tracy cried and cried and only became pacified when his daddy told him they would dig a grave for Lassie and give him a proper funeral.

Lorene remembered Doris telling how much Tracy was missing Lassie, in the days that followed. Lassie had been his constant companion for all the years they had had him since he was a pup. He and Tracy had grown together, long before Tracy was of school age, Lassie followed right beside Tracy as he made trip after trip up and down the hill in his pedal car he got for Christmas one year.

Those nights as Lorene lay reminiscing, her thoughts often times turned to little Mike. She would chuckle as she remembered the time two of their neighbors helped Kelsie clean out the cistern. The two neighbors were lowering Kelsie down into the cistern with a rope as Mike and Doris watched. Well, little Mike became very frightened for his daddy and began screaming. No amount of explaining would quiet down Mike. Finally, the men had to pull Kelsie back out of the cistern and wait until Doris took Mike for a ride in the old blue pickup before they could lower Kelsie down into the cistern.

Those incident's, as well as a lot of others that took place when her own children and the grand children were little, seemed only like yesterday to Lorene. "How time has passed. How things have changed. What will the future bring?" Were usually the words Lorene spoke, quietly as sleep overcame her.

Well, time continued speeding by and life went on for Lorene. The part of her that went when Lawton died continued to be missing; nothing or no one could ever fill that spot. Lorene had resigned herself to that fact, so, she continued filling her days with mending and altering clothes for her customers, along with, quilting, making clothes, crocheting and knitting. Her hand work, along with friends and family dropping in, were the elements that kept her going during those days, weeks and month's of adjusting to the loss of her companion of fifty two years.

The Eighties gave way to the Nineties and Lorene's mother, Duck had undergone some serious health problems. Two years prior, Duck had gone into the hospital for a routine check up before under going cataract surgery, only to discover she had breast cancer. The doctor, at that time, removed a large tumor, which was malignant, but did not encourage chemotherapy or radiation, because of Duck's age. When she healed from the biopsy, she returned for cataract surgery. Duck was able to continue living by herself there in Cadiz, on Glenn Dale and she even kept mowing her own lawn. Lorene could see her mother's health steadily, going down hill after the first year of her surgery. Duck began to realize she shouldn't be driving her car for she had developed a cataract on the other eye, but refused to have it removed, so, she finally consented for her car to be sold and for Lorene to drive her to the grocery and the doctor.

One of her routine checkup's with the doctor who had done the breast biopsy, revealed she had cancer in the other breast. Surgery was not encouraged because of her age and her reluctance to have it done. Lorene and the others did not argue the issue.

Duck was nearing ninety one when she began to stumble quite often and on two occasions, she received hard falls. It was then, Lorene, Guy and Reba Nell convinced her she must have someone to stay with her. Things went quite well for several months, then Duck began getting weaker. The children confronted her with going to the Trigg County Manor, which was a facility that kept only the elderly who were able to be up and about. Duck knew she needed specialized help and since she knew several of the residents of the Manor, agreed to go. She had only been at the Manor for a few months when she contracted the flu, which ran into pneumonia and she had to hospitalized. When she had recovered enough to leave the hospital she could not return to the Manor because she was bedfast. Guy Crittenden, Lorene's younger brother and his wife Faye were living in Murray and they were able to get Duck into the West View Nursing Home there in Murray.

Five generations: (left to right) little Tracy, Doris, Lorene, Duck, and Grandma Birdsong.

She stayed in West View for almost two years, but she was not happy any of the time she was there, so Reba Nell, Lorene's younger sister, who lived in Calvert City and had worked at the Calvert City nursing home some years prior, was able to get her in the nursing home close to her. Duck's condition continued to decline and after a little over two years she died in the Calvert City Nursing Home at the age of Ninety four. Two days later, Duck was laid to rest beside Ed in the little Turner cemetery near Turkey creek. Lorene, again, experienced another loss. She could not grieve because each had laid down their earthly, painful bodies, but she grieved because of the loneliness of continuing her life without them.

Lorene and her remaining siblings went through Duck's personal belongings and plunder, distributing the contents among themselves and their children, then put the neat little house on Glenn Dale on the market. The cloud of gloom engulfed Lorene, once again. And once again, she threw herself into the one thing that seemed to bring her piece of mind, her seamstress work. Not only did keeping her hands busy, enable her to have courage, but the interaction with her customers, her friends gave her the encouragement she needed so badly during the trying time.

Lorene's old hip injury she incurred in the car wreck that hot July afternoon in 1948 as she and the children returned to Golden Pond from a visit to Ed's store, was beginning to cause increasing pain. Sometimes she could hardly raise from her chair when she finished with mending a garment, either at the sewing machine or her chair in the living room. It was also causing stiffness in her back and leg, hindering her from doing the heavy cleaning and yard work she had always been used to doing. This degree of disabling was very frustrating to Lorene. She had always loved a clean house and a neatly clipped lawn with flowers. Now, she had to hire someone to do her deep cleaning and mow her lawn. She was, now only able to set a few blooming plants in the brick planter beneath the picture window. She would think of the many beautiful plants, shrubs and bloomers she had in the yard at Golden Pond as she placed the few tiny plants in the planter there at the house on Warton Road. "How times and things have changed," she'd mumble as she would slowly straighten her back there in the warm, spring sunshine.

Well, all of the excitement hadn't gone from Lorene's life, completely, for one Sunday afternoon, the next spring, following her mama's death, Lorene retired to the living room after lunch, to do some, long over due mending. As she sat there with her mending on her lap and listening to the television, she noticed it was getting awfully dark outside. After awhile, she could hear the wind rising, sharply and she had to turn on additional light to be able to see her work. In a few more minutes, lightning flashed and thunder began to roll so closely it rattled the picture window behind her. Then, she began to feel the house jar as the fierce wind thrust against it. She laid her mending aside and looked out the front door. The street lights were on, revealing, trees, whose limbs that were bending to the ground as the sheets of rain pelted heavily against them. Cans, chairs and other small objects, not anchored, were flying through the air. Quickly, Lorene closed the front door and went to the window to continue viewing the terrible spring time storm. As she was watching, a terrible thud, then the sound of tearing metal was heard toward the end of house, which held the garage! She made her way to the kitchen as fast as her bad hip would let her go, and flung open the back door! To her amazement, the strong wind had, somehow caught the bottom of the garage door and had torn it from the runners on either side that allowed it to raise and lower. She feared from what she could tell from her view, standing in the kitchen door, that it was bent and twisted, beyond repair. "Oh, my Lord!" She said, aloud. "What next?"

Well, when the storm finally subsided, she along with the neighbors were all, outside viewing the damages, at which time her fears about her garage door being beyond repair, were confirmed. Her car, which was inches from the, misshapen door was unharmed. This, she had, to be thankful for. Later that afternoon, she was able to contact Doris, at which time, they got in their car and came right over. They had been in Hopkinsville during the time of the storm and were not aware of it's severity until they returned home. Nothing was damaged at their house. Only some buckets and lawn chairs were scattered over their yard.

Kelsie looked the situation over and suggested Lorene get in touch with her insurance agent. So, the next morning she got on the phone. The insurance company sent out an adjuster and the following morning, she contracted a local carpenter to order and install the garage door.

Now, some few weeks later another unexpected phenomena occurred, which, in a round about way, involved the previous instance brought on by the terrible storm. The carpenter who installed the new garage door left behind the large cardboard box in which the garage door was stored. He had leaned it against the outside wall at the end of the house and Lorene had been meaning to get Kelsie or one of the boys to haul it off, but it kept slipping her mind. So, one warm Sunday afternoon Lorene decided to drive over to Golden Pond to the old home site and maybe on to the cemetery. She opened the garage door to get out her car and, in so doing, she thought of the large cardboard box that had been taking up space at the end of the garage for several weeks, now. Well, she backed her car out of the garage, got out, opened the trunk and put the box inside. There was a large gully in a small thicket near the road just above the old home site where she and Lawton had thrown numerous, unwanted items in years past. In fact, the last time Lorene had visited the old home site, someone had pushed an old car off in the gully. So, Lorene thought she would just, "kill two birds with one stone" that sunny, autumn afternoon. She would visit her very favorite spot in the whole world and get rid of the unsightly, cardboard box that had been leaning against the end of her garage. She eased her car onto the wide shoulder of the road just above the gully and got out. When she was getting the box from the trunk of the car, she noticed a state trooper car coming slowly up the road, while the man driving kept looking in her direction, but she gave it little thought and proceeded getting the box from the car and carried it the short distance to the gully, then threw it in. She had just reached for the door handle of her car when she saw the same vehicle coming toward her at a much faster rate of speed than when it had passed her going in the opposite direction, only moments earlier. She froze in her tracks, her hand still on the door handle, "Oh, Lord! What now?" She whispered through clenched teeth, but she did not proceed to open the door. The young man driving wheeled the car on to the shoulder of the road right in front of hers, coming to a jolting stop, and jumped out of the vehicle, leaving who she figured was his family in the car. "Lady, what do you think you're doing? Don't you know that littering is against the law?" he asked, walking briskly toward Lorene.

"To answer your first question. What I'm doing, is throwing a cardboard box in MY ditch! And, to answer your second question, yes, I know littering is against the law, but, I understand that a person can put what he wants to where he wants to on his own place and I lived right here on this property for nearly thirty years! I consider that my ditch, and who the hell are you anyway?" was Lorene's stern reply, as she pointed to the gully and looked the young man right in the eye.

"I happen to be a state trooper, and I'll have you know Mam, this property now belongs to TVA." he said quietly as he began to try and reason with Lorene.

"Well, I'm not the first person to throw something in that ditch? Look at that car down there. Why didn't you catch the person who put something big as a car in there instead of picking on somebody who just threw a piece of cardboard. Besides, my brother was a state trooper for years, and I happen to know it is against the rules to be carrying your family in a trooper car," Lorene was saying as he interrupted.

"Mam, I didn't drive by and catch who ever put the car in there and I did drive by and see you throw the cardboard box in there. As for who rides in my car, that's between me and my supervisor. It is no concern of yours," the young officer answered, still in a low tone of voice.

Lorene opened her mouth to say more, but the state trooper beat her to it. "You leave me no choice but to write you a citation, Mam, I'll need to see your driver's license, please," he stated as he reached for the small pad in his shirt pocket.

Lorene drew a long breath and jerked the car door open. She could feel the heat of anger on her face as she bent over her purse to get her wallet and she wanted to scream out in a rage as to how unfairly she had been treated, not just to this cocky, young state trooper, but to TVA and the government, how this very sight still seemed like her home even though bulldozers had pushed to the ground the house, her first home, to the ground and how her heart had been crushed to the core along with it. But, she knew she could not...The state trooper was already beginning to write the citation and she had common sense enough to know if she let the things out that were bearing on her mind and heart that it would do her more harm than good. She took the citation when he handed it to her and he mumbled, "I'm sorry Mam." Then he turned and walked back to his unit. At least that's what she thought he said. Hot tears burned her eyes as he pulled around her and went on down the road. She got into her car and sat looking out over the spot where her house once set. How long she sat there, she didn't know, but she finally started the motor and proceeded down the road to find a place to turn around. Her afternoon had been ruined and she had no desire to go on to the cemetery.

Chapter Twenty:
Failure or Victory?

Flakes of snow fell from dark, low, clouds that Christmas Eve of 1996. The temperature was too warm for any accumulation, besides, the flakes were few. The slowly, falling flakes did, however, add to the music, jingles and Ho, Ho, Ho, along with, the hustle and bustle of the season, Lorene guessed. She sat in her living room with her knitting on her lap. She was finishing a vest she planned to give as a present. She did not experience the enthusiasm she once did, over the holidays. It seemed to overwhelm her...All of the shopping, cooking and visiting. There was too much from which to choose in the stores. Too many gourmet dishes served any more, in comparison to the basic holiday meals she used to enjoy pre-paring for her family. Too much running from here to there trying to make all of the engagements, along with all of the entertaining the different ones who dropped in. "Hem, I sound like Scrooge," she mused to herself, but, why couldn't people just spread some of the giving, cooking and visiting, throughout the year and reserve a little more time at Christmas to think on the real meaning of the season?" These were the things Lorene contemplated as she continued with the project on her lap.

"Law, law, things have changed a heap in my Eighty three years on this earth," she mumbled, as she stared at the television which boasted of elaborate advertisements for the millions of items available, for a price, of course, which were to bring people, what they thought, was happiness. How she wished the present, commercialized, society of youngsters could experience the simple, satisfying and happy Christmas' of her childhood days.

A lot of water had gone under the bridge since Lorene's childhood days, some tumultuous, for a fact. Those childhood days, tho, were days she remembered and cherished. Many of the people who had touched her life down through the years, came to her mind as she reflected on the past. Uncle Joe and Aunt Rhodie, had long since gone. Ed and Duck, too. Little Clyde and fair haired Jewel had not lived long enough to enjoy many Christmas'. Shaw, who had lived in Cadiz, died over ten years ago, while Guy lived up until two years past. George, the youngest, passed on in 1990 and his wife Grace went shortly after. There was only three of the Turner clan left. Reba Nell, the youngest, who was still in Calvert City, Kentucky, Viona Katherine, four years older than she and widowed for some twenty years, was still in Houston Texas, and Lorene, the oldest of the whole Turner bunch, who would turn eighty-four in April, was still residing in the yellow, brick house, on Warton Road, in Cadiz; still knitting, crocheting, piecing and hand quilting quilts, along with the alteration and mending of garments for her many customers. She kept going on with the hand work she had always loved to do, in order to supplement her income and keep her hands and mind occupied.

Ma Annie, Lawton's mother, had long since gone, and over the last several years, Lawton's sisters, Clara, Buina and Dora May had died.

Virgil and Shirley were now living in West Land, Michigan, a suburb of Detroit. Virgil had retired from his job with the Ford Motor Company, several years prior, after putting in forty-seven years. He, like his daddy, Lawton, suffered from high blood pressure and circulatory problems.

Timothy, Virgil and Shirley's oldest, and his wife, Lois, also live in Michigan close to Shirley and Virgil. Matthew and his second wife, Patty, reside in Michigan. Their son, Matthew, also now resides in Michigan. Lori, Virgil and Shirley's youngest, married Rodney Bailey and they live some one hundred miles from Virgil and Shirley, in Cold Water, Michigan. They have three sons, Rodney, Jr. who is thirteen, Stephen, eleven and Tad Jacob, "Jake," six.

Doris and Kelsie still live in Cadiz in the white brick house Lorene and Lawton had built and moved into upon leaving Golden Pond. Kelsie is employed as a security guard at Johnson Control industries in Cadiz, while Doris works during the tourist season, at Lake Barkley State Park in the Gift Shop.

Tracy, Kelsie and Doris' oldest son, lives in Florida and is pursuing his career in interior decorating, while Mike and his wife, Janet, reside in Hopkinsville, Kentucky. Mike is in business for himself and Janet is employed as Mortgage Loan manager at the City Bank. They have three children, Nicholas, fourteen, Lauren, eleven and Zachary, three.

Lorene, having re-traced the genealogy of she and Lawton's family and their where-abouts in her mind, paused from her knitting to glance to the dozen or so portraits hanging on the wall across the room. They were, all, beautiful, baby pictures of her grandchildren and great-grandchildren. She smiled and said, aloud, "My pride and joy."

The sound of a vehicle pulling in her driveway, startled her back to the present. With some effort, she rose from her chair, laid her knitting where she had been sitting, and looked out the window. Doris was getting out of her car. She knew Doris' reason for coming by. She was on her way to Hopkinsville, and had come by to get Lorene's grocery list to pick-up a few items she needed for preparing some of her traditional, Christmas treats which she planned to take with her to Mike's house, where the family had all been invited for Christmas Day dinner. Lorene opened the door to let Doris in. A blast of cold air hit her in the face and she noticed the snow flakes had increased and were coming faster.

Renie's "Pride and Joy", November 1997.

"It's looking real "Christmasy" out here, Mom, and feeling real wintry. It's really turning cold fast," Doris said as she rushed inside.

"Then, you'd better make your trip to Hopkinsville in a hurry before the roads get slick." Lorene answered, closing the door. I've got my list right here on the table," Lorene continued, making her way to the small table that set next to her chair. "Kelsie not going with you?"

"Naw, he had to work awhile this morning. I'll be alright, Mom. I've only got a few things to pick up, then I'll be coming right back," Doris answered, taking the list and check Lorene handed her.

Lorene grunted, then bent to pick up her knitting as Doris headed for the front door. "Oh Mom, I almost forgot. I've got something I want you to read. Knowing you, and how well you like to read, you'll probably get it finished before the day's over," Doris said, as she reached in her purse and pulled out a small, paper back book. She handed the book to Lorene, then added, "this book is in the gift shop at Barkley. I was thumbing through it the other day, and got interested in it, so I brought it home and finished reading it. You know how you've always said you'd like to tell your life's story to somebody and have them put in book form? Well, I believe the woman who wrote that book could do just that. She lives close by, in Princeton. Here, read it and see what you think."

"Well, I don't imagine I'll have time to get it read today or tonight. I like a little on this vest, and I've got to get my treats fixed for tomorrow, but I'll get to it, soon as I get a chance," Lorene said, examining the cover of the book Doris had handed her.

Lorene was too busy the remainder of that Christmas Eve day to even think of picking up the book Doris had handed her. She usually took her reading material to bed to her, but, tonight, she was too tired, come bed time, to read. She had gone to bed early and fallen immediately, asleep. It just seemed, being on her feet for any length of time, not only brought on intense pain in her hip, it also brought total exhaustion on her.

Lorene, along with the rest of Doris' family, had a wonderful dinner and afternoon at Mike's house on Christmas day. Gifts were exchanged and the adults were entertained by the youngsters as they showed off their surprises from Santa. Lorene's greatest pleasure, in her older years were the grand children and the great grand children. Truly, they were her "Pride and Joy." Lorene's only regret of the day was that Virgil and his family would not be with them. Although, she had talked to him earlier in the day, it would have been very nice to have shared the whole day with he and his family.

Two days after Christmas, Doris came by to pay Lorene a short visit. The skiff of snow that had fallen on Christmas Eve was still on the ground and the frigid temperatures that had blown in with the snow, were beginning to moderate. The sun had driven the dark clouds away that had sent a threat of more snow for the past two days. Lorene had been busy all morning, catching up on the garments she had laid aside for the past several days, when Doris arrived.

"Well Mom, I figured you'd have that book finished by now," Lorene said, when she saw the book still laying on the table.

"Law Doris, I have been so far behind on my work to read any in the daytime and I've been too tired at night, but things will slow down, now, and I'll get around to it in a day or two," Lorene answered.

"Well, I really think the woman that wrote the book would be able to write one for you," Doris added.

"Well, I've always said I'd like to let people know just what we went through when TVA made us move out from between the rivers, and I would like to leave some of the

165

old times and old ways that we used to live by for you and Virgil and the kids and their kids, but, who else, in the world, would be interested in all of that?" Lorene asked.

"Mom, you'd be surprised how many people would buy and enjoy reading a book about life between the rivers and moon shining and all of that. You'd just be surprised," Doris answered, encouraging her. "Why, Kelsie says Golden Pond is known all over the United States."

"Well, we'll see. I'll get the book read one night soon, then we'll talk about it," Lorene answered.

And, that she did. Two days before the first of the year, Lorene got her seamstress work caught up and after she finished supper, she sat down in her chair and picked up the book which had laid on the table for the past week. The book was the autobiography of the woman who lived near the neighboring town of Princeton. She had experienced quite and unusual childhood and as Lorene, she was encouraged by her family to leave her legacy for them. Since the woman enjoyed writing, she decided to try her hand at putting her stories in book form herself. The small book was easy to read and the flow of the story easy to follow. It was informative on the habits and customs practiced in the various rural communities practiced, many of which, were, now a lost art, same as the life style of by-gone days between the rivers. There was some sadness in the book, as well, as happiness and a lot of humor. A little intrigue and romance, mixed with detailed description of the sights and sounds of the outdoors, which depicted the beauty of the Western Kentucky region, kept Lorene reading on. The actual theme, or main point, being expressed by the writer, as she unveiled her, inner most self, was how she, with the strength of her maker, overcame many obstacles in her young life, victoriously.

Well, Lorene finished the book in two nights and remarked to Doris and Kelsie that she did enjoy it. She, too, thought the writer could write her story to please her, but, she still had reservations as to venturing into having a book published. Doris and Kelsie kept encouraging her to go through with it. Virgil and Shirley even got in on the act of coaxing Lorene to look into getting the writer from Princeton to write her story. Still, Lorene was reluctant to go through with it. But, the following Saturday, "the straw that broke the camel's back," came in the form of a phone call by Mike, along with Tracy, backing him up. They told "Nanny," Lorene, they would be so proud if she would have the story of her life written to leave as a legacy for them, their future children and all of the other generations to come. Now, Lorene had never had a problem with saying no to Virgil and Doris when she set her mind to do so. But, the grandchildren were a different story. So, she consented for Doris to contact the writer in Princeton and see if she would be interested in hearing her mama's story. Well, the writer expressed interest in writing Lorene's story and a date was set, two weeks from the following Sunday, for an interview with Lorene at her house, with no obligation on the part of Lorene or the writer if, either chose not to proceed with the venture.

Many thoughts began racing through Lorene's mind as she pondered the, up coming, interview. "Am I being silly, going through with getting a book written? Do I want to dig up all the old stuff that I've experienced in my life? Who would want to read about how poor I was, and Lawton's moonshinin' and bootleggin,' and the terrible time we all experienced over Virgil's handicap when he was little? Would anybody want to read about how the government, through TVA, forced us out of our homes and took away from many a family, all of the land between the rivers? I just don't know. It'll be such an expense, and I'm on a fixed income. I just don't know about it all." Then her thoughts would focus on the positive. "Maybe, people would like to read about all of that. I know the kids would, and the grandkids, and Reba Nell and Viona, and all of Lawton's people, and Kelsie's too. Then too, I know there's a lot of the people who've grieved over losing their places when TVA took over that would be interested. So, I guess if the woman from Princeton who wrote her story is interested in writing mine and she doesn't charge an arm and a leg, I'll try to go through with it."

So, having set her decision in her mind, Lorene began, "digging up bones," as she called it, in reverence to the title of a song, which perfectly described her frame of mind for the days that followed. Much to Lorene's surprise, many stories of the past came to her mind; stories of excitement, such as, the day she and Lawton was chased and supposedly, shot at, by the law, as they were transporting a hundred and ten gallons of moonshine to Murray. And, the narrow escapes when they were raided by the revenuers and local sheriff at Ma Annie's, as well as their house in Golden Pond. Then, there were the heart warming stories that evolved around her own childhood and also, that of her children and grand children. Stories of heartbreak, some of which included the death of close family members, Virgil's handicap and Lawton's declining health, along with, having to give up her home, of almost Thirty years, in Golden Pond. Stories of humor, associated with growing up in a large family, then marrying at the tender age of fifteen, moving in and adjusting to the family life of her moonshinin' husband and his family. Then, there were stories she could tell of how she managed to survive on a day to day basis as she wrestled with the hurdles she was forced to face. Yes, Lorene guessed, soon after she began "digging up bones," that she, more than likely, had enough stories to fill the pages of a book.

Two weeks later, on a bright and sunny Sunday afternoon, Lorene met the writer who was to put her story into the written text. Yes, the interview went well. The initial details of the business contract were discussed, agreed upon and sealed, verbally. The writer, with a small tape recorder, along with pencil and pad, then relaxed and spent a pleasurable afternoon listening, as Lorene began revealing the interesting and entertaining contents of her book.

Lorene kept on "digging up bones," for nine months, while the writer mailed or delivered each chapter as it was finished. Lorene, along with Doris and Kelsie, Virgil and Shirley, in addition to the grandchildren pointed out needed changes and corrections, as the project continued until completion.

Soon after the project began, word got around that Lorene Turner Higgins, an ordinary gal from the Fenton community or Turnerville, in the land between the rivers, was telling her life story. Lorene is amazed continually at the number of people who are expressing their excitement and eager anticipation of reading and owning the finished product. Well, the finished product is almost ready for it's debut. Yes, Lorene still experiences doubts, sometimes, as to whether many people will be interested in reading her story. Her writer smiles at her and tells her she is in for many more surprises.

Renie and Lawton, late 1960s.

Renie Higgins, photo taken in mid-1950s.

Lorene is now eighty-four years old and still resides in Cadiz, Kentucky on Warton Drive. Lorene, because of her age and declining physical condition, is no longer able to do many of the things she did years past. She even wonders, many times, how she endured the numerous, traumatic events she has incurred throughout her life. She ponders the last statement for a moment, however, and concludes; the Lord just wasn't through with her yet, or she wouldn't have. The old adage "if a bad situation doesn't kill a body, it will strengthen a body," has proven true in Lorene's case. Lorene is a very strong person; strong in faith, strong in spirit and strong in will. She has been, down through the years, and continues to be, a pillar of strength for her family, an encouragement to her many friends and a delight to new acquaintances. Lorene has touched many lives throughout her eighty-four years and has left on each a vivid impression of warmth and fairness, yet honesty toward all.

When asked, based on her many years of experience, what Lorene would like to leave, as a word of advice, to her reading audience, she chuckled, tilted her chin, shook her head and replied, "Well, I don't know if I'd had the sense years ago to change the things I look back now and wish I had, but, I don't advise any girl to get married at fifteen years old, an' I would tell her to run fast if she finds out he's a moonshiner. I'd advise any woman to stand by her family, regardless of the situation, for blood's thicker than water, and, families stickin' together is strength. I'd tell young people to "make do an' be satisfied and proud of what they've got, watch their money, an' I'd tell older ones, when their kids are grown an' gone an' have families of their own to keep their minds occupied and not to give up on life. Here I am in my mid '80s, an' I'm not able to do as I used to, an,' no, I don't like it none, but I've not give up yet. Some days my ol' bones won't hardly let me get around, but I can still fix your pants."

Every day Lorene Turner Higgins continues to wrestle with the hurdles of this life, along with the inevitability of a life to come, just as we all do. She has fears, suffering and emotional trauma, mixed with a measure of joy, laughter and peace of mind; the elements, both the good and the bad which are imposed upon us all, for they are essential in the maintenance of balance that enables us to live this earthly life, which in essence, is just a dressing room for eternity…

Printed in the USA
CPSIA information can be obtained
at www.ICGtesting.com
JSHW082209140824
68134JS00014B/516

9 781681 625911